WALKING THE 12 STEPS WITH JESUS CHRIST

A Christian, Bible-based Study Guide for use in recovery from addiction to substance abuse, emotional strongholds, and codependency.

Compiled by: Ray Geisel

COPYRIGHT 1996 - Christian 12 Step Ministry, Inc.
COPYRIGHT 2016 - Christian 12 Step Ministry, Inc.

Please note - Copyright restrictions

This study guide has been compiled to help those who struggle with various forms of addictions and codependency problems. This material has been compiled from various sources including the 12 steps of the Alcoholics Anonymous program that is used by permission from Alcoholics Anonymous World Services, Inc.

Any reproduction of this material in whole or in part is expressly prohibited.

Scripture quotations are taken from the Today's English Version, Second Edition. Copyright 1966, 1971, 1976, 1992, American Bible Society. Used by permission.

First Printing - June 1993
Second Printing - November 2016
Third Printing - May 2017
Fourth Printing - November 2017

As of November 2017, over 178,000 copies of
"Walking the 12 Steps with Jesus Christ" have been printed and distributed.

Additional copies may be obtained by writing our office or visiting our website:
Christian 12 Step Ministry, Inc.
PO Box 4321, Ocala, FL 34478-4321
www.christian12step.org
Phone: (352) 732-0877 · Fax: (352) 402-0177
Physical Address: 415 NW First Avenue, Ocala, FL 34475
Please send all mail to the PO Box above.

Walking the 12 Steps with Jesus Christ

The 12 STEPS

THE ORIGINAL 12 STEPS OF ALCOHOLICS ANONYMOUS

1. We admitted we were powerless over alcohol - that our lives had become unmanageable.
2. Came to believe that a Power greater than ourselves could restore us to sanity.
3. Made a decision to turn our will and our lives over to the care of God as we understood Him.
4. Made a searching and fearless moral inventory of ourselves.
5. Admitted to God, to ourselves and to another human being the exact nature of our wrongs.
6. Were entirely ready to have God remove all these defects of character.
7. Humbly asked Him to remove our shortcomings.
8. Made a list of all persons we had harmed and became willing to make amends to them all.
9. Made direct amends to such people wherever possible, except when to do so would injure them or others.
10. Continued to take personal inventory and when we were wrong promptly admitted it.
11. Sought through prayer and meditation to improve our conscious contact with God, as we understood Him, praying only for knowledge of His will for us and the power to carry that out.
12. Having had a spiritual awakening as the result of these steps we tried to carry this message to alcoholics and to practice these principles in all our affairs

THE 12 STEPS OF AA, AS USED IN THIS STUDY GUIDE

1. I admit that (by myself without Jesus) I am powerless over my addiction; that my life has become unmanageable.
2. I came to believe that a power greater than myself (Jesus Christ) could restore me to sanity.
3. I made a decision to turn my will and my life over to the care of God as I understood Him.
4. I made a searching and fearless moral inventory of myself seeking to identify the wrongs of my past.
5. I admitted to God, to myself, and to another human being the exact nature of my wrongs.
6. I was entirely ready to have God remove all the wrongs of my past.
7. I humbly asked Him to remove these wrongs.
8. I made a list of all persons I had harmed and became willing to make amends to them all.
9. I made direct amends to such persons whenever possible, except when to do so would injure them or others.
10. I continue to take personal inventory daily, and when I am wrong, I promptly admit it.
11. I seek through prayer and meditation to improve my conscious contact with God, as I understand Him, praying only for knowledge of His will for me and the power to carry that out.
12. Having had a spiritual awakening as a result of these steps, I try to carry this message to others with addiction and to practice these principles in all my affairs.

The 12 Steps are reprinted and adapted with permission of Alcoholics Anonymous World Services, Inc. (AAWS) Permission to reprint and adapt the 12 Steps does not mean that AAWS has reviewed or approved the contents of this publication, or that AAWS necessarily agrees with the views expressed herein. A.A. is a program of recovery from alcoholism <u>only</u> - use of the 12 Steps in connection with programs and activities which are patterned after A.A., but which address other problems, or in any other non-A.A. context, does not imply otherwise. Additionally, while A.A. is a spiritual program, A.A. is not a religious program. Thus, A.A. is not affiliated or allied with any sect, denomination, or specific religious belief.

Walking the 12 Steps with Jesus Christ

TABLE OF CONTENTS

The 12 Steps with Related Scriptures	iv
Welcome	v
Study Guide Order Form	vi
Instructions	1
Student Correspondence Course	2
Student Correspondence Course Introductory Lesson	3
Discussion Guidelines	5
Overcomers Daily Prayer	6
The Road Map	7
30 Common Addictions	8

Introductory Lesson
- First Things First 9
- The Four Stages of Recovery 12

STEP 1: Admit Powerlessness Lesson 1 14
- Lesson 2 15
- Lesson 3 *Step 1 MEDITATIONS* 20

STEP 2: Believe God Can Lesson 4 23
- Lesson 5 28
- Lesson 6 *Step 2 MEDITATIONS* 30

STEP 3: Turn to God Lesson 7 34
- Lesson 8 36
- Lesson 8 **Understanding Salvation** 40
- Lesson 9 *Step 3 MEDITATIONS* 41

STEP 4: Searching and Fearless Moral Inventory Lesson 10 45
- Lesson 11 51
- Lesson 12 56
- Lesson 13 *Step 4 MEDITATIONS* 59
- Lesson 14 62
- Step 4 **Personal Inventory Check List** 66

Growth/Strength ACTIVITY STEP 4 -*PRAYER* Lesson 15 70

STEP 5: Share Our Story Lesson 16 73
- Lesson 17 *Step 5 MEDITATIONS* 78
- Lesson 18 81

Growth/Strength ACTIVITY STEP 5 -*BIBLE STUDY* Lesson 19 85

STEPS 6 & 7: Get Ready – Ask God to Remove Wrongs Lesson 20 90
- Lesson 21 *Steps 6 & 7 MEDITATIONS* 94
- Lesson 22 97
- Lesson 23 100
- Lesson 23 **Soul Tie Breaking Prayer** 104
- Lesson 23 **Healing a Memory** 105
- Lesson 23 **Healing Prayer for Abandonment** 106
- Lesson 24 *Steps 6 & 7 MEDITATIONS* 107

Growth/Strength ACTIVITY STEPS 6 & 7 -*ACTIVELY INVOLVED* Lesson 25 110

STEPS 8 & 9: Make a List – Make Direct Amends Lesson 26 113
- Lesson 27 *Steps 8 & 9 MEDITATIONS* 117
- Lesson 28 120
- Lesson 29 *Steps 8 & 9 MEDITATIONS* 124

STEP 10: Daily Personal Inventory Lesson 30 128
- Lesson 31 *Step 10 MEDITATIONS* 132
- Lesson 32 136
- Lesson 32 **My Daily Inventory Chart** 140

STEP 11: Improve Conscious Contact with God Lesson 33 141
- Lesson 34 *Step 11 MEDITATIONS* 145

STEP 12 & Growth/Strength ACTIVITY STEP 8 -*SERVICE STEPS* Lesson 35 148
- Lesson 36 *Step 12 MEDITATIONS* 151

Postscript 153
References 154
Who does God say that I am .... Inside Back Cover

The 12 Steps with Related Scriptures

Step 1—I admit that (by myself, without Jesus) I am powerless over my addiction; that my life has become unmanageable.
Romans 7:18, "I know nothing good lives in me, that is, in my sinful nature; for I have the desire to do what is good, but I cannot carry it out."

Step 2—I came to believe that a power greater than myself (Jesus Christ) could restore me to sanity.
Philippians 2:13, "For it is God who works in you to will and to act according to His good purpose."

Step 3—I made a decision to turn my will and my life over to the care of God, as I understood Him.
Romans 12:1, "Therefore, I urge you, brothers, in view of God's mercy, to offer your bodies as living sacrifices, holy and pleasing to God—which is your spiritual act of worship."

Step 4—I made a searching and fearless moral inventory of myself seeking to identify the wrongs of my past.
Lamentations 3:40, "Let us examine our ways and test them, and let us return to the Lord."

Step 5—I admitted to God, to myself, and to another human being the exact nature of my wrongs.
James 5:16, "Therefore, confess your sins to each other and pray for each other so that you may be healed."

Step 6—I was entirely ready to have God remove all the wrongs of my past.
James 4:10, "Humble yourselves before the Lord, and He will lift you up."

Step 7—I humbly asked Him to remove these wrongs.
1 John 1:9, "If we confess our sins, He is faithful, and just and will forgive us our sins and purify us from all unrighteousness."

Step 8—I made a list of all persons I had harmed and became willing to make amends to them all.
Luke 6:31, "Do to others as you would have them do to you."

Step 9—I made direct amends to such people whenever possible, except when to do so would injure them or others.
Matthew 5:23-24, "Therefore, if you are offering your gift at the altar and there remember that your brother has something against you, leave your gift there in front of the altar. First, go and be reconciled to your brother; then come and offer your gift."

Step 10—I continue to take personal inventory daily, and when I am wrong, I promptly admit it.
1 Corinthians 10:12, "So, if you think you are standing firm, be careful that you do not fall."

Step 11—I seek through prayer and meditation to improve my conscious contact with God, as I understand Him.
Colossians 3:16, "Let the Word of Christ dwell in you richly."

Step 12—Having had a spiritual awakening, as a result of these steps, I try to carry this message to others with addiction and to practice these principles in all my affairs.
Galatians 6:1, "Brothers, if someone is caught in a sin, you who are spiritual should restore him gently, but watch yourself, or you also may be tempted."

WELCOME

Dear Overcomer,

Christian 12 Step Ministry has distributed over 170,000 copies of "Walking the 12 Steps with Jesus Christ" throughout all 50 states and several foreign countries. Recognizing God as their "Higher Power" has helped those with all kinds of addictions to overcome and live Spirit-filled lives.

With Jesus Christ at the center of this study, it is His power at work that enlightens, strengthens, and transforms those who apply the teachings to their own lives. In God's Word, Philippians 4:13 states, "For I can do everything through Christ, who gives me strength." (NLT)

Please visit our website at www.christian12step.org. You will find more information about our ministry including videos that share our history and testimonies from those who have participated in this study in a group setting.

Our Founder, Mr. Ray Geisel, personally experienced healing from his own addiction through the power of Jesus Christ. He witnessed hundreds of people healed by becoming "new creations" through the power of the gospel message. He believed that life was God's gift to us and what we do with our life is our gift to Him.

It is our sincere prayer that you, too, will find new life in Jesus Christ as you walk these 12 steps with Him. May God bless you, strengthen you, and completely heal you from your addictions. May His victory be yours.

Serving you,
The Staff and Board of Christian 12 Step Ministry, Inc.

> "I would like to express to you with the deepest sincerity of my heart that this has been a humble, joyous task given to me by the Lord Jesus Christ. I have tried to be a simple vessel of His grace and healing. I give Him all the honor, praise, and glory. What you hold in your hand as you read this study guide is not my work, but the work of God's Holy Spirit."—Ray Geisel, Founder of Christian 12 Step Ministry, Inc.

THANK YOU

We would like to thank all of the volunteers who make this program possible. Some have helped with the writing, arranging, editing, and revising of the study guide. Others read and comment on lessons for the Student Correspondence Course or facilitate this study in group meetings. Still others assist with office duties or serve on our Board of Directors. This program is truly the work of many different people who are led by the Spirit of God to do His work.

We cannot do what we do without our volunteers. Volunteers are truly the heart of our ministry and we appreciate you all.

STUDY GUIDE ORDER FORM

WALKING THE 12 STEPS WITH JESUS CHRIST
PO Box 4321, Ocala, FL 34478
Ph: (352) 732-0877   Fax: (352) 402-0177
www.christian12step.org

FOR OUR STUDENT CORRESPONDENCE COURSE:
- Instructions can be found on page 2.
- To begin this course complete and return the Introduction Lesson found on page 3.

TO PREVENT DELAY, PLEASE PRINT CLEARLY.

Name: _____ Inmate# _____ Date: _____
Institution: _____
Address: _____
City: _____ State: _____ Zip: _____
Male / Female   Age: _____ Occupation: _____

Please describe the recovery programs you have been in: _____
_____
How did you learn about this program? _____
_____

Study guides are FREE to incarcerated *individuals* and *must be requested by the individual*. To accommodate large groups, we do request donations. We may be contacted at the above address, phone or website for group orders. We are a designated 501(c)(3) corporation solely funded by the giving of individuals, businesses and churches.

STUDY GUIDE ORDER FORM

WALKING THE 12 STEPS WITH JESUS CHRIST
PO Box 4321, Ocala, FL 34478
Ph: (352) 732-0877   Fax: (352) 402-0177
www.christian12step.org

FOR OUR STUDENT CORRESPONDENCE COURSE:
- Instructions can be found on page 2.
- To begin this course complete and return the Introduction Lesson found on page 3.

TO PREVENT DELAY, PLEASE PRINT CLEARLY.

Name: _____ Inmate# _____ Date: _____
Institution: _____
Address: _____
City: _____ State: _____ Zip: _____
Male / Female   Age: _____ Occupation: _____

Please describe the recovery programs you have been in: _____
_____
How did you learn about this program? _____
_____

Study guides are FREE to incarcerated *individuals* and *must be requested by the individual*. To accommodate large groups, we do request donations. We may be contacted at the above address, phone or website for group orders. We are a designated 501(c)(3) corporation solely funded by the giving of individuals, businesses and churches.

Walking the 12 Steps with Jesus Christ

INSTRUCTIONS

Walking the 12 Steps with Jesus Christ is a Bible-based study guide for Christian living. This guide is intended to: reinforce your regular 12 Step meeting, give you a Biblical basis for Jesus Christ as your "Higher Power," help you heal from hurtful life events, and strengthen your Christian walk. It is not intended to replace your regular 12 Step meeting.

The material in this study guide is meant to be studied carefully. It is very important to apply it to your life and practice it whenever possible. Immediate application and practice will help you retain what you learn and bring forth the changes in your character and life that you so desire. Persistence is key.

You will notice that some lessons are identified as "Meditations." "Meditations" are short writings based on Scripture to encourage and increase your faith in God. We believe you will find them easy to understand and relate to. Always begin the "Meditation" by looking up and studying the verse that is referenced. Read a little before and a little after the referenced verse so you can clearly understand what it is saying. Each "Meditation" is designed for the specific step in which you find it.

You will also notice that some pages contain a section marked "Scripture Study." These scriptures are intended to be used to deepen your study of God's Word. Again, look up and study each verse being sure to read a little before and a little after it to understand what it is saying. Answer the following question for each verse: "How does this scripture apply to this step?" It will probably be helpful to do this on a separate sheet of paper. "Scripture Study" can be repeated again and again because God's Word is living and active. This means that it will speak to us in different ways depending on the situations we find ourselves in and what we are seeking from God at any particular time.

Remember, this study guide is a tool to assist you in your transformation through Jesus Christ. You will get out of it as much as you put into it. If you invest very little, you will gain very little. If you invest much, you will gain much.

It is our deepest desire to reach as many people as possible. Therefore, we have purposefully tried to keep the language and wording more simplified and untechnical. Questions and comments regarding this material are always appreciated and considered. They may be addressed to Christian 12 Step Ministry, PO Box 4321, Ocala, FL 34478-4321 or sent by email to renee@christian12step.org. We will do our best to reply promptly.

We would like to reiterate that this study guide is free to those who are confined to a correctional institution anywhere. To obtain a copy, the confined person needs only send a written request to the address above. For all others, we simply request a donation of $15.25 to cover the costs of printing and shipping. Christian 12 Step Ministry, Inc. is a non-profit, 501(c)(3) corporation and we are solely funded by donations from individuals, businesses, and churches. Donations are necessary in order to keep copies free for those incarcerated.

Again, it is our sincere hope and prayer that you be healed and delivered from any substance abuse, emotional stronghold, or codependency. May God bless you, strengthen you, and may you be transformed.

The Staff and Board of Christian 12 Step Ministry, Inc.

The first mile of a long journey - begins with a single step.
-Lao Tzu

When we surrender to our Higher Power, the journey to recovery begins.
-Anonymous

Whoever goes to the Lord for safety, whoever remains under the protection of the Almighty, can say to Him, "You are my defender and protector.
You are my God; in you I trust." He will keep you safe from all hidden dangers and from all deadly diseases.
He will cover you with his wings; you will be safe in His care;
His faithfulness will protect and defend you.
-Psalm 91:1-4

Walking the 12 Steps with Jesus Christ

CORRESPONDENCE COURSE

Christian 12 Step Ministry, Inc.
PO Box 4321
Ocala, FL 34478-4321
(352) 732-0877
Visit us at: www.christian12step.org
"Like" us on Facebook

Student Correspondence Course Available

Thank you for your interest in "Walking the 12 Steps with Jesus Christ," the study guide of Christian 12 Step Ministry, Inc. In addition to this study guide, a Student Correspondence Course may be requested. The Student Correspondence Course consists of insightful questions that thoroughly cover The 12 Steps. A Certificate of Completion will be issued at the conclusion of this course. The Introductory Lesson for this course can be found on page 3 of this study guide.

How to begin this course in order to receive a Certificate of Completion:

From within a correctional facility, submit the following to the address at the top of this page: your completed Introductory Lesson which can be found on page 3 of this study guide. Please note that this study guide and course is free to those incarcerated. Also upon your request, we will send a letter to your classification officer to include in your jail/prison file.

Outside of a correctional facility, submit the following to the address at the top of this page: (1) your completed Introductory Lesson which can be found on page 3 of this study guide, and (2) a self-addressed, stamped envelope for its return.

Upon the receipt of your Introductory Lesson, it will be reviewed and comments may be added that will encourage you in your recovery journey. It will be returned to you along with the following lesson.

For Group Meetings or Classes, donations are requested for our study guide. Please visit our website, www.christian12step.org, for purchasing information or contact our office at (352) 732-0877.

Facilitator Training Correspondence Course

Those who complete the Student Correspondence Course and demonstrate genuine recovery with a sincere desire to carry the message to others are invited to further participate in the Facilitator Training Correspondence Course. To begin this course, submit a request for it in writing to the address at the top of this page. This course consists of 10 lessons using the same study guide and the same procedure for submitting lessons as described above. Upon the review of the final lesson of the Facilitator Training Correspondence Course another Certificate of Completion will be issued.

We highly recommend this course for the following reasons:

- This course presents you with questions that will help you evaluate how well you know the material and have applied it to your own life. This is extremely important for effectively presenting it to others and helping them apply it to their own lives.
- This course also presents you with a few questions that may come directly from your group that are of an antagonistic nature so that you may be prepared in advance for how you would handle those questions within a group setting.

> Please print clearly to prevent any delay.

Name: _____
Inmate # (if applicable): _____
Institution: _____
Address: _____
City/State/Zip: _____

CHRISTIAN 12 STEP PROGRAM
"Walking the 12 Steps with Jesus Christ"
Introduction – Pages 8 through 11

Instructions: Please read the above referenced pages carefully. Spend some time in prayer thinking about what you read and how it applies to you. Answer to the best of your ability and return your lesson to us. Your lesson will be reviewed, some comments may be made, and it will be returned to you with the following lesson. Follow this procedure for all lessons. At the receipt of your final lesson, you will be mailed a Certificate of Completion. Feel free to use a separate sheet of paper if you need more room.

---

1. How would you define <u>addiction</u>? How do you recognize it?

2. What is the cause of addiction in most people?

3. What do you think is the cause of your addiction?

4. How would you define an <u>emotional stronghold</u>? How do you recognize it?

5. What <u>emotional strongholds</u> are you living with? What do you think caused them?

Introduction Continued

6. What is <u>codependency</u>? How do you recognize it?

7. Describe how you or someone you know acts out codependent behavior.

8. According to this study, what does the word <u>drunk</u> mean?

9. What are the 3 attitudes that you need to adopt now?

10. Which of the 3 attitudes will be the most difficult for you to adopt?

11. Explain why this attitude will be the most difficult for you to adopt.

12. Is Romans 12:1-2 essential to your recovery? Please explain why.

CHRISTIAN 12 STEP MINISTRY, Inc.—
Discussion Guidelines

*Please note: These guidelines are included should you be participating in a group or class setting. Should you desire to begin a new group or class, please contact our office (352) 732-0877 or visit our website, www.christian12step.org.

Meeting Format: Everyone's time, attention, and participation are highly valued. Therefore, the following meeting format is suggested each week:

- We will begin promptly at _____
- We will recite the "Overcomer's Prayer" on page 6 together, out loud
- We will only have time to cover the highlights for each step—it is ALL very helpful information, be sure to read whatever we are not able to cover in class

As we cover the material, anyone who would like to ask a question or comment about *their own* personal experience, strength, and hope is welcome to do so. However, <u>*at this time, comments/questions should be kept short and relate specifically to the material we have just covered*</u>. If a lengthier question or comment comes to mind, please jot it down in your book or on a separate sheet of paper so you won't forget it. We can address these more deeply after class. If you need something repeated, please just ask.

Discussion Guidelines:

- **Confidentiality**: Whatever is shared in group needs to stay within group. This is extremely important to promote a safe environment for sharing. **Exceptions**: Information disclosed that indicates someone may be a threat to themselves, to their minor children, to any other, and any reports of abuse must be reported.
- We should avoid preaching, giving advice, and talking directly at each other. We will not hurt or destroy another's reputation.
- Sharing needs to stay focused on *our own* thoughts and feelings. Use "I" messages instead of "You" messages whenever possible. Examples: "I have a difficult time with…because…", "I've not understood…", "How can I…", or "…is difficult for me because…". We are the ones seeking healing/recovery, so everything is about us!
- Please remember this is *not a counseling session*. Many details about situations are not fully disclosed. People only share what they are comfortable sharing. Only God knows all and has promised to lead us when we seek Him with our whole heart.
- Avoid cross talk—when two or more people engage in a conversation during group time which excludes all others. Lengthier discussions of any kind should occur outside of class to respect everyone's time and feelings. No one likes to feel left out.
- We should speak respectfully to one another and be careful not to shame ourselves or others. Remember, some people are more sensitive than others. Choose words carefully and watch facial expressions when you can. Avoid profanity and other harsh or inappropriate talk--think of group time as a fast from these habits.
- We will not stay in offense. If we become angry with or feel hurt by anyone in our group, we will seek help to resolve any conflict. We will not keep our anger or hurt to ourselves, neither will we talk unkindly about the person whom we perceived cause it.
- We will speak one at a time, monitoring the time we take.
- We may respectfully remind each other of these guidelines if we begin to stray from them. Our code word for doing so is _____.

OVERCOMERS DAILY PRAYER

Lord Jesus Christ,
I abandon myself to you.
I give myself to You just as I am,
the good, the bad, and the indifferent.
I hold nothing back.
I give you my fears, my resentments, and my anger.
I give you my powerlessness, my failures, and defeats.
I make you Lord over all of me.
I renounce everything that is not from You or of You.

Give to me the power and grace to love You
and to serve You.
Fill me with Your joy and Your peace.
Have mercy on me and help me this day.

Lord Jesus,
if I should change my mind later about all this,
then do it anyway in spite of me.
I give You my will, change it as You see fit.
Deliver me from my self-seeking.
Make me into one who helps others,
and desires to do YOUR WILL!

Amen - so be it!

Prayer inspired by the Holy Spirit and written by Bill Godfrey

Walking the 12 Steps with Jesus Christ

THE ROAD MAP

Road Map to Recovery

THE FOUNDATION STEPS

STEP 1: I admit that (by myself without Jesus) I am powerless over my addiction; that my life has become unmanageable.
STEP 2: I came to believe that a power greater than myself (Jesus Christ) could restore me to sanity.
STEP 3: I made a decision to turn my will and my life over to the care of God, as I understood Him.

THE ROAD TO HEALING THE PAST
The Discovery & Healing Steps

STEP 4: I made a searching and fearless moral inventory of myself seeking to identify the wrongs of my past.
STEP 5: I admitted to God, to myself, and to another human being the exact nature of my wrongs.
STEP 6: I was entirely ready to have God remove all the wrongs of my past.
STEP 7: I humbly asked Him to remove these wrongs.
STEP 8: I made a list of all persons I had harmed and became willing to make amends to them all.
STEP 9: I made direct amends to such people whenever possible, except when to do so would injure them or others.

THE ROAD TO GROWTH & STRENGTH FOR TODAY
The Building Stage - Growth/Strength Activities (G/S Steps)

ACTIVITY **STEP 4:** I made a daily effort to pray:
a. Believing in Jesus Christ as my personal Lord and Savior,
b. Accepting Him into my heart and life,
c. Asking Him for what I need to come closer to Him and not for what I want.
d. Praising and thanking Him for the gift of the new life He is giving me.
e. Listening to His word in my spirit.
ACTIVITY **STEP 5:** I made a conscious effort to study the Bible at least one hour per day.
ACTIVITY **STEP 6:** I became actively involved in a church fellowship—attending services and Bible studies each week.
ACTIVITY **STEP 7:** I made a diligent effort to fast from food at least one meal, three times a week, drinking only water during that time.

STEP 8: I make a daily effort to give the healing and strength, which I have received from the Holy Spirit, to those in my life. I make a daily practice of loving others as Jesus loves me.

THE OVERCOMING IN JESUS STEPS

STEP 10: I continue to take personal inventory daily, and when I am wrong, I promptly admit it.
STEP 11: I seek through prayer and meditation to improve my conscious contact with God, as I understand Him, praying only for knowledge of His will for me and the power to carry that out.
STEP 12: Having had a spiritual awakening as a result of these steps, I try to carry this message to others with addiction and to practice these principles in all my affairs.

Walking the 12 Steps with Jesus Christ

30 COMMON ADDICTIONS

ALCOHOL 	ANGER 	SEX 
CAFFEINE 	GAMBLING 	SEXUAL ABUSE 
SPORTS 	LOVE 	SHOPPING 
CHRONIC ILLNESS 	CO-DEPENDENCY 	INTERNET 
COMPULSIVE LYING 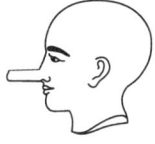	MONEY 	JUNK FOOD 
CHURCH 	NICOTINE 	TALKING 
CREDIT CARDS 	OVER EATING 	CELL PHONE & TEXTING 
	PAIN 	
DRUGS 	PHYSICAL ABUSE 	TELEVISION 
EMOTIONAL ABUSE 	PRESCRIPTION MEDICATION 	GAMES 
PORNOGRAPHY 		WORK 

Christian 12 Step Ministry, Inc — *Walking the 12 Steps with Jesus Christ*

FIRST THINGS FIRST

Before we begin our study of addiction, emotional strongholds, and codependency, let's take a look at some basic facts and definitions of these terms:

ADDICTION - What is it and how do we recognize it?

Addiction is a habit that has taken control of us over which we have little or no control. We find ourselves in a position of being unable to break that habit. The cause of addiction is basically a sickness of man's inner being which we choose to call spirit.

1. Addiction - A spiritual sickness. Something hurts deep inside the inner person and causes great pain. This pain may come from past, childhood days, or from events of the recent past, or both. Something happens in the form of a life crisis that opens up the wounds of the past and causes us to hurt deeply inside.

2. Pain - We seek to put out the fire of that hurt. When we experience this tremendous hurt inside ourselves, we desperately try to put out the fire of that intense pain. Pain is against our basic human nature, so we search for a way to kill the pain inside and obtain relief. This causes us to look around to see what others are doing with situations like this. We ask ourselves, "How is my friend handling a problem that is similar to mine?" Quickly, we find ourselves tempted to try the same solution as our friend. Most people become introduced to drugs through a "friend". At this point, we become very open and vulnerable to the temptation to try our "friend's" solution. We are very "down" in our spirit, and the devil is at our door with all sorts of evil solutions. In our desperation to find some relief from our pain, we listen to him and fall prey to some sort of chemical or behavioral habit that, in time, turns into an addiction leading us into out-of-control, compulsive behavior. We tend to walk away from God, and our sanity, into a dream world looking for the solution, an escape from our inner problem, and then we find ourselves addicted.

The Bible deals with temptation. In James 1:13-15 we read: "...and He (God) tempts no one. But we are tempted when we are drawn away and trapped by our own evil desires. Then our evil desires conceive and give birth to sin; and sin, when it is full-grown, gives birth to death." In our desperation, we are tempted to keep trying solutions that lead us into sin. The reading above tells us that sin leads to death - spiritual and sometimes physical.

3. Addiction - Leads to compulsive behavior. As we chase our habit in a desperate attempt to put out the fire of our inner hurt, we wind up with a compulsive habit we cannot stop and our lives spin more and more out of control. If not corrected, this downward pull of our inner self can, and will, eventually lead us to spiritual death. We are slowly dying on the inside -in our spirit. Drastic steps need to be taken to correct this situation. Physical death can and often does occur.

4. Addiction - Leads us to insane, out-of-control behavior. We recognize this compulsive habit by the out-of-control behavior it causes. When we get drunk in our addictive habit, we act in an insane manner that we are totally unable to stop. At this point, we can be certain that our addiction has us by the throat.

EMOTIONAL STRONGHOLD

An emotional stronghold is the habit of dark, negative thinking that comes from lies we believe that hurt and confuse us. Emotional strongholds cause ongoing spiritual, emotional, and/or behavior problems. They can be attitudes that cause us to act against the will of God. We can be born again and genuinely sincere in our faith, yet struggle with certain thoughts, emotions, and habits. (Corn, J)

Think of a stronghold as a fortress the enemy has built in your mind. Many emotional strongholds are rooted in sin, either our own, or the sins of others that have affected us. Strongholds of this nature can be broken by genuine repentance, asking for and extending forgiveness, knowing and practicing God's Word, and healing prayer which will be discussed later. Some strongholds may be physiological in nature, caused by a chemical or hormonal imbalance or some other lacking in our physical bodies.

Examples of emotional strongholds are out-of-control anger, anxiety, depression, worry, fear, insecurity, loneliness, rejection, resentment, bitterness, and unforgiveness. These strongholds cause us to think negative, dark thoughts about all kinds of things.

Scripture referring to this kind of stronghold is 2 Corinthians 10:3-5, "We are human, but we don't wage war as humans do. We use God's mighty weapons, not worldly weapons, to knock down the strongholds of human reasoning and to destroy false arguments. We destroy every proud obstacle that keeps people from knowing God. We capture their rebellious thoughts and teach them to obey Christ." Romans 8:5-6 says, "Those who are dominated by the sinful nature think about sinful things, but those who are controlled by the Holy Spirit think about things that please the Spirit. So letting your sinful nature control your mind leads to death. But letting the Spirit control your mind leads to life and peace." See also Mark 7:20-22 and Romans 12:2.

Introductory Lesson

What is: Addiction, Emotional Stronghold, and Codependency

Walking the 12 Steps with Jesus Christ

Introductory Lesson

What is: Addiction, Emotional Stronghold, and Codependency

FIRST THINGS FIRST

CODEPENDENCY - What is it and how do we recognize it?

Codependency is a situation in which we find ourselves close to someone who is severely addicted and acting in out-of-control behavior. The most common codependency situation occurs between husband and wife. If one person is severely addicted, the partner must decide to either live with that situation or to remove him or herself from it. When the partner decides to live with the addicted person, almost always the partner allows the addicted person's problem to become theirs. The partner adjusts their life to the addiction of their spouse. Codependency is a situation in which we allow another person's problem to become ours. I begin to live the problem of my spouse. This situation creates a very painful reality for the partner. The spouse becomes infected by the spiritual sickness of their mate and finds the relationship deteriorating at a rapid pace, totally unable to stop or correct the situation. The partner will eventually become addicted to the sick partner's behavior and a "family war" almost always breaks out. To learn about the solution to the problem, it is extremely important that the affected spouse seeks help from a counselor and becomes involved in an Al-Anon program for codependent spouses. Persons who live with an addicted spouse need to learn all that they can with regard to the sickness of addiction and to experience the support from Al-Anon group members. Codependent persons may develop an addiction to:

PEOPLE - By assuming the role of rescuer or victim.

BEHAVIOR - Such as work, anger, sex, or perfectionism.

THINGS - Such as alcohol, drugs, money, food, etc.

A codependent person is one who has allowed an addict close to him to pull him down into the trap of addiction and its out-of-control behavior.

HOW TO IDENTIFY AN ADDICTED OR CODEPENDENT PERSON

1. They are driven by one or more compulsive (can't stop) habits.
2. They are bound and tormented by the way things were in their original family relationships.
3. They have a very low self-image. Often their maturity level is also low.
4. They have the notion that their happiness depends on another person.
5. They have severe difficulty getting along with others. They are unbalanced in their relationships- seeking total dependence on another or total independence from others.
6. They are masters of denial - unable to recognize reality the way it is, and constantly lie to cover up their addiction and its behavior.
7. Codependents constantly try to control others- trying to make them act against their will for the codependents' benefit.
8. Their life is full of way out, extreme behaviors.
9. They worry uncontrollably about things they cannot change and totally ignore the things that they can change. They try to change things in all sorts of strange, dishonest, and devious ways. They become masters of manipulation.
10. They are constantly searching for something that is lacking, or missing, in their life.
11. They will do, or give up, anything to satisfy their addictive appetite. They are totally unable to stop their habit even though they cry out and want to do so.

TERMS DEFINED

In this study guide, I will use a number of different terms in connection with addiction. At this point, I would like to define these terms as I have used them in this study guide.

THE THREE "C's" OF ADDICTION

1. Craving - An addicted person finds himself or herself with a huge appetite for a substance, relationship, thing, or place that consumes them and results in their addictive behavior.
2. Control - An addicted person will lose control of their sanity and act in out-of-control behavior as a result of practicing their addiction.
3. Continued use - An addicted person becomes a "slave" to a substance or habit and develops an uncontrollable desire to continue on its path of destruction. In their spirit, they want to stop but cannot.

SOME COMMON TERMS DEFINED

DRUNK - Drunkenness applies to all forms of out-of-control behavior resulting from practicing an addiction. The term applies to all forms of addiction, not just alcoholism.

INSANE - The out-of-control behavior resulting from the practice of an addiction produces a state of temporary insanity. This results in a total inability to think rationally and act responsibly.

SANITY - Having a sound, healthy mind; showing reason, sound judgement, or good sense.

SOBER - This is a person who is not under the control of a substance or condition which causes insane, drunken behavior; an in-control, rational person.

FIRST THINGS FIRST

Introductory Lesson

What is: Addiction, Emotional Stronghold, and Codependency

- **WRONGS** - Any negative behavior that causes a break in the love relationship described by Jesus in His commandment to "love one another". This can be any behavior directed by another toward us or behavior directed by us toward another. The result of these wrongs causes inner pain and hurt.
- **ABUSE** - This is another term having the same basic meaning as wrongs. Abuse also causes hurt and pain in others and us.

SOCIOPATHIC BEHAVIOR - What is it?

All forms of addiction include some element of sociopathic behavior. This form of temporary insanity is caused by the person's desire to be totally in control of himself and others. To sum it all up - he has declared himself god and he goes about asserting that authority. Let's take a look at him for a moment:

A sociopath is a person who lacks social and moral responsibility. He knows that what he is doing is wrong, but does not care in the least. He lives life only for himself with total disregard for the presence of another. He is totally self-centered. He has extreme difficulty getting along with others and, at times, does not even care to get along. It is always the other guy's fault in his social relationships. He sees no fault whatever in himself.

The sociopath loves to have no boundaries. "Don't fence me in with rules and discipline!" is his motto. His value system is a momentary one that changes to suit his fancy, and his wants. He loves to lie and steal. He will often lie merely because lying is more fun to him. He is mischievous in his behavior because that gives him "a bang" inside. He cheats others even when it would be just as easy for him to get the same results by earning it.

He enjoys living in the fear of "getting caught". This produces a "high" for him and picks him up. He likes the way it feels to cheat people and take advantage of them, especially if they remind him of the parents who spoiled and overindulged him and gave him complete "freedom". He is acting out what he learned in childhood. This is the life of the sociopath.

As we begin our walk with Jesus Christ, it is extremely important that we check our mental attitudes. In order to break the strangle hold that our addiction has over us, we must check ourselves to eliminate the "stinkin' thinkin'" of our past. We must learn a new, healthy way of thinking about our addiction problem and ourselves. We must also change our attitude toward our spouse, family, friends, and everyone we meet. Beginning right now, I urge you to adopt three new attitudes in your daily life. When you find yourself thinking the wrong way, STOP, and pray about how you think. Be aware that your thinking is not "on target" and begin to change. This may require considerable effort on your part, but let me assure you, it is well worthwhile and is the key to healing your addiction.

Three new attitudes are:

STOP BLAMING

Please, stop blaming yourself or anyone else in your life right now. Blame keeps us locked up in the prison of self, or other condemnation. As a result, we cannot identify our problem and deal with it. We are too busy blaming ourselves or someone else or both.

By ceasing to blame others and ourselves we do not deny our guilt. Yes, we have done many sinful things in our lives, but blaming others or ourselves will not correct that. Rather, we need to stand up, become individuals responsible for our own actions, and begin to change our actions now and in the days to come.

Blaming keeps us chained to condemnation and prevents us from dealing with the problem. Let us take charge of our problem, admit our guilt and begin to deal with and correct it. That is healthy thinking. Blame and condemnation are addictive thinking.

BE HONEST

Honesty with self and others is absolutely essential to recovery. Lying or hiding the problem will continue to rob us of recovery. Healing and recovery are impossible when covered with lies and the failure to deal with ourselves as we really are. Lying is, in itself, an addiction. If we persist in this habit, we will reach a point when we will no longer be able to distinguish between right and wrong, fact and fantasy, fiction and reality. Total honesty is absolutely essential to recovery from addiction.

BE WILLING - WANT TO - AND DO IT!

DO WHAT? - CHANGE ME!

Running from the problem of addiction, or any other problem, will not solve it. We have problems in our life simply to show us what we are doing wrong – where we need correction. If we fail to see the problem in a positive manner and run from it, we will never be able to correct the problem because we refuse to deal with it.

Therefore, we must stand up and openly, honestly admit that the only person I can change is ME. My recovery and new life depends on changing me; for I am the only person I can change. I have come to realize that I have no power to change anyone other than myself, and will only change when I come to the Lord Jesus Christ. Therefore, I openly and courageously declare that I will begin to change my life with the help of Jesus Christ.

"The place to improve the world is first in one's own heart and head and hands."
 - Robert M. Pirsig

For as he thinks in his heart, so is he.
 -Proverbs 23:7 (NKJV)

When the going gets tough, the tough get going.
 -Robert Schuller

Religion may inform and reform, but only Christ can transform.
"Christ is the door to the cage of sin." - Amen!
 -Larry Zapp

Walking the 12 Steps with Jesus Christ

Introductory Lesson

THE FOUR STAGES OF RECOVERY

RECOVERY STAGES

This study guide is based upon the twelve steps of the Alcoholics Anonymous program. In compiling this study guide, I have incorporated a Bible study along with the application of the twelve steps of recovery. This results in a Christian, Bible based twelve-step walk with Jesus Christ very similar to the AA program.

Four clearly distinct stages of recovery have resulted in this process and are described as follows: (Note: Please refer to the outline on page 7 for the exact wording of each step.)

STAGE ONE
- THE FOUNDATION STAGE

This stage of the program includes Steps 1, 2 and 3 at the top of the outline page. Throughout this study guide, the concept of building a new house, a "NEW ME" is developed. The Bible refers to this concept in the idea of a "New Creation" and the "born again" experience. Paul speaks of dying to the old self and coming to new life in Jesus. During this stage of the program, we begin the process of laying the foundation for our new house, the new house in which we are going to live. As with any building in the physical realm, the building is no stronger or secure than the foundation upon which it is built. So it is with our spiritual house. It must be built upon the Rock of Jesus Christ. The first three steps lead us into that experience of building our new house on the Rock of Jesus Christ.

In Step 1, I admit that, BY MYSELF WITHOUT JESUS, I am powerless over my addiction, that my life has become unmanageable. I can't overcome my out-of-control, addictive behavior by myself. I have tried and failed over and over again.

In Step 2, I come to believe that God in Jesus Christ can correct this situation. The concept of "Who is God to me?" is developed in this study guide. I come to know Jesus in a more intimate way.

In Step 3, I make a decision to give my total will and life over to the care of Jesus, as I understand Him. At this time, we learn what our will and life are and we experience the process of giving them to Jesus.

As we complete this stage, we build a solid foundation for our spiritual home on the Rock of Jesus Christ. We lay the foundation for the steps that follow when we will build a new life in Jesus. We understand that this foundation must always be kept in tact and in a strong condition. If it should weaken, the whole house will fall and we will be back to our old spiritual sickness again. We will have fallen back into addiction.

STAGE TWO
- THE DISCOVERY/HEALING STAGE

This stage begins with a searching and fearless moral inventory in Step 4, which results in our discovery of the causes leading to the hurt in our spiritual life. This hurt ultimately led us to our addictive behavior. We seek to identify and bring out the causes of the wrongs from our past life that have resulted in our spiritual pain and hurt.

Once we have identified the causes of our spiritual pain, our next step is to bring that hurt and pain to Jesus Christ for healing. During this time, we begin to understand and appreciate that Jesus came specifically to save us from our sin and the results of that sin. He came to save us; hence, He is called our Savior. This salvation is the process in which we are forgiven and healed from our past sins. In Step 5, we admit to God, to ourselves, and another person the exact nature of the wrongs of our past. The cleansing process begins and continues in Steps 6 and 7 when we become ready to come to Jesus for the healing and we do so. These two steps are the central theme or core of the entire recovery program. This is the time when we open our hearts and come to Jesus to receive His healing, forgiveness and grace. We finally begin to get rid of the pain and hurt from our past.

The final phase of this stage is Steps 8 and 9 in which we seek to mend those personal relationships from our past that have been victimized by our addictive behavior. We ask forgiveness from those we have hurt and we forgive those who have hurt us. These two steps complete the healing of our past.

STAGE THREE
- THE BUILDING STAGE

In this portion of the recovery process, we recognize that the most important time of our life is today. The AA program stresses the motto - "ONE DAY AT A TIME!" The Bible tells us in Psalm 118:24, "This is the day of the Lord's victory; let us be happy, let us celebrate!" In this stage, we concentrate on building new habits into our spiritual lives. From people who are out-of-control in behavior and discipline, we now begin to learn habits of responsible, in-control behavior. These steps are called the Growth/Strength steps on the outline page.

In G/S Step 4, we learn about the essentials of an effective prayer life. We examine the elements of good communication with our God, Jesus Christ. We begin to see our Lord Jesus as a true friend, always ready to lift us up and help us on the road of life, just for the asking.

Walking the 12 Steps with Jesus Christ

RECOVERY STAGES

Introductory Lesson

THE FOUR STAGES OF RECOVERY

In G/S Step 5, we study the importance of the Bible as our spiritual food. We begin to learn why the Bible is so important to our spiritual health and how Bible study will help us find the answers in life.

In G/S Step 6, we learn about the importance of sharing our lives with our Christian family - the Church. We learn to reach out to others in a healthy environment. We learn how to raise our children in the presence of the Lord Jesus Christ in order to prevent their spiritual sickness later in life. We find new friends and new strength in "The Body of Christ", the Church.

In G/S Step 7, we begin to understand and appreciate the discipline of our physical body through fasting. We learn how undisciplined our body can be in driving us into all sorts of insane and sinful behavior. We learn that fasting is a very effective way to control the appetites of the fleshly body.

The four steps that make up the building stage of this program are taken from the Bible itself. Jesus practiced these steps and calls us to follow His example in practicing them in our own lives. We are building a new house in which to live healthy, holy lives in the future. These steps are the building process of our new house in Jesus Christ.

STAGE FOUR - THE OVERCOMING IN JESUS STAGE

In the AA program, this stage is called the maintenance stage - the rest of our lives as we maintain our sobriety.

In this program, I have chosen to call this final part the "Overcoming in Jesus" stage. In the past steps, we have learned to walk the walk with Jesus. Now it is time to put it into practice in our daily lives.

Now that we have traveled this road, admitting our addiction, giving our will and life to Jesus, healing the past and building the present, we begin to concentrate on the process of maintaining our present, and short term, in-control behavior. During this final stage of the program, we learn that "self-control" is available to us only through the power of God's Holy Spirit. This self-control must be received by and through the power of walking with the Holy Spirit and putting that into practice in our daily lives. Our first step in this process is our daily personal inventory, which is described in Step 10. During this time, we learn how to keep track of our daily life with a constant eye on any future addictive problems that may come, or the resurrection of an old problem that may want to return and haunt us. We keep a watchful eye on our spiritual progress day by day. As problems come, we see them as signposts along the way that tell us that we need work in certain areas of our spiritual life. We deal with each problem as it presents itself in the manner described in the program. We have learned to take everything to Jesus, and with His help, solve the problem in His time and in His way. We learn how to keep our spiritual life "clean" in Jesus Christ.

In Step 11, we experience and develop a new closer prayer relationship with Jesus in meditation and contemplation.

In Step 12, we begin to realize the importance of maintaining our spiritual walk with Jesus by reaching out to others in need and helping them as well.

Finally, in G/S Step 8, we learn the true meaning of love - the Jesus way - and we begin to practice that love toward others.

When we entered the program, we found ourselves pre-occupied with "OUR problem" and that problem seemed to consume us. All of our time and energy was spent in dealing with our addiction. Now, we have learned a great deal about our addiction; we have seen that we are not alone in our struggle; we have learned how to open up to God, to ourselves and to others. We have experienced the healing and rebuilding of our lives the Jesus Christ way. As we prepare to reenter the world, we see ourselves as healed and we become more concerned with helping others to also experience this same healing. We truly have been transformed by the power of God. We are no longer alone; God walks with us.

This study guide is designed to help the addicted person understand himself more completely and to come to Jesus for healing. In so doing, he learns to recognize his problem, apply the solution and live in that solution today and in the days to come. A complete transformation takes place from a ME centered person to an OTHER centered person. In so doing, the addict becomes healed in spirit and becomes a healthy functioning part of the solution to our society's problem of addiction. God has truly worked a miracle in his life and he is very happy because of it. As a result, our world is also a better place in which to live.

In closing this brief description of the four stages of this study guide, I would like all to understand that no permanent healing is possible without the presence and healing touch of our Lord Jesus Christ. We are called by God's Holy Word to live by the power of HIS HOLY SPIRIT. When we do, miracles will and do happen. May God bless you in your search for your miracle.

Step 1 Lesson 1

"I admit that (*By Myself -without Jesus*) I am powerless over my addiction, that my life has become unmanageable."

Action Word: ADMIT

STEP 1

In our next lesson, we will begin our journey through the 12 step program in the scriptures with Jesus Christ. In preparation for this journey, I would like to ask you to answer the following questions on a separate sheet of your own paper. Please give each question careful thought and answer them as completely as possible.

What are the persons, places, relationships or substances in my life that I am powerless over?

What have I allowed to happen in my life that has made it unmanageable?

List each one separately and describe it as fully as possible. Please be honest with yourself. This is your book. No one will see your answer unless you show it to him or her. Start first by putting today's date in the box provided.

The answer: Today's date: _____

Write out the above questions and number them accordingly. Then:

- List your talents - the things you like about yourself and are good at:
- What do others like in me?
- What do I like about myself?
- What do I want to improve or eliminate in my life?
- How has God blessed me in my life to this day?
- Find at least five scriptures in the New Testament and five in the Old Testament that describe what kind of a person you want to become. Example: Colossians 1:21-23 - I want to become a friend to God through Jesus Christ the Son.

SCRIPTURE STUDY:

The following scriptures are related to Step 1 as indicated on the first page of this lesson. Look up each scripture and read before and after it. Study the scripture and, on a separate sheet of paper, write down the answer to the following question:

How does this scripture apply to Step 1 of this lesson?

- ☐ Psalm 5:1
- ☐ Psalm 18:27
- ☐ Proverbs 14:12
- ☐ Psalm 6:6-7
- ☐ Psalm 22:1-2
- ☐ Proverbs 18:14
- ☐ Psalm 10:14
- ☐ Psalm 22:11-13
- ☐ Proverbs 26:12
- ☐ Psalm 12:5
- ☐ Psalm 25:16-18
- ☐ Proverbs 28:26
- ☐ Psalm 13:1
- ☐ Psalm 28:1-2
- ☐ Mark 4:35-41
- ☐ Psalm 16:4
- ☐ Psalm 69:33
- ☐ Ephesians 2:1-5
- ☐ Psalm 18:6
- ☐ Psalm 88:1-4
- ☐ Peter 2:19

> "The Lord who created you says,
> Do not be afraid - I will save you.
> I have called you by name -
> you are mine.
> When you pass through deep waters,
> I will be with you;
> Your troubles will not overwhelm you.
> When you pass through fire,
> you will not be burned;
> the hard trials that come will
> not hurt you.
> For I am the Lord your God, the holy
> God of Israel, who saves you."
>
> -Isaiah 43:1-3

Walking the 12 Steps with Jesus Christ

STEP 1

ADDICTION - A DEADLY TRAP

To admit that we are powerless over our addiction is totally against most of the messages we receive from the world around us each day. The world tells us - "Be strong! You are the master of your own life! You can make it on your own! You don't need anyone to help you!" To admit that we are powerless (have no power) over something as painful as our addiction conflicts with the messages we hear from the world and from our past.

On top of all this, our habit tells us, "You've got it all under control! You can use more of me; you can handle it!" What a trap we are caught up in. We listen to the world around us; then we hear the voice of our habit inside of us and finally we see the terrible consequences of our life. It is in ruins, a real mess.

Finally, in desperation, we cry out, "What is the right way anyway? I'm all messed up and can't stand myself! Where is the right path? How can I be saved from this mess, this trap that I have fallen into?"

OUR POWERLESSNESS

The central and most important theme of the 12 step recovery program is to admit to myself first, and then to others, that "I am powerless over my addiction - that it has me by the throat and that my life is out-of-control as a result of it!" To make this admission and to BELIEVE IT is the first, important step toward recovery. To refuse to believe it, or to play mind games with this fact, is to continue to be trapped in addiction. Further, our refusal to stand up and make this statement before others, and believe it, will continue to lock us up in the prison of our addiction. If we cannot or will not make this admission to ourselves, and to others, we will continue to think that we can "handle it". That is not true, as our past life has so strongly demonstrated. This attitude is the very reason we have fallen into the pit of our habit. If we could handle it, we would have already done so and would not be in the situation we are in today.

We are powerless over our habits and today is the day to admit it and to begin the process of healing and recovery.

HOW ADDICTION WORKS - The Cycle

In order to break the bondage of our addiction, we must first understand what an addiction is and how it controls our lives. The following five steps describe the cycle or process of addiction:

1. **PAIN IN THE INNER SPIRIT** - Deep within, some thing is very wrong. We are troubled and confused. Nothing in life seems to come out right and we can't seem to find the problem or fix it. As a result, we experience inner pain and hurt and may not know why.

2. **WE SEEK RELIEF FROM THIS PAIN** - The pain becomes unbearable and so we desperately look for some way to put out that hurt. We reach out to a substance or some behavior that will make us feel better.

3. **WE USE - OR WE DO IT** - Finally we find something that will help to put out the fire of our unhappiness and we use or we do it. We medicate ourselves and we wind up becoming a very different person - gradually we become a slave to a compulsive substance and/or habit.

4. **WE GET DRUNK** - In our search for relief, we finally get drunk - we retreat into an addictive fantasy that relieves our pain. It's a dream world that seems to make us feel better inside. BUT, that fantasy also creates an out-of-control person who is acting in a very difficult and insane manner. We find ourselves drunk and totally out-of-control.

5. **WE HIT BOTTOM AND, OUT OF NECESSITY, WE SOBER UP** - Sooner or later, our bodies cannot stand the strain and our wallets are empty. We have reached the end of the road. It's time to sober up; but oh, what a mess we have made of our lives. The hangover is bad enough, but then we look at the wreckage of our own lives and the lives of the people around us. Our situation is worse, much worse, than when we started, and now all we want is to retreat back into our drunken state to escape the consequences and pain again.

Such is the insane cycle of addiction. It makes no difference who we are, how intelligent or powerful we are, we are now totally out-of-control as a result of the habit which has made us a prisoner of its power.

ADDICTION - ITS CAUSES

In the preceding section, we have seen just how addiction affects us once we step forth and become involved. In paragraph 1, we notice that we find ourselves with severe pain and hurt in our inner person - we feel down and totally unable to function.

The first and most basic cause of addiction is pain in the inner self. We don't have a good image of ourselves and we struggle with problems in our life that seem to overwhelm us. This hurt and pain is the single most prominent cause of our addiction. What causes this hurt and pain, and the method of healing that pain, will be studied in future lessons. For now, we need to acknowledge that this pain is

---

Step 1 Lesson 2

"I admit that (*By myself -without Jesus*) I am powerless over my addiction, that my life has become unmanageable."

Action Word: ADMIT

Step 1 Lesson 2

"I admit that (*By Myself -without Jesus*) I am powerless over my addiction, that my life has become unmanageable."

Action Word: ADMIT

STEP 1

the primary cause that drives us to medicate ourselves in a desperate effort to put the fire of that pain out.

The second cause of addiction is the influence or pressure we can receive from our peers and the world around us. We sometimes allow people we know to indirectly influence us toward addiction and unhealthy behavior. We see how they use crack cocaine, alcohol, marijuana, or any other substance and it seems to work for them. We start to consider that maybe it will work for us. We see their methods of coping with worry, fear, anger, anxiety, relationships, and difficult situations and we decide to try those methods ourselves. Then there is the friendly, direct invitation we can sometimes receive to try something new. Our need for relationship, acceptance, belonging, and love will many times cause us to cross the thresholds of doors that we would otherwise keep closed.

The third cause of addiction is our tremendous appetite for pleasure along with our hatred of boredom. The entertainment industry and internet are flourishing like never before. At times, music, videos, television, computers, smart phones, movies, magazines, and social media can seem to push us towards unhealthy ways of expressing ourselves and feeling good. The assault on our senses and the appeal to our emotions is ongoing. We can have immediate access to substances, illicit lyrics, pornography, and all kinds of inappropriate material that can fan the flame of our normal appetites way beyond our control. Marketing and advertising tactics convince us that we are incomplete, inadequate, and unfulfilled. We begin to practice what we see and we start seeking the products that will no longer leave us lacking. A balanced amount of pleasure and entertainment within the boundaries God has set for us is healthy, but obsession with the pleasures of life is addiction.

These three causes of addiction become a part of us. Please take some time right now and think about the following questions:

1. Do I hurt inside over something(s) that happened to me in the past - something that I cannot seem to let go of?
2. Have I practiced my habit because I am trying to keep up with my friends? Do I feel pushed by them into practicing my addiction?
3. Have I become hooked on the pleasurable "high" which I get from practicing my addiction?

BY MYSELF - I AM POWERLESS OVER MY ADDICTION.

The good news is that there is an answer to this problem. But that answer does not come by continuing to try to fix this problem by ourselves. By ourselves, we will NEVER be able to correct this problem. Our addiction will destroy us. Yes, kill us in the end if we persist in trying to fix it ourselves.

The good news is that our Savior Jesus Christ came to save us from this mess. In John 10:10 Jesus says, "The thief (devil) comes only in order to steal, kill, and destroy. I have come that you might have life - life in all its fullness." If we rely upon our own power, we will get steadily worse and die from our habits. If we come to Jesus and receive His life, we will recover, be healed and live a Holy Spirit filled life.

ADDICTION LEADS TO DESTRUCTION

Our past behavior and experience with our habits teach us that they don't get better on their own. We may have short temporary "clean times", but sooner or later, we fall again and again. This causes us to experience the frustration and hopeless feelings that continue to fuel our addiction more and more. We wind up doing more of it than before instead of less. This is our insanity, our out-of-control behavior.

An important question that we must constantly ask ourselves is this, "If I can handle it myself, why haven't I already done so? Why is my life such a mess?" Over and over again we must "talk to ourselves" and admit and believe that we are powerless (we have no power) over our addiction - that, by myself, I can't stop.

This requires patience and determination. How easy it is to slide back into the old me. How difficult it is to stand up and admit that I can't do it by myself, only with Jesus Christ can I change my life.

THE FEAR OF WITHDRAWAL

There are two factors that tend to keep us locked up in the prison of our addiction. The first is fear, which is our inner feeling of hopelessness and frustration. We become afraid to want to make the change that is so necessary in our lives. We have lived under the deception of our addiction for so long that it becomes a very, very hard habit to break. Down deep in our subconscious mind, we fear walking away from this familiar, comfortable way of handling our problems. We may even get to the point of saying that we "like" our addiction - if only the after affects would go away.

STEP 1

Step 1 Lesson 2

"I admit that (*By myself - without Jesus*) I am powerless over my addiction, that my life has become unmanageable."

Action Word: ADMIT

Deep in our mind, we have gotten used to handling our problems in this way and the thought of a new way, over which we have no control, frightens us.

There seems to be a struggle going on in our mind. One part says that it is OK to handle the problem in the way we have always done it. Sure it causes problems, but it does relieve the pain and we won't let go until we find a new and better way. Another part of our mind tells us that our past has been a real mess and that something drastic needs to be done to correct the situation. It's time to deal with the problem now.

If we fall into the trap of listening to our old habit, we will continue in our insanity and drunkenness. Old bad habits die hard, but die they must. It is time to stand up and admit that BY MYSELF I can't correct the problem. I need help, and only Jesus Christ can help me. Only He can heal me and bring me back to being a normal person. That is the only way to lasting and real recovery.

The devil, the father of lies, will tenaciously tempt us to retreat back into our old life. As the scripture states in John 10:10, the devil is a thief, a murderer, and a destroyer. Beware of this trap and know that Jesus Christ stands ready to help us all overcome our past addictions and sins.

DENIAL - PROJECTION

The second factor that keeps us locked up in our addiction is denial and the resulting tendency to project fault for our addiction onto another person or situation.

Denial is a mind game in which we refuse to accept life the way it actually is and change it mentally to suit our addictive fantasy. Instead of dealing with life around us the way it actually is, we try to change that reality into some fantasy situation that makes us look and feel better inside. We say to ourselves - "This situation isn't really this way; rather, it is some other way." We tend to blame others for our problems; and, we look for ways out of the mess that our addiction has created.

This attitude blinds us and shields us from taking an honest look at our problem. We are hiding behind our contrived fairytale to escape from the real source of our problem, our spiritual sickness. Instead, we look for an easy way out and wind up fueling our addiction. This results in an emotional and mental roller coaster ride that just won't quit. We are either up really "high" or way down in the dumps.

Some of the common denial messages we tell ourselves are:

"I can stop anytime I want to. Things aren't really that bad."

"I only practice my addiction because I want to. It's the "in" thing to do. I need my friends, etc."

To take this denial one step further, we begin to transfer, or project, the blame for our behavior over to someone else. Here are some examples of that problem:

"You make me do what I do! It's all your fault. If you weren't this _____ way, I wouldn't have a drug/alcohol problem."

"If my boss wasn't this _____ way, if he would only do it my way and see my point, I would stay sober."

Denial is failure to face the problems that are within me. Since we, alone, are unable to face the problems within us, we project them onto some other person or situation outside of ourselves. We end up using someone or blaming someone else for our problem when, in reality, the problem lies deep within us.

HITTING BOTTOM

Breaking out of this attitude of denial generally requires a painful encounter with the consequences of our addictive life style. These consequences are called "hitting bottom". "Hitting bottom" forces us to take a long careful look at ourselves from the inside out. It causes us to ask, "Hey, just who do we think we are and what are we doing to ourselves?" "Hitting bottom" forces us to admit our powerlessness over our addictive life style and to look at ourselves the way we really are. We have been stopped "dead in our tracks" and forced to take a good look at our life. Some "hitting bottom" places are: a detox center, a mental institution, a hospital bed, a wheel chair, a jail cell or prison, a physical sickness or disability caused by the addiction. Anything that confines us and prevents us from freely moving around is a "hitting bottom" situation. We have been caught in our own trap, the prison of our own addiction. We are being forced to look at ourselves just the way things really are.

Our next question is to ask - "Where do I go from here?" We now find ourselves totally powerless over the area of our life that involves our addictive habit. We are powerless over that which controls us. We seem to be caught in a hopeless trap in which there is no way out.

The answer - we must surrender our lives to a power greater than ourselves. We have to surren-

Step 1 Lesson 2

"I admit that (*By Myself -without Jesus*) I am powerless over my addiction, that my life has become unmanageable."

Action Word: ADMIT

---

der again and again as we admit our powerlessness over our lives. The "Higher Power" we seek is God - the God of Jesus Christ, the God of the Holy Bible, for He is the ONLY one who can help us to successfully overcome.

In my own life, it took nearly 50 years of addiction and painful struggle to learn that God is the answer. God spoke to me and told me that if I were able to heal myself, He would have given me that power. But since I could not do it myself, nor could anyone else for that matter, then He did not give me the power to heal myself. Instead, He calls us to Himself for our healing.

MULTIPLE ADDICTIONS

Chances are very good that we suffer from a combination of addiction problems - not just one. These problems come from our past life and will be discussed later on in this study guide. In Lesson 1 you were asked to identify all habits or addictions over which you have no control. Our task, for the moment, is to recognize and admit that we are powerless over some people, places, substances, and situations. We must actually let those things go, to release them from our inner lives and thinking. The Good News of Jesus Christ is that He heals all of our addictions at the same time regardless of the type of addiction. In this regard, we have this beautiful prayer by Reinhold Niebuhr:

THE SERENITY PRAYER

GOD, grant me the serenity to accept the things I cannot change - (others);
the courage to change the things that I can - (me);
and the wisdom to know the difference -
(Your way Lord)!

SWITCHING ADDICTIONS

If we do not, or will not, release to God each problem in our life over which we have no control, we will probably end up switching addictions from one kind to another or acquire a new addiction in addition to the old ones. Our drive to find an answer for our hurt inside will cause us to try one addiction after another in a hopeless quest for the answer. The solution is not to find another addiction; but rather, to bring out that hurt and pain and give it to Jesus Christ, who will heal it. As we do this, we will heal inside; the hurt and pain will subside; and we will have no further need for the medication of our addiction to cover up the hurt or make it feel better. It will have been healed by and through the power of Jesus Christ. Switching addictions is not the answer - Jesus Christ is.

THE ADDICTION ROLLER COASTER

For those of us who are addicted, control, or lack of it, is at the core of every part of our lives. When we begin to admit and bring out our powerlessness, healing begins to take place. When we are addicted, we behave in extremes of under or over control. Our behavior becomes out of balance; we have gone off the deep end. When we admit our powerlessness to God, to ourselves and to another, we open the door for the great healer, Jesus Christ. Only He can create a healthy balanced life in which we can lessen and eliminate the addictive behavior we have acquired. We can and will begin to experience greater positive control in our life as we become healed. We will then become a person in control rather than an insane addict out of control.

HAVE COURAGE - JESUS CHRIST HEALS

We should not fear admitting our powerlessness. Rather than feeling inadequate and down, our admission helps us to feel relief that we finally have come to grips with our problem. It takes a strong person to face God, themselves, and another in a serious effort toward change and growth in life.

Anyone can run from the problem. Admitting our powerlessness leads to submitting our will to God's will so that we can be healed and become the most effective and complete person that He created us to be. When we finally give up on "my way" and begin to live "God's way", we sense a wonderful feeling of freedom and peace. We begin to receive new life in Jesus Christ just as the Bible promises. See John 11:25-26.

We no longer need to lie to self or another (denial). We need not fear withdrawal; nor play "head games"; nor sink to the "bottom" of life. Rather, we have come to God's holy mountain and we are climbing out of the bottom of the pit of despair to the top of that mountain by His help and grace. We are being healed.

Remember, God did not create you and me to get through this life successfully without Jesus. In John 14:6 Jesus tells us - "I am the way, the truth, and the life; no one goes to the Father except by me". Trying to get through life successfully without Jesus is impossible and most miserable. He calls us to come to Him. When we do, we are healed; and we find the right way.

STEP 1

Step 1 Lesson 2

"I admit that (*By myself -without Jesus*) I am powerless over my addiction, that my life has become unmanageable."

Action Word: ADMIT

SCRIPTURE STUDY:

The following scriptures are related to Step 1. Look each scripture up in your Bible and carefully read around it, before and after the verse given. Study this scripture - pray and reflect on it. Then answer this question for each scripture: How does this scripture speak to me regarding Step 1 and my powerlessness over my addiction. Please write the answers on a separate sheet of paper.

- ☐ Numbers 11:10-17
- ☐ Psalm 30:10-12
- ☐ Psalm 116:1-11
- ☐ Psalm 31:9-10
- ☐ Psalm 147:10-20
- ☐ Psalm 31:22
- ☐ Jeremiah 9:23-24
- ☐ Psalm 34:18
- ☐ Mark 5:21-29
- ☐ Psalm 38:1-9
- ☐ Luke 13:10-13
- ☐ Psalm 39:4-5
- ☐ John 15:5
- ☐ Psalm 40:17
- ☐ Romans 5:1-6
- ☐ Psalm 42:6-8
- ☐ 2 Corinthians 1:9
- ☐ Psalm 44:15-16
- ☐ 2 Corinthians 10:3-4
- ☐ Psalm 55:4-8
- ☐ Ephesians 3:16-18
- ☐ Psalm 69:1-4
- ☐ Hebrews 11:32-34

> Doubt sees the obstacle,
> faith sees the way.
> —*Anonymous*

> Jesus said - "I am the vine, and you are the branches. Those who remain in Me, and I in them, will bear much fruit; for you can do nothing without Me."
> —*John 15:5*

> I can't handle it Lord, you take over.
> —*Anonymous*

> God said to us humans, "To be wise, you must have reverence for the Lord. To understand, you must turn from evil."
> —*Job 28:28*

Walking the 12 Steps with Jesus Christ

Step 1 Lesson 3

"I admit that (*By Myself* -without *Jesus*) I am powerless over my addiction, that my life has become unmanageable."

Scripture:
MEDITATIONS

MEDITATIONS

The following daily meditations regarding this step are provided for your study, reflection, and prayer. Be sure to read before and after the scripture given. Please study at least one meditation each day during the coming week. Meditate on each scripture and the written commentary. Reflect on it and let it sink into your mind and spirit.

DAY ONE - Study Matthew 9:36

In this step, we are asked to look at ourselves squarely in the eye. We are asked to recognize our powerlessness, declare it, and to see clearly the unmanageability of our addicted lifestyle. We find ourselves in a very strange condition - the more we try to compulsively control ourselves and others around us through the practice of our addiction, the more out of control we become.

Basically, we are very insecure persons trying desperately to find our way in life. We have become totally confused and lost. We struggle to find security and purpose in life by hiding our hurts and acting out the pain of our problems in drugs, alcohol or some other extreme thinking behavior. We may become occupied with health, bodily, or sexual functions in a search for some kind of physical "heaven". Or, we may try to prop up our own broken-down self worth by allowing a love partner to become everything to us.

The reading today describes our helpless state of affairs. We are caught up in compulsiveness and we are like "lost sheep". We are weary and scattered - torn apart and separated from the flock by the "hell" we have slipped into. Yet, in verse 35, we see Jesus going about visiting the people, preaching about the Kingdom, bringing the Good News and healing every kind of disease and sickness. We see the True Shepherd, Jesus Christ, bringing His great love and compassion to heal the lost sheep. He is always right there to help us and save us from the mess we have created. This 12 step walk with Jesus shows us how to deal with our addiction/powerlessness and resulting unmanageability. We are on the road to recovery.

DAY TWO - Study Romans 7:18-20

Two symptoms of our addiction are: 1) The gradual loss of our sense of who we are; and 2) The progressive throwing away, or loss, of our sense of self worth. This scripture describes our situation - "I am no longer the one who does it; instead, it is the sin that lives in me" (Verse 20)

In looking at our problems and ourselves, we ask: "Is the dog wagging the tail, or is the tail wagging the dog? Just who is in control here; is it me, or is it the sin in me?" Sober, Jim is a hard working honest man who loves his wife and children. Drunk, Jim is out of control - a man who steals, lies, gets violent, cheats on his wife, and is a "bear" to live with. Sober, the dog is wagging the tail. Drunk, the tail is wagging the dog.

Suddenly, I see a big red warning sign that asks this question: "DO I DO WHAT I SHOULD NOT DO? Am I in control or out of control of my life?" To recognize that I am out of control is the beginning of the awareness of our addiction. To admit that I am powerless over this out-of-control behavior is my first step. When I make this admission and STICK TO IT, I am on the road to recovery.

DAY THREE - Study Psalm 6:2-4

It is our human nature to want to be (and to believe that we are) in complete control of our lives and the circumstances around us. Fortunately, some people come to a point in their lives when they realize that this is just not possible or even desirable. These people are fortunate. They have not fallen into the pit of addiction and its consequences. They admitted, long before reaching "bottom", that they were powerless and had come to the end of their own physical resources.

Walking the 12 Steps with Jesus Christ

MEDITATIONS

Step 1 Lesson 3

"I admit that (*By myself -without Jesus*) I am powerless over my addiction, that my life has become unmanageable."

Scripture: MEDITATIONS

Many of us, who are stubborn and have failed to admit our powerlessness over our habits and attitudes, have continued to sink into the pits of the hell of our addiction. The scripture talks of this as it says: "I am worn out, O Lord; have pity on me! Give me strength; I am completely exhausted and my whole being is deeply troubled." (Verse 2) Here is King David, a strong valiant warrior, admitting his weaknesses, his emotional collapse. His life has become out of control and he is deeply troubled.

But instead of being defeated by his problem, David has actually placed himself in the strongest possible position when he says: "Come and save me, Lord; in your mercy rescue me from death." (Verse 4) Without God, David admits that he will die. Can you admit that you will die if you continue on the road that you have taken? Can you cry out to the Lord for help? Like David, you can be free to overcome the emptiness and unhappiness of your addiction. But first, you must admit your own powerlessness over your life. You must surrender trying to manage things yourself - in your own strength. You must recognize, "I can't do it myself!" and mean it. When you can do that, you are on the road to recovery.

DAY FOUR - Study Psalm 31:9-10

David cries out: "I am completely worn out!" (Verse 9) For those of us who have fallen victim to our crippling addictions, such a cry is necessary if we are to fully surrender our broken lives to Jesus.

We may think that to admit our brokenness, powerlessness and helplessness is to admit defeat. In reality, however, if we can admit to this condition and BELIEVE IT, we have taken the first, important step toward healing, recovery, and victory. The strange fact of our condition is that we must give up in order to win.

Usually, we cannot admit our powerlessness until we have first taken a good look at the size and horror of what our addiction has cost us. Maybe we should make a list of the losses we have suffered as a result of this problem. This list might include such things as: loss of our job or career, loss of a high school diploma or college education, loss of close family relationships and friends, loss of our spouse or a person we love very dearly, loss of the children we have borne, or loss of our relationship with God. Only as we look back and begin to appreciate the full grief and impact of these losses, can we approach the total surrender, the "I give up" required of us by Step 1 of this program. Only when we acknowledge our guilt and failure, and take responsibility for it, can we hope to be healed. To admit our failure and defeat is not our death; rather, it is the very act that will allow us to be healed and saved. In practice, it will bring us "New Life". This is exactly what David did in our reading today. He came to the Lord and pleaded for mercy, admitting his powerlessness, and was eventually healed. (Verses 21-22) We must do the same. When we believe and confess this first step and mean it, we have a new life ahead of us. We are on the road to recovery.

DAY FIVE - Study Psalm 38:1-15

In Acts 13:22, God calls David "the kind of man I like, a man who will do all I want him to do." We would think that such a man, so close to the heart of God, would do everything God wanted him to do; and live his life in oneness with and perfect obedience to God. In short, you would think that David would have had his life "all together".

But this Psalm shows us that David did not live up to that image and experienced periods of sin and despair. David fell into the addiction of sexual lust, which led to a murder plot. As a result, David had to go back to "square one". In this Psalm, he mourns over how messed up his life has become. He has drifted away from God and has fallen into the clutches of the devil himself. David "did it his way". Because of this, he admits that he is foolish (verse 5); and, that he is crushed by his own behavior (verse 4). He is in great spiritual pain (verse 8). In verse 9, he calls out to the Lord. Still, surrender does not come easily for King David. Maybe you can identify with King David as you read these 15 verses. Is David's prayer your prayer?

Walking the 12 Steps with Jesus Christ

Christian 12 Step Ministry, Inc

Step 1 Lesson 3

"I admit that (*By Myself -without Jesus*) I am powerless over my addiction, that my life has become unmanageable."

Scripture :
MEDITATIONS

"A sinner is one who follows the way of sinfulness;
A saint is one who follows the way of Godliness."
-Ray Geisel

But it is the spirit of Almighty God that comes to us and gives us wisdom.
-Job 32:8

Old habits die hard.
-Anonymous

I trust in the Lord for safety.
-Psalm 11:1

MEDITATIONS

As with King David, the difficult part of this struggle with addiction is letting go of the things that cause us misery. Like David, we have struggled long and hard in our addictive lifestyle. David struggled with his problem for 14 verses. His heart was greatly troubled - but - in verse 15 he turns to the Lord. What a wonderful hope belongs to David and to us - "But I trust in you, O Lord; and you, O Lord my God, will answer me". (Verse 15) It's only by admitting and believing, that we are powerless over that which controls us, that we can open the door to our healing. We must take this first step very firmly and never deny it. When we do, we have made a healthy beginning on our road to recovery.

DAY SIX - Study Psalm 44:13-16

Our sense of shame is one of the most poisonous emotions we can ever experience. This sense of shame drives us deeper into our addiction in an effort to escape or compensate for the loss of our self-worth. Thousands of years ago, David speaks of the shame that he suffered when his neighbors "mock us and laugh at us". (Verse 13)

What is this shame that can cover us and paralyze us? We may feel shame about turning our back on God. We may harbor shame feelings about our inability to overcome our addiction or compulsive behavior. We may feel shame because of the hurt and pain that we have caused those we love the most. We may feel shame about some of the "bad stuff" that happened to us in our childhoods.

In Step 1 of our journey we face a turning point. Will we allow this flood of guilt and shame to overtake, drown, and drive us back into our addictions and compulsions? Or will we give up and admit that we are powerless and helpless over this "thing" in our lives? Can we begin to look outside of ourselves to a power much greater than ourselves for the solution? We have the choice - it's ours to make.

Are you willing to let go and admit that you tried to correct the problem and failed; that you cannot correct the problem; that you are now ready for help? Can you let go and begin to turn to God? Can you admit your powerlessness and reach out for healing? When you do - and only then - will you be on the road to recovery. When you take it back and say: "I can do it myself!" then you will be the loser. What is your choice? Only you can answer that. It is only in saying, "I give up!" that you can be healed and begin down the wonderfully exciting road to recovery.

DAY SEVEN - Study Psalm 72:12-14

Pretending that we are strong and able and "in control" of our lives, keeps us from gaining physical, emotional, and spiritual healing and freedom. The wise King Solomon wrote today's psalm. In this psalm, he shows us that God is ready to rescue any who would humble themselves to cry out to Him for help. We can be delivered from our addiction only when we acknowledge (before our God, ourselves and another) that our lives are unmanageable - that we are out of control. As long as we stay locked up in our pride and we fail to make this admission, we will not begin to see God work in our lives. In fact, our failure to let God into our lives by our stubborn attitude prevents us from being healed. WE, OURSELVES, are the very reason we cannot be healed.

Even when we begin to open up and deal with the problem, we may find ourselves looking to friends and relatives to save or rescue us from the problem. We may even get really "holy" and check into a "program" for 30, 60 days or even six months thinking that the "program" will cure us. This is all a lie of the evil one. There is no one or nothing that can save us from our condition except the mighty power of our God, Jesus Christ. Only when we come to face this fact - that Jesus alone is our final and total source of healing - can we begin to recover and be healed. We must first admit that we are sick in our spirit and cannot heal ourselves. We must turn to Jesus Christ - only then are we on the road to complete recovery.

STEP 2

Step 2 Lesson 4

"I came to believe that a power greater than myself (Jesus Christ) could restore me to sanity"

Action Word: BELIEVE

WHERE DO I GO FROM HERE?

In Step 1, we admitted that, by ourselves without Jesus, we were powerless over our addiction; we were out of control. We also came to understand that there is a solution to our problem since many others have traveled our same path and have overcome. So we ask ourselves - "Who or what is the solution to my problem?" Again, we look to those who have gone before us for the answer. In order to overcome this powerlessness, we must reach out to some power greater than ourselves, and that power is our "Higher Power - the God of Jesus Christ".

At first, the struggling addict may come up with the following thought:

"Look at what you people have done to me! You have convinced me that I am an alcoholic or a drug addict, etc., and that my life is totally out of control - unmanageable you call it. You have reduced me to a state of absolute helplessness, and now you tell me that none but a Higher Power can remove my addiction from me. Maybe I won't believe in this God - or maybe I can't bring myself to believe that this God even exists. I may also have no faith that He will perform a miracle that heals me."

In order to understand the "Higher Power" in this lesson, we will take a good look at some of the attitudes and understandings we have about this God of Jesus Christ. In the next lesson, we will ask ourselves "Who is this God anyway?"

OUR ATTITUDES TOWARD GOD -
Here are some examples:

THE SELF MADE PERSON

First, let's look at the person who just won't believe. He is in a state of mind that is best described as primitive, cave man style. His whole idea of life is that HE IS GOD, and he glorifies himself each moment of each day.

"There's nothing I can't do by myself", he growls when confronted. It's bad enough, he thinks, to admit that an addiction has him down, but now he is faced with something really impossible. If we ask him to step down from his godly throne and take a back seat to God, he'll retort, "Why you guys are nuts!" You see, he is so in love with himself that he has made himself into a god; and now, he cannot and will not admit his helplessness. To submit his life to a "Higher Power," he will have to admit that he is helpless and powerless over the situation. Since his attitude is always one of controlling the situation and his pride and ego are driving him - he will stay "stuck in the mud" of his addiction.

In Exodus 20:3 and Deuteronomy 5:7, God gave Moses the Ten Commandments. God commands Moses, "Worship no other God but Me!" When our pride and ego get in the way and we make ourselves our own god, we are disobeying the first commandment of God. As we walk in this disobedience, our lives will fall apart in complete failure. The only lasting solution is to make the God of Jesus Christ number one in our life. Give Jesus the rightful place and we will overcome.

THE PERSON WHO HAS LOST FAITH

Let us now consider the condition of the person who once had faith in God; but, that faith is now cold. Something may have happened along the road of his life; and God did not help him when he needed it, or the way he wanted it.

Now he finds himself rejecting God and even speaking against God. In the past, he tried God and found Him wanting. The way of faith and the way of no faith have failed him, he thinks. He is bitterly disappointed and confused about God. For many of these people, grasping the 12 step program is more difficult than for those who neither knew Jesus nor had any faith. They have tried the way of faith and the way of no faith and found them both empty and powerless. They are lost and seem to have no place to go for the solution to their problems. They may believe like the atheist who denies there is a God or like the agnostic who says, "God cannot be proved." These people suffer from mass confusion. They are totally lost and wander through life with no purpose or direction. They have nothing and nobody but themselves to believe in. They float through life getting kicked around by one storm after another.

Many of these people were introduced to God in their childhood, but the ways and pleasures of the world lured them away from God. They began to become self-made and they either did not care about God or they rejected God completely. Life was a "blast", so they thought, and they were out to get all they could out of it. All they seemed to care about was the here and now. "Who cares about tomorrow -let's just live for today." THEN, along came drugs, alcohol or some other out-of-control habit. It always happens with this type of attitude. As a result, they are dragged down to the pits of hell by the very stuff that was supposed to make them happy and set them on top of the world. Finally, when their scorecard hit zero and they saw that one more strike would cost them their very life, they had to look for their lost faith. It is then, that discovering the AA 12 step program would bring them to sanity and recovery. And so it can for you also.

Step 2 Lesson 4

"I came to believe that a power greater than myself (Jesus Christ) could restore me to sanity"

Action Word: BELIEVE

THE INTELLECTUALS

Then, there are the intellectuals, those who are too smart for their own good. They use their education to blow themselves up into a prideful balloon that seems to piously float above the rest of us. Secretly, they think that brainpower can solve any problem. These are the folks that say, "I can handle it." Their brain told them that that they could do ANYTHING. Their knowledge was all-powerful. Intellect could conquer their human nature. The god of their intellect replaced the God Jesus Christ. Again, this person takes a nosedive right into alcohol, drugs, or some other addiction and winds up an addict- a slave to some habit. His intellect, his "smarts", did not and will not save him. He is out of control and at the bottom of his life. The only hope for him is to reconsider his thinking and make the God of Jesus Christ his first priority. The God of Jesus Christ must come before anything in his life, especially his intellect. He must submit, become humble, and make Jesus Christ number one in his life.

PEOPLE TURNED OFF BY RELIGION

These people are just plain "turned off" by religion and its entire works. They think that the Bible is just a bunch of nonsense. They call it the morality of a bunch of screwball, fanatic religionists. They are quick to point out all of the mistakes of the "Christians" and try to prove that God and religion are just a fake, a business. Again, these people are all hung up on their ego, pride, and intelligence. They have made themselves God, and again, like all of the others, find themselves a slave to some habit that controls them. Self-righteousness and pride have been their downfall. They have bottomed out in their drunken state. Their only hope is the God of Jesus Christ. It is a proven fact that the outstanding trait of addicts is DEFIANCE. They set out on a mad course to "do it my way regardless" and they do not want to change under any circumstances. So it is not strange that they defied God along with those close to them who love and care about them so much. They stubbornly and blindly stand their ground in doing it the way they see it. This bondage of defiance is the very thing that holds them bound to their addiction. They must break the strangle hold of defiance in their attitudes and come to the God who created all of us and came to "save us" from ourselves. They must believe in Him. Belief means RELIANCE ON GOD-not defiance of Him. The whole key to the success of the 12 step recovery program is BELIEF AND SURRENDER TO GOD. Over the past seventy plus years of the AA program, millions of people have been healed of their addiction by believing and surrendering to the power of God. You can too. But surrender to Him you must -we all must, if we are to be healed and expect to succeed.

THE FAITH FILLED PERSON WHO STILL FALLS

Now let's take the person who is full of faith, but still gets drunk on his addiction. He's stuck on God and his religious practice is nearly perfect. But, he still gets drunk, high, or demonstrates some other insane behavior. He seems to be doing everything right in his life except that he still gets high or drunk at times. He tries to fight his addiction imploring God's help but help does not seem to come. What then can be the matter?

To almost everyone around him -ministers, doctors, counselors, friends and family -this is a heartbreaking problem. But to those in this program with the same problem, it is not. The answer has to do with the-QUALITY OF FAITH rather than the QUANTITY OF FAITH. This was his blind spot. He imagined that he possessed humility when, in reality, he did not. He supposed that he was serious about his relationship with God when, in reality, he was not. He was playing games with God, "head games", and his heart got hurt. He may have become all wrapped up in emotionalism and mistook it for true spirit-filled feelings. The fact was, that he had not cleaned house in his inner, spiritual life so that the Grace of God could enter him and expel the compulsiveness of his addiction. He had not gotten really serious in his spirit about cleaning house and coming to the God of Jesus Christ as his Higher Power. He had been playing "head games" with God, himself and those around him. He did not understand or experience the loving, healing touch of God because he had not given into the God of Jesus Christ. He had not turned his ENTIRE SELF over to God. Therefore, he remained self-deceived and was incapable of receiving the grace or help of God to restore him to sanity. Even though he went through all the motions externally, he had not gotten right with God deep down inside.

Few of us are able to admit how irrational and insane we really are under these situations. We have become masters of deception and denial. We call ourselves "problem" or "borderline" drinkers, druggers or addicts. We must admit that we are out of control in our thinking -we suffer from a spiritual or mental sickness.

"Sanity" is defined as soundness of the mind. When we admit that we have "blown it" and we turn to our "Higher Power" -Jesus Christ -for healing, we have taken the most important step to recovery, which results in sanity and soundness of the mind.

STEP 2

Step 2 Lesson 4

"I came to believe that a power greater than myself (Jesus Christ) could restore me to sanity"

Action Word: BELIEVE

THE ROAD TO NEW LIFE

1. Get sober and stay sober. Don't try to swallow the 12 Step program all at once. Take your time, working through the 12 Steps slowly and carefully.

2. Have an open mind. Regardless of how you have believed up until now, you can believe anew, "I believe! Constantly help my weakness of faith!"—Mark 9:24, Amplified Bible. Understand and accept that you don't have all the answers. Be determined to search for them and find them.

3. Step 2 is the beginning of a turning point. With a true and humble heart, come to believe that the power greater than yourself is Jesus Christ. Believe that He will restore you to sanity, a sound mind. Begin to listen and learn from Him. You will overcome and be healed as your faith grows.

UNDERSTANDING THE BATTLE— BODY, SOUL, & SPIRIT

We have just examined some attitudes that we may have towards God. Now we will take a look at why we are sometimes ruled by these attitudes instead of the Holy Spirit. The areas of the body, the spirit, and the soul have been studied by many and in great depth. Our intention is to keep the explanations brief, but helpful so you are able to better understand the battle you face.

The following explains how you exist as body, soul, and spirit:

Body—"Don't you realize that your body is the temple of the Holy Spirit, who lives in you and was given to you by God? You do not belong to yourself." (1 Corinthians 6:19)

Think of your body as the container for your soul and your spirit. The five senses of hearing, seeing, smelling, tasting, and touching are part of your body. Your senses help you discern and understand your environment. Your body desires things such as food and sexual pleasure. Your body will follow the rule of your soul. This is why it is so important that we allow our spirit to be filled with the Holy Spirit and rule our soul. Your body can be healthy, sick, or injured. When it is sick or injured, it requires the proper attention to restore its health.

Soul—"Now, may the God of peace make you holy in every way, and may your whole spirit and soul and body be kept blameless until our Lord Jesus Christ comes again. God will make this happen, for he who calls you is faithful." (1 Thessalonians 5:23-24)

The soul consists of your mind, will, and emotions. Your mind includes your thoughts, thinking processes, imagination, intentions, reasoning, and rationalization. Your will includes your wants, desires, and wishes which influence the decisions and choices you make. Your emotions include your feelings and affections and are often stirred by your five senses. Emotions can also be stirred by our thinking, which is why it is so important we become disciplined in our thinking and thought processes.

Our soul is often not fully set on or yielded to the things of God. The conflicts within our soul cause the majority of our problems. Just like the body needs the proper care when it is sick or injured, the soul also needs the proper care and attention when it is sick, injured, or functioning outside of God's will.

Spirit—"For the word of God is alive and powerful. It is sharper than the sharpest two-edged sword, cutting between soul and spirit, between joint and marrow (a reference to the body). It exposes our innermost thoughts and desires." (Hebrews 4:12)

When "spirit" is written in the Bible with a capital letter, it refers to the Holy Spirit of God. When "spirit" is spelled with a lowercase "s" it may refer to the spirit of man or it can indicate an evil spirit such as any agent of the devil. Here, we are discussing "spirit" as it refers to the spirit of man. (Strauss, 2004)

Your spirit consists of your intuition, conscience, and the part of you that is able to commune with God. **Intuition** is a sensing to do or NOT to do something that seems to occur without a reason or cause. **Conscience** points out and convicts you of sin, but it also points out and approves when you're acting righteously. **Communion** is intimate communication with God. (Nee, 1993, 52-64)

In Romans 10:9 we are told that when we openly declare that Jesus is Lord and believe in our heart that God raised him from the dead we are saved. It is at this time that the Holy Spirit comes to reside within our spirit. At this time, our spirit is resurrected from death (an eternal separation from God) to life with God forever through Christ. Colossians 1:12-14 tells us, "…He has enabled you (us) to share in the inheritance that belongs to His people, who live in the light. For He has rescued us from the kingdom of darkness and transferred us into the Kingdom of His dear Son, who purchased our freedom and forgave our sins."

With this brief understanding of the body, spirit, and soul, hopefully you can see that although you may have the Holy Spirit residing in your spirit, your soul may not be fully submitted and ruled by the Holy Spirit. Once you have accepted Christ as your personal Lord and Savior, it is important to

Step 2 Lesson 4

"I came to believe that a power greater than myself (Jesus Christ) could restore me to sanity"

Action Word: BELIEVE

ask the Holy Spirit to *fill* your soul that you may be: **transformed**—"Don't copy the behavior and customs of this world, but let God transform you into a new person by changing the way you think. Then you will learn to know God's will for you, which is good and pleasing and perfect."—Romans 12:2, **renewed**—"Put on your new nature, and be renewed as you learn to know your Creator and become like him."—Colossians 3:10, **restored**—"Lord, your discipline is good, for it leads to life and health. You restore my health and allow me to live!"—Isaiah 38:16 "Restore to me the joy of your salvation, and make me willing to obey you."—Psalms 51:12 "For since our friendship with God was restored by the death of his Son while we were still his enemies, we will certainly be saved through the life of his Son."—Romans 5:10, and **preserved**—"For the glory of your name, O Lord, preserve my life. Because of your faithfulness, bring me out of this distress."—Psalms 143:11 "You gave me life and showed me your unfailing love. My life was preserved by your care."—Job 10:12

WE CAME TO BELIEVE

In this step, we finally get to the point where we "come to believe." This "coming to believe" process that we must go through is essential to us on our continuing road to recovery. A portion of the tradition of the twelve steps program defines this coming to believe as a three part unfolding. First, we admit that we are powerless over our addiction; second, we come to believe in a power greater than ourselves; third, we finally embrace and surrender our will and life to that God of power Jesus Christ.

In the unfolding of our new life:

1. We admit our powerlessness, that is, we showed up and stumbled in the door of our first AA type meeting.

2. We came to believe in God. We came to our senses and sobered up and began to experience emotional sobriety. We began to relate to God as the one who can and will heal us.

3. We surrender ourselves to the God of Jesus Christ. We came to believe in God and released ourselves to his power in our lives.

This begins our real recovery process and spiritual growth. This method of spiritual growth is the same method demonstrated by the life of Jesus Christ of the Holy Bible. It is the born-again experience which Jesus describes in John 3:5, and is the description of our recovery process. It is the process of our spiritual rebirth by water and the coming of the Holy Spirit that will be described in future lessons.

STEP 2

Step 2 is a very logical outgrowth of Step 1. In Step 1, we admit our powerlessness; therefore, it is quite logical to seek after some "Higher Power" that becomes a new source of strength and power to change us and bring us to sanity. This is Step 2. For some people, spiritual conversion, this change in direction, is as dramatic as it was for the apostle Paul, described in Acts 9. But for most of us, however, it is a very gradual process. As we grow and mature emotionally, we also grow spiritually. Conversion, or change of direction, is a learning process. This learning comes through study, experience, example, and teaching. So be patient, you have the rest of your life to arrive at your new self.

OUR SPIRITUAL HOUSE-CLEANING

Before we can welcome in a new power Jesus Christ, to restore us to spiritual wellness, we will probably have to engage in some emotional and spiritual house cleaning.

1. We need to ask God to help us to identify and give up all of the objective agents and behaviors that we have used to meet our deepest cravings and desires.

We need to be willing to give up the alcohol, drugs, sex and other addictions that we have acquired over the years. We need to be prepared to give up anything that controls us over which we have no power. We need to get these things and this behavior off the pedestal that we have placed them on. They must no longer be worshipped as our god. Instead, we must be totally dedicated to overcoming this problem.

2. We need to rise up over the god of our intellect and reason. In other words, we must quit worshipping God with our mind only and begin to worship Him with our heart and spirit.

3. We need to renounce our tendency to play God. We need to admit that we are not God and that we must never again give in to that temptation. If we do, we will be back to our old ways. We will think that WE are in control when, in reality, we are totally out of control. We will have gone right back to our own addictive habits.

4. We need to renounce putting other people or human institutions in the role of God. The God of Jesus Christ is our only source of strength and healing. We must NEVER put anyone or any program over our God. 12 step recovery and overcomer's programs are very helpful but they are intended only to point the way to God and are not to be used instead of God.

Not only do we need to rid ourselves of false gods in our life, we must also overcome old sources of bitterness and anger toward Him:

STEP 2

Step 2 Lesson 4

"I came to believe that a power greater than myself (Jesus Christ) could restore me to sanity"

Action Word: BELIEVE

1. We may have identified God or blamed Him for an abusive parent.
2. We may have had negative experiences with the church or one of its ministers. Our experience with church may have been bad; it may have caused us to blame God for what human clergy or other Christians may have caused.
3. We may have struggled with a sense that God has failed us -that he has allowed us to fall into this pit of addiction.
4. We may be angry that God has not, in an instant, healed us of our addictive illness. We are people who want instant answers to the problems and addictions in our lives.

DEDICATION TO A LIFE OF RECOVERY

As we commit ourselves to a lifetime of recovery, our starting point may be the teaching and instructional literature that we receive. That teaching and literature makes a valuable contribution toward the opening up of our spiritual door so that healing and overcoming can take place. But if we really want to break down the barriers that keep us in bondage to an addiction, we need to turn to the ultimate source of God's word and discover what the scriptures have to tell us. By exploring the Bible, we will learn more about Jesus, we will draw closer to Him, and we will discover more about His will for us. We have opened the door that leads to freedom, our spiritual freedom. John 8:36 -"If the Son sets you free, then you will be really free." And when the spirit is free, so shall the body be free; in fact, the whole of that person is free by the mighty power to which he has reached out -the saving power of Jesus Christ.

To refrain from sin doesn't make us holy; but holiness makes us refrain from sin.
Holiness is living our life -God's way.
-Anonymous

To gain self control, give Jesus Christ control.
-Anonymous

God's spirit made me and gave me life.
-Job 33:4

The Lord said, "I will go with you, and I will give you victory."
-Exodus 33:14

"Go, then, to all peoples everywhere and make them My disciples; Baptize them in the name of the Father, the Son, and the Holy Spirit, and teach them to obey everything I have commanded you and I will be with you always, to the end of the age."
-Matthew 28: 19-20

Walking the 12 Steps with Jesus Christ

Christian 12 Step Ministry, Inc

Step 2 Lesson 5

"I came to believe that a power greater than myself (Jesus Christ) could restore me to sanity"

Action Word: BELIEVE

STEP 2

In Lesson 4, we took a good look at our "Higher Power" who we called the God of Jesus Christ. We examined some of the various concepts and ideas that we might have as we look at God. We looked at many of the "head games" that we play with God that prevents us from having a personal relationship with Him.

WHO IS GOD, JESUS, AND THE HOLY SPIRIT?

Throughout the Bible we read about God as God the Father, God the Son (Jesus), and God the Holy Spirit. We need to understand that God is not three different people, but rather one person experienced three ways. Our intention is not to overwhelm you with a full study of this aspect of God, but to help you better recognize how you may experience Him.

Since we are people and we live and work with people we may tend to see God the same way that we see ourselves or others. We may have a difficult time relating to God as our perfect, heavenly Father if our own earthly father hurt or disappointed us. It is quite possible that our earthly father did not know how or was not able to love us the way we needed to be loved. Therefore, we may be limiting God because we view him through a lens or filter that distorts who He really is.

God is:

Omnipresent—present everywhere at the same time. "God is Spirit", John 4:24, and cannot be confined to a human body or any particular place. "There are not parts of Him spread out in every location. Rather, everything is immediately in His presence. This should be a constant source of comfort, His presence may be experienced at any time or any place. No one can escape God's notice." (www.blueletterbible.org) God existed before anything was and He will exist after everything is gone. He is eternal, without beginning or end, lasting forever. (See Psalm 139:7-12, Proverbs 15:3, Jeremiah 23:23-24, Matthew 18:20, and Hebrews 13:5-6)

Omnipotent—all powerful, having very great or unlimited authority or power (See Genesis 1:1, Job 37:23, Job 42:2, Isaiah 40:28-31, Isaiah 44:24, Jeremiah 32:27, Daniel 2:20-22, Daniel 4:35)

Omniscient—all knowing, having complete, unlimited knowledge, awareness, or understanding (See 1 Chronicles 28:9, Job 28:23-24, Psalm 139:1-6, Psalm 147:5, Jeremiah 1:5, Hebrews 4:13, and 1 John 3:20)

God is experienced as:

God the Father: "Yet for us there is [only] one God, the Father, Who is the Source of all things..."—1 Corinthians 8:6, Amplified Bible. God determined and planned everything from creation to the redemption of man to the day Christ comes for His church and throughout eternity. He is the Creator, author, and originator of all truth and how it affects us. He created us because He wants a relationship with us—He loves us and wants our love in return. "Even before He made the world, God loved us and chose us in Christ to be holy and without fault in His eyes. God decided in advance to adopt us into His own family by bringing us to Himself through Jesus Christ. This is what He wanted to do, and it gave Him great pleasure...And this is the plan: At the right time He will bring everything together under the authority of Christ—everything in heaven and on earth,"—Ephesians 1:4-10. Though God desires to be in a relationship with us, He will not force us into that relationship. We will discuss more about a relationship with God in Step 3.

God the Son: Jesus is God the son. Jesus is called Emmanuel, which means God with us. John 4:24 tells us that God is spirit. In John 6:46 Jesus says that no one had ever seen God, "Not that anyone has ever seen the Father; only I, who was sent from God, have seen Him." Jesus was sent from God and given a body like ours to walk the earth to reveal God to the world. "Christ is the visible image of the invisible God,"—Colossians 1:15. "For in Christ lives all the fullness of God in a human body,"—Colossians 2:9. Jesus says, "I have made Your name known to them and revealed Your character and Your very Self, and I will continue to make [You] known..."—John 17:26, Amplified Bible. Jesus was a clear example of God's love by the way He spoke to, dealt with, and instructed sinners and also by the way He loved the Father, doing His will by dying on the cross that we could be redeemed. "For I have come down from heaven to do the will of God who sent me, not to do my own will...For it is my Father's will that all who see His Son and believe in Him should have eternal life. I will raise them up at the last day."—John 6:38-40. "God sent His Son into the world not to judge the world, but to save the world through Him."—John 3:17. Jesus lived love so we would know how to live love.

God the Holy Spirit: God lives in us as the Holy Spirit. In John 15:26 Jesus tells the disciples that He will send them the Spirit of Truth and in John 16:7 He tells them that the Spirit of Truth will not come unless He goes through the crucifixion, resurrection, and returns to the Father. On the Day of Pentecost, 50 days after Christ's resurrection, the Holy Spirit became available to all who believe. In Acts 2:38 Peter says, "Each of you must repent of

STEP 2

Step 2 Lesson 5

"I came to believe that a power greater than myself (Jesus Christ) could restore me to sanity"

Action Word: BELIEVE

your sins and turn to God, and be baptized in the name of Jesus Christ for the forgiveness of your sins. Then you will receive the gift of the Holy Spirit." Peter says this after an address to a large crowd whose hearts were pierced because they recognized the error of their ways. 3,000 people were added to the church that day showing us that the Holy Spirit is readily available to us through Christ. The Holy Spirit has the mind, will, and emotions of God. The Holy Spirit also has the power of God. Once we turn our will and our life over to God by accepting His son, Jesus, as our Lord and Savior we receive the gift of the Holy Spirit to live in us. Therefore, we now have the power we lacked to overcome. We overcome to the degree that we remain in His strength and His ways and not our own. Paul prays that the Christ followers in Ephesus will "…understand the incredible greatness of God's power for us (them) who believe in Him. This is the same mighty power that raised Christ from the dead and seated Him in the place of honor at God's right hand in the heavenly realms," Ephesians 1:19-20. We need to understand that power is available to us today.

WHO IS GOD TO ME?

In order to stir your thinking and help you see God, see the following list of names for God that can be found in the Bible. Reflect on these names by asking yourself, "Who is God to me? How do I see Him?"

Remember that God is experienced three ways: God the Father, God the Son, and God the Holy Spirit.

God is:

Jesus	Righteous Judge	Advocate	Comforter
Son of God	Emmanuel - God is with us	Resurrection and the Life	Protector
Guider	Lamb of God		The "I AM"
Prince of Peace	Light of the world	God of the Impossible	Healer
Shepherd and Bishop of our souls	Leader	The Way	Provider
	Prince of Life	Governor	Encourager
Forgiver	Head of the Church	Strengthener	Justifier
Messiah	Teacher	The Truth	Redeemer
Savior	Lord God Almighty	The Alpha and Omega	Light of our Way
Way-shower	Morning Star	Renewer	Grantor of Freedom
Mighty God	Sustainer	The Life	Rescuer
Chief cornerstone	Lion of Judah	Lord of Lords	Mighty King
Word of God	Son of Righteousness	Our Victory	Father - Abba - Daddy
Wonderful Counselor	Sign - the Rainbow	Dayspring	Our Best Friend
King of Kings	Author and Finisher	Holy Spirit	The Father's only Son
The Good News	Chief Shepherd	Servant	The Source of our Life
Holy One	All Powerful	Lord of All	To be Praised

Walking the 12 Steps with Jesus Christ

Step 2 Lesson 6

"I came to believe that a power greater than myself (Jesus Christ) could restore me to sanity"

Scripture:
MEDITATIONS

MEDITATIONS

The following daily meditations regarding this step are provided for your study, reflection, and prayer. Be sure to read before and after the scripture given. Please read at least one meditation each day during the coming week. Try to meditate on each scripture and the written commentary. Reflect about it and let it sink into your mind and spirit.

DAY ONE - Study Matthew 12:18-21

What a beautiful picture of Jesus given to us through the prophet Isaiah. (Isaiah 42:1-4). The Father is revealing to us a wonderful description of His Son - Jesus Christ.

In this reading, the Father describes His Son as the Beloved Servant chosen by Him to bring the Father's love to man on earth. The Spirit of the Father will rest upon and in Jesus, and the Father is well pleased. In verses 19 and 20, we read a description of the beautiful gentleness and power of Jesus. In verse 21, we read of the promise of our hope in the Son - Jesus.

Jesus is the Beloved Servant of the mighty God and Father. He came into this world to bring the Father's love to us, His greatest and closest creation. Jesus is so compassionate and concerned about us that He cares for us constantly in a number of ways. He heals our wounded spirits and bodies. He feeds us with the abundance of His creation; He rescues us from our sinfulness and addictive habits; He raises us from death (both physical and spiritual); He calms the storms of our lives and provides for our every need. In addition, Jesus is a gentle and compassionate Savior. He does not force us but calls us gently and faithfully to Himself. And yet, we see the awesome power of Jesus in His command over the sea and the storm.

The same power that the Father gave to Jesus is also available to us through the Holy Spirit of Jesus. Our loving, Father God desires nothing more than to rescue us from the living death of our addiction and dependencies and give us a whole and happy life filled with His precious gifts. However, in order to receive what the Father wishes to give us, we must come to Him through Jesus Christ, His Son. "Will you open your heart and ask Jesus to come into your spirit to heal me?" Only you can do that. What will be your answer?

DAY TWO - Study Mark 9:17-27

We get "stuck" in our damaging addictions and habits. Over the years, we find ourselves chained up and in prison inside over these situations and wonder if we will ever be able to break out and become free again. We are like the young man who was demon possessed. It seems to become a most impossible situation to us. But the words of our Lord through the angel in Luke 1:37 tells us: "For there is nothing that God cannot do!"

In this reading today, we see a frightened and doubting father experience the reality and truth of the words of Luke 1:37. He brought his son, filled with an evil spirit, to Jesus for healing. In words of desperation (verse 22) and at the "end of his rope ready to give up", he pleads with Jesus to heal his son - and a loving and compassionate Jesus does so. In verse 23, Jesus encourages the father to have faith saying, "Everything is possible for the person who has faith!"

The father's response to Jesus was -"I do have faith, but not enough. Help me have more!" Is the cry of that father our cry? Do you hurt inside and want to be healed? Just how much faith is necessary? Let's look at Luke 17:6. We find Jesus speaking to the apostles about faith. He tells them that all that is necessary is faith "as small as a mustard seed". All we need is a little bit of faith in our turning to Jesus. He does the rest!

When we truly want to believe in God's great power to deliver us, He will be there ready to release us from our lack of faith and help us to overcome our bondage. A simple reaching out to receive the hand of Jesus as our best friend is all that is necessary. Are you ready to trust Jesus and begin to let go of your struggle with your addictions? Reach out your hand and heart to Him now. Only He is the answer.

"The will of God will never take you where the grace of God will not protect you."
-Anonymous

The person who loves God is known by Him.
-1 Corinthians 8:3

Walking the 12 Steps with Jesus Christ

MEDITATIONS

Step 2 Lesson 6

"I came to believe that a power greater than myself (Jesus Christ) could restore me to sanity"

Scripture :
MEDITATIONS

DAY THREE - Study Luke 13:10-13

The New Testament contains many accounts of the healing Jesus provided people with all sorts of physical and spiritual sicknesses. This was the sign of the Father's unmistakable and total love for His people, you and me. As in the days of Jesus, our Father still seeks to heal us from the sickness of both our bodies and our spirits. However, in order to be healed, we must bring our sickness to Jesus as the woman did in the reading today.

Since the time of Jesus to the present day, this same loving Jesus, who lives in our midst by the power of His Holy Spirit, has delivered many people from their sicknesses. Not everyone is healed in the same way. Some have received miraculous, instantaneous healing while others have had a slow gradual path of recovery. But the fact remains, whoever sincerely seeks the healing of the Lord Jesus Christ will receive it in time.

While healing from our spiritual and physical sickness is very important to you and to me, it is not the most important goal in our lives. The most important goal to us all is to live in the fullness of the spiritual life that Jesus desires to give us (See John 10:10). We are called into a deeper, more meaningful oneness with our Father through Jesus. There is an old saying that states, "There is a hole inside of our inner spirit large enough to drive a tractor trailer through. Only the love of Jesus Christ can fill that hole for us." You and I are not complete unless the hole in our inner spirit is filled with the love of Jesus. The healing of our addiction is only a stepping stone to a complete and full life in touch with and filled by the love of Christ. Are you willing to accept this Son of the Father, Jesus, into your life as your personal Lord and Savior? Only you can answer that question.

DAY FOUR - Study John 6:63

The terms addiction and codependency are defined by many as an unhealthy reliance on the control of exterior things or people in order to cover up or fill the inside needs of our spirit. In other words, we seek to put out the fire of pain in our spirit by picking up a compulsive, addictive habit that goes about masking and hiding the pain we feel inside. This reading today warns us to beware of seeking the solution to our problems in man's power. The reading clearly states that - "Man's power is of no use at all." The desires of the flesh will not satisfy or heal our spiritual hurts. To believe that satisfying the flesh will heal our spirits is a special form of spiritual insanity. It is a lie of the devil and it is pushed upon us to kill us in the end. Belief in it will pull us down farther and farther into the pits of hell itself.

Step 2 promises us that we shall be restored to sanity (soundness of mind) as we give up the ways of our flesh and turn to the spiritual healer - the God of Jesus Christ. When we take this step and believe in it, we will experience a spiritual rebirth. The old self will have died and a new, beautifully healed self will emerge.

The AA recovery literature describes this rebirth and in-filling of the Holy Spirit in the following way, "As we felt new power flow in, as we enjoyed peace of mind, as we discovered we could face life successfully, as we became conscious of His presence, we began to lose our fear of today, tomorrow or the hereafter. We have become reborn." (Alcoholics Anonymous) Are you willing to let go of yourself into the loving, forgiving healing arms of Jesus Christ to experience a new life? It is your decision - you alone must decide.

DAY FIVE - Study John 12:46

Light and darkness - Jesus speaks of it many times. Just what is He trying to tell us? If you or I, as a little child, are hidden away in the darkness, what would our reaction be when we finally came into the light? I believe that our eyes would be severely impaired and it would be nearly impossible for us to see. In addition, we would see things for the first time that are totally unknown to us. Most of what we now see we would not recognize or understand.

Walking the 12 Steps with Jesus Christ

Step 2 Lesson 6

"I came to believe that a power greater than myself (Jesus Christ) could restore me to sanity"

Scripture : MEDITATIONS

MEDITATIONS

In much the same way, those of us who have struggled with hurts and wrongs from the past may be totally unaware of the extent and the impact of these wrongs now that we are adults. Because of what has happened to us earlier in our lives, we may now find ourselves defiant, resentful, angry, out of control or living in some sort of fantasy world. We don't really recognize or understand why we do the things that we do. We have learned to cope with the difficulties of our past and we have built up an addiction to "get off the hook" of our feelings towards our past. We have learned to use this addiction to protect ourselves from further pain and suffering. In short, we have been living our lives in total darkness. We have learned to cover up this hurt by using an addictive behavior to give us temporary relief from having to deal with our inner self. We become people who are hiding from the stuff that is inside that bothers us in the blackness and despair of our addiction.

The reading today tells us that we must step out into the light of Jesus and when we do we "should not remain in the darkness". Walking in darkness is confusing and gives us a lost feeling. When we come out into the light of Jesus we experience His power and love. We no longer have to hide from ourselves in that crippling darkness. When we step out into His light, He fills us with His love and we can begin to accept ourselves just as we are. We no longer have to hide from others and ourselves. In His light, we can and WILL BE HEALED. We call this light of Christ - Eternal Life. We have truly been born again from the darkness of sin and death into the Light of Christ - Eternal Life. Would you like to leave the darkness of your past life behind you and come into the Eternal Life of Christ? You can, you know. It's your choice and it is free for the asking.

DAY SIX - Study Psalm 18:1-3

In Steps 1 and 2, we are involved in a process called ego/pride deflation. In our lives up until now, we have depended on our own strength and knowledge. Now, we are called to admit that we are out of control in a certain area of our lives. In the past, we have tried, without success, to control and run our lives. Our own efforts have failed miserably to control the enemy of addiction and dependency. Our ego and pride are worthless to us and we now find ourselves at the "bottom of life".

We find ourselves having to make a serious decision. On the one hand, the old self, with its addictions and habits, calls to us and promotes the lie that the practice of alcohol, drugs etc. will give us joy and happiness. On the other hand, we hear the promise of Jesus Christ calling us in this psalm. What shall we do? Our old habits have failed to provide the answer to life and have caused misery and severe pain. Shall we listen to Jesus and come to Him? As we continue to consider the decision, we see two extremes: 1) Our old self leading us to death; 2) Jesus leading us to life. Along with many others around us, we have discovered that our old self and its addictions have failed. There seems to be no other choice but to give up on them and to come to Jesus.

And so, we listen to the Psalmist, David, as he celebrates a God who is "my strong fortress". He turns to the Lord who he calls "my defender". David speaks of God as his protection and "with Him I am safe". David calls to God who "saves me from my enemies". David, like you and I, was brought to the "bottom" of life by an addiction. David sinned in the addiction of sexual lust and resultant murder. David gives up his powerlessness by coming to the Lord and trusting in Him. David realizes that only God can save him.

Our God - Jesus Christ, is calling to you also. He is standing at the door to your heart and knocking. He is asking you to let Him into the very center of your life so that He can help you. (See Revelations 3:20) Are you willing to go to the door of your heart, open it wide and let Jesus in? You don't have to be perfect, for we all have sinned and fallen short of the glory of God. All we have to do is to be WILLING. Are you willing to let Him in? Only you can answer that question.

MEDITATIONS

Step 2 Lesson 6

"I came to believe that a power greater than myself (Jesus Christ) could restore me to sanity"

Scripture :
MEDITATIONS

DAY SEVEN - Study Psalm 142

In this reading, David is surrounded by his enemies. He knows that he cannot escape and that the cave he has hidden in will not save him. His enemy is too strong. David turns to the Lord in this psalm. He looks for the protection of the Lord and asks for deliverance from the danger.

As you and I struggle with our addictive habits and resulting behaviors, we feel that we are facing an impossible enemy, that we are imprisoned in a cave like David. We have been caught in the prison of guilt, fear, frustration, blame and pain. Our very inside is caught up in a tornado of confusion and threatens our very sanity (soundness of mind). We are like a runaway freight train unable to regain control.

In this psalm, David sees the cure for his problem. In verses 5 to 7, he shifts the center of his thought from the problem to the cure, the power of the Lord. He opens his spirit to the presence of God and places his entire faith and trust in the power of the Lord to overcome his enemies. In verse 7, he says, "I will praise you because of your goodness to me". David yields his entire body and spirit to the power of the Lord God, and David is victorious. Likewise, you and I can yield totally to our God - Jesus Christ - for strength, comfort, guidance, and healing. In this way, like David, we too will be victorious. Are you willing to go to the Lord as David did? The enemy of addiction is stronger than you are. You cannot fight it alone and win. Are you willing to admit your helplessness in the face of this enemy and seek the Lord to rescue you with His strength and power? Unless you come to Jesus, you will continue to fight a losing battle against your enemy. Only Jesus can give you the victory. Are you ready to turn to Him? Only you can answer that question.

SCRIPTURE STUDY:

The following scriptures are related to Step 2. Look up each scripture in your Bible and read the verses before and after it carefully. Study this scripture, pray and reflect on it. Then answer this question for each scripture. How does this scripture speak to me regarding Step 2 and my call to believe in the "Higher Power" of Jesus Christ? Please write the answer on a separate sheet of paper.

- ☐ Matthew 9:12-13
- ☐ Philippians 2:13
- ☐ Matthew 20:29-34
- ☐ Colossians 2:13-14
- ☐ Mark 5:35-36
- ☐ Hebrews 2:14-18
- ☐ Luke 1:37
- ☐ Hebrews 7:24-25
- ☐ Luke 11:5-13
- ☐ 1 John 4:10
- ☐ Luke 18:35-43
- ☐ Psalm 18:16-19
- ☐ John 3:14-18
- ☐ Psalm 20:7-8
- ☐ John 6:28-29
- ☐ Psalm 27:11-14
- ☐ John 6:68-69
- ☐ Psalm 46:1-3
- ☐ John 7:37-39
- ☐ Psalm 71:1-3
- ☐ John 8:12
- ☐ Psalm 107:27-31
- ☐ John 10:9-10
- ☐ Psalm 107:41-43
- ☐ John 11:25-26
- ☐ Psalm 109:21-27
- ☐ Acts 3:16
- ☐ Psalm 119:123-125
- ☐ Acts 4:12
- ☐ Psalm 119: 162-166
- ☐ Acts 16:31
- ☐ Psalm 121
- ☐ Romans 8:38-39
- ☐ Psalm 130
- ☐ 1 Corinthians 1:18-25
- ☐ Psalm 139:1-16
- ☐ 1 Corinthians 15:20-22
- ☐ Psalm 149:4
- ☐ 2 Corinthians 1:8-11
- ☐ Proverbs 1:7
- ☐ 2 Corinthians 5:21
- ☐ Proverbs 2:2-15
- ☐ Galatians 1:4
- ☐ Proverbs 13:16
- ☐ Ephesians 2:4-5
- ☐ James 1:17-18

God, after all, is love unlimited.
-Elizabeth-Anne Vanek

The only part of our faith in God that is real - is what we express in our daily walk. What we believe we will practice.
-Ray Geisel

Obedience is the greatest free decision one makes for God.
-Leonardo Boff

God is ready - the moment you are.
-Emmett Fox

If we could earn our salvation, Christ would not have died to provide it.
-Our Daily Bread

To love ourselves in Jesus, is the only way to find ourselves.
-Richard J. Foster

Walking the 12 Steps with Jesus Christ

Step 3 Lesson 7

"I made a decision to turn my will and my life over to the care of God as I understood Him."

Action Words:
DECISION TO TURN

STEP 3

> In the beginning the Word already existed; the Word was with God, and the Word was God.
>
> From the very beginning the Word was with God.
>
> Through Him God made all things; not one thing in all creation was made without Him.
>
> The Word was the source of life, and this life brought light to people.
>
> The light shines in the darkness, and the darkness has never put it out.
>
> The Word became a human being and full of grace and truth lived among us. We saw His glory, the glory which He received as the Father's only Son.
>
> -John 1:1-5; 14

OUR NEW FOUNDATION

In this step, we complete the building of the foundation of the new house that is "ME". In Step 1, we admitted that we are powerless over our addiction, that our lives are out of control, and that by ourselves we can do nothing. In Step 2, we began to reach out to a power greater than ourselves to restore us to sanity. We also began to see that we must renounce all of the false gods of our lives, including self, and begin to search for the God of Jesus Christ, as we understand Him. Now, in Step 3, we can see this God of Jesus Christ as our "Higher Power" and we ask Him into our lives to take over the total care of our inner self, something we have been unable to accomplish in the past.

TURN IT OVER

This 12 Step program teaches that we must "Turn it over!" For those of us who are addicted, that simply means that we need to turn our ENTIRE LIVES over to the care of God, as we understand Him. It means turning all of the little problems of our day over to Him -all of our moment-by-moment frustrations which we all experience each day. These frustrations may be with our spouse, children, boss, work, driving a car, too many bills to pay, etc. In the face of all these frustrating problems as well as our addiction, we say to ourselves, "Turn it over! Turn it over! Turn it over!"

GETTING "UNSTUCK" ON OURSELVES

To those involved in addiction, we have learned that we are very "stuck" on ourselves. If we admitted the truth to ourselves, we would find a deep sense of insecurity and fear as a result of the deep spiritual pain inside. Something is "bugging" us down deep inside resulting in a great sense of uncertainty, fear, insecurity and frustration. We try to hide this insecurity with our pride and ego. We become very ego-centered and self-centered. In the language of the professional, we are "an egomaniac with an inferiority complex". Step 3 invites us to get out of the center of our universe, as we see it, and hand that place back to the God of Jesus Christ. As we move further into any addiction or dependency, we tend to become more self-centered, self-absorbed and pre-occupied with self, in trying to address the pain driving our addiction. This pre-occupation with self simply drives us deeper into our addiction. We tend to become more self-centered and pre-occupied with self as we seek to address the pain; yet, this action results in more pain, loneliness and isolation, in addition to what we already have. This addiction cycle pulls us down more deeply in to our pain. In order to overcome this cycle of pain, ultimately, we must step out of ourselves and look beyond ourselves for the answer. This answer is Jesus Christ.

WHAT ABOUT OUR PAST HURTS?

In breaking the bondage of our pride and ego, does that mean that we deny or ignore our hurts? Certainly not! In fact, the reverse is true. When we discover healthy new God-given and God-directed ways to handle our needs, we become less selfish and prideful. We begin to develop a healthy dependence on our God who is Jesus Christ. By giving ourselves over to the care of the God of Jesus Christ, we are strengthened and guided in our daily lives. We trust Him to heal our hurts and show us the way. We no longer live in our own selfish will but we live by the grace (help) of God. By turning our needs over to God, we actually become released from our bondage and we enter a new balanced "in-control" lifestyle. Turning our will and lives over to Jesus will become the greatest and most unselfish act of our lives. We cease to "handle it my way". Instead, we "handle it God's way". We trust Jesus to take care of our spiritual, emotional and physical needs as He sees fit. We begin to understand that our addictions, the way we handled things before, was a false, counterfeit way of meeting our basic needs. Now, with God's help, we can find the right way to meet our needs. He is the only Power that can help us and restore us to our sanity, and we turn to that Power.

Do we want to turn ourselves over to the God of Jesus Christ now? How do we get out of the driver's seat and turn our lives over to Him? The key to all of this is willingness. If we open the door just a little bit, then God will direct us in the process.

GOD'S INVITATION TO COME AND LIVE IN US

Revelation 3:20 says: "Behold I stand at the door and knock. If anyone hears My voice and opens the door, I will come in to him and eat with him, and he with Me."

This Third step is an excellent way to open the door to Jesus in your life. The door referred to in this scripture is the door to our hearts. Are you willing to open that door to Him now and invite Him in to have supper with you? Only you can answer that question. Why not pray the following prayer to Him now and mean it from the bottom of your heart.

> *"Dear Jesus, I offer myself to You - to heal me and do with me just as You will. Relieve me of the prison of self-pride, so that I may better do Your will. Take away my addictions and hurts. Give me victory over them so that I may bear Your witness to those who need help by Your power, Your love, and Your way of life. Lord help me to do Your will. Help me to put it to use in my life this day and each day for the rest of my life - AMEN!*

STEP 3

Step 3 Lesson 7

"I made a decision to turn my will and my life over to the care of God as I understood Him."

Action Words:
DECISION TO TURN

We have studied the first three steps in this 12 step recovery program. Please answer the questions given below to the best of your ability. There are no right or wrong answers, just your answers. These answers will tell you something about where you are in your 12 step walk and how you see this program. Please do not seek help. We want to know what YOU think. Thank you.

1. What does the term "powerlessness" mean to you?

2. What have you learned from this Twelve Step program regarding YOUR "powerlessness"? In what areas of your life have you been "powerless"? (Please share only what you feel comfortable sharing. We are not asking you to give information about yourself that you are not comfortable about giving or information that could incriminate you.)

3. Study Matthew 9:9-13. Why do you think that Jesus ate with the sinners and outcasts of His day? If you were present at this meal, how would you feel about Jesus coming to eat with YOU?

4. In the reading in question 3, Jesus says that the healthy do not need a doctor - only the sick. How do you feel that Jesus can heal you and bring you to righteousness in your life?

5. What does it mean to you that your life is unmanageable? Are you out-of-control in that area of your life? How do you know that your life, in this area, is out-of-control or unmanageable?

6. Study Romans 7:14-8:2. How does Paul describe the unmanageability of his life? How was his life out-of-control?

7. Paul had a problem doing what was right and good in his life. How does this compare with the experiences of your life?

8. Why do you think it is important to admit that you have lost control and that your life is unmanageable?

9. What verses in the study in question 6 tell us about the freedom of Christ over our powerlessness and unmanageability? How do you think Christ can set you free from the sin in your life?

10. We are people who struggle with self-control in our lives. How do you think admitting that you are out-of-control affects the healing and recovery from your addiction?

Write a prayer to Jesus. What would you like to say to Jesus, who does not condemn you for your behavior, even though you have been out-of-control? See yourself sitting at a table with Him in the reading in question 3. How would you speak to Jesus? Please write your prayer below.

Walking the 12 Steps with Jesus Christ

Step 3 Lesson 8

"I made a decision to turn my will and my life over to the care of God as I understood Him."

Action Words:
DECISION TO TURN

STEP 3

WILLINGNESS - THE KEY TO OPEN THE DOOR

In our last lesson, we talked about opening the door of our spirit, which has been and may still be closed and locked tight. In order to open this door, all we need is the key and that key is called WILLINGNESS. Once we insert the key and turn it, the door opens almost by itself. Once the door opens, Jesus is there inviting us to follow Him. His way is the way to recovery and a faith that overcomes the problems of life.

I NEED A "HIGHER POWER" TO SAVE ME

In our previous two steps, we looked at ourselves and reflected on our past life, the life that brought us to this point. We finally concluded that our addiction has brought us down to the "pits" and that we are powerless over it. We also began to see that there is a solution to the problem and that solution is our personal relationship with one greater than we are- our "Higher Power". We realized that it is necessary to have faith in this "Higher Power" in order to overcome our addiction. This conclusion required faith as we progressed - but it now requires action to accept this fact. The fact is, "I need a power greater than myself to return me to sanity and that power is the God of Jesus Christ. I now turn my will and life over to Him as I understand Him!"

Before we begin that process of turning our will and life over to Jesus, we need to take a good look at the question, "Just what is my will and my life?"

WHAT IS MY WILL?

The answer to this question can best be given by asking ourselves another question, "Just who am I?" As we look inside of ourselves, we see that the answer comes in our belief system. We are who we believe we are at the moment. In Proverbs 23:7 we read, "For as he thinks in his heart, so is he." (KJV) Our belief comes from our past experiences in life. In asking ourselves what we think about a certain issue, we automatically draw on our past experiences and our belief system to answer that question. Therefore, our will and who we are, is determined by our past life and what we believe to be our thinking on that matter today.

WHAT IS MY LIFE?

If what we think about an issue today is determined by our will, then how we act out that issue becomes our life. How we live our life day by day becomes who and what we are.

The only part of our faith in God that is real to us is what we practice in our daily walk. What we believe in is exactly what we practice.

Therefore, in this step when we declare that we are turning our will and life over to the care of God, we are simply turning over who we are and how we live our lives to the care of God as we understand Him. These two parts of us, our thinking (will) and behavior (life), we give over to the care of God for Him to guide us and show us the way.

TIME FOR ACTION

So now it's time for action. We have recognized the problem and brought it out into the open. It is no longer hidden down deep inside of us; however, faith alone is not enough. Action on our part is now required. Action that will cut away the self-will that has blocked Jesus Christ from our lives and kept us in the prison of our addiction. We have come to understand that faith alone cannot do it all. We can have faith and yet keep Jesus out of our lives. Now, our question is, "Just how and what specific means shall I use to be able to accept Jesus into my life?" This step gives us what may be the first opportunity ever to do this. The effectiveness and success of this 12 step walk will depend on how well and completely we are able to "turn our will and lives over to the care of God as we understand Him".

DOES THIS SOUND HARD TO YOU?

Maybe this all sounds very complicated and almost impossible. It isn't at all, so have courage dear friend. Let's look at just how practical it really is. When a person enters a 12 step recovery program and intends to stick with it, they have, without realizing it, made a beginning on Step 3. Simply by coming to a 12 step meeting, the person has decided to find a solution to the problem. In accepting and believing the first two steps, they have decided to give their lives over to the care of that program.

They trust the program to show them the way to recovery. In so doing, they have acquired a willingness to cast out their own will and to give up their own ideas in favor of a successful, proven program and to turn over their will to the direction of that program. So, for the moment, this 12 step program may be your guide and your protector and director. However, this concept will not stay this way as we grow in the solution to our problem. Our attitude will broaden and we will come to recognize the central power of the program, JESUS CHRIST. The point is, that we have already begun to let go of our lives and turn them over to the guidance and direction of this Christ centered 12 step program. So, in a very definite and recognizable way, we

STEP 3

Step 3 Lesson 8

"I made a decision to turn my will and my life over to the care of God as I understood Him."

Action Words:
DECISION TO TURN

have already begun the 3rd step by being here and opening our minds and hearts to the teaching set forth in this program.

DEPENDENCE vs. INDEPENDENCE

We are already beginning to do away with our independence based on our self-will. We are recognizing our position of powerlessness. We are deciding to seek the Higher Power upon whom we can depend for direction in finding our way.

We understand that the word dependence is a difficult, distasteful word to us and others who are addicted. We are becoming aware that there are many wrong forms of dependence and we are seeing how we have experienced them. For example, no one should depend too much on another person such as a parent, girlfriend/boyfriend, boss, pastor, etc. What then is healthy dependence?

The outstanding truth of this program is this—the more we become willing to depend upon our Higher Power, God, the more independent we actually become from our addictions and those things which control us. Dependence on God creates independence from other people and sinful addictions. Dependence on God is healthy dependence and He will direct us to those who He knows can help us when we do need others.

For a moment, let's take a look at this idea of dependence in our everyday living. Just what does this idea of dependence mean? In this area it is a real revelation to discover how dependent we really are and how unconscious we are of that dependence. For example, every building in our land has electricity. We take this for granted. But let an electrical storm shut off the juice and everything comes to a complete stop. By accepting our dependence on this marvel of science, we find ourselves becoming more independent of our helplessness and we open up our lives to doing things that would be impossible without electricity. The same might hold true for our automobiles. We become totally dependent upon that "set of wheels". When it breaks down, we find out how difficult life can be. Yet by depending upon the automobile, we actually become free to do and accomplish many more things in our life than would be possible without the "wheels". Not only are we more independent, we are even more comfortable and secure in our life style. Power and convenience flow just where they are needed. By our dependence on electricity and the automobile, we actually become independent to accomplish many tasks that would otherwise be impossible. Silently and surely, electricity meets our simplest daily needs and our most desperate ones too. Ask the surgeon in the hospital how important electricity is to saving lives.

WHAT ABOUT THE DECISIONS IN MY LIFE?

But wait, the moment our mental or emotional independence is threatened, how differently we begin to think and behave. We stubbornly claim the right to decide by ourselves just what we will think and just how we will act. Maybe we'll listen and weigh the pros and cons of every problem. Maybe we'll listen politely to another's advice, but after all is said and done, all the decisions will be made by "ME". We strongly declare, "Nobody, but nobody is going to deprive me of making the decisions of MY life. It's my life and I alone will decide! I'll not be pressured by anyone!" In addition, we think that there is only one I can really trust and that is "ME". We are sure that our intelligence, backed by our own will power, can give us the right answers in our inner lives and guarantee us success in the world we live in. This brave, stubborn attitude, in which we play god in our lives, sounds good when we speak and think it. But when we put this kind of attitude to the test, just how well does it actually work? One good look at our problems and ourselves will give us the real answer. All we need to do is ask ourselves - "Am I really happy - down deep inside? Have I been successful in reaching my goals in life? Have I been in control of my life?" The answer to these questions will show us just how successful our lives have been.

TAKE A LOOK AT THOSE AROUND US

Should our own image in the mirror be too awful to look at, we might first take a look at the results "normal people" are getting around us from their self-directed lives, doing it their own way. Let's look around us. Everywhere we see people filled with anger and fear, marriages falling apart, abortion, murder, drugs, violence, homeless children, stealing from Washington all the way down to our own hometown and just a vast amount of sinful living all over the place. Every person out there says, "I'm right and you are wrong." We have groups of people running around fighting with other groups. One tries to force another into their way of thinking, which is "ALWAYS RIGHT". This is also done among individuals. The result of all this is more fighting and less and less peace and love. There is little or no brotherhood among men in our day. Each person is out for what he can get. The result of all this, the Bible teaches, is total loss, ruin and a living Hell.

WE ARE BLESSED - WE RECOGNIZE OUR PROBLEM AND ARE WILLING TO TAKE ACTION TO CORRECT IT

Those of us who are addicts can consider ourselves very fortunate. We are blessed because we can

Walking the 12 Steps with Jesus Christ

Step 3 Lesson 8

"I made a decision to turn my will and my life over to the care of God as I understood Him."

Action Words:
DECISION TO TURN

STEP 3

recognize our problem and we have the courage to stand up and do something constructive about it.

I know, down deep in my heart, that the problem is MINE, and the only way I can correct my problem is to CHANGE ME. This is true for all of us. Aren't we all looking for a better way? We have been called into the 12 step program because we know that it is the oldest and only program that succeeds for the vast majority of people. We succeed in this program in direct proportion to the effort and belief that we put into coming to the "Higher Power" of that program, Jesus Christ. We have failed on our own. Now is the time to come to the faith and commitment of this program and to make that decision to turn our will and life over to the God of Jesus Christ.

JUST HOW DO I TURN MYSELF OVER TO GOD?

When you came into the 12 step program and made a beginning, you started this process. By now, chances are that you have become convinced that you have some other problems in addition to alcohol or drugs. You also know that some of these "other problems" seem to refuse to be solved by the sheer, personal determination, struggle and courage that you can muster. These "other problems" simply will not budge; they have made you desperately unhappy and threatened your newfound sobriety. You may still be the victim of guilt or shame when you think of your yesterdays. Bitterness and sick feelings still overpower you when you brood over those you still envy or hate. Your finances are a wreck or your marital relationship worries you sick. Panic takes over when you think of all the bridges to safety that your addiction blew up. And how shall you ever straighten out that awful jam that cost you the affection of your family and separated you from your loved ones? Your lone courage and unaided will cannot do it. You've tried to correct the problem many times in the past and have failed. Surely you must now depend upon someone or something else to save you.

YOUR SPONSOR/PRAYER PARTNER - A CLOSE FRIEND

At first, when you realize your helplessness, you may turn to a close friend. This friend is called a sponsor or prayer partner as we call them in this program. Your friend points out that your other troubles, brought about by alcohol, drugs, and can also be solved using this 12 step program. But the healing takes time, just as the healing of your drug or alcohol problem. Just the admission of your powerlessness and your attendance at the 12 step meetings will not totally accomplish the healing. You are a far cry from permanent sobriety and a contented, happy and useful life. This is where the remaining steps of the program come in. Nothing short of continuous action upon these as a WAY OF LIFE can bring the much desired result, which is a new life in Jesus Christ.

STEP 3 - A WAY OF LIFE

It is very important to understand that the remaining steps of the 12 step program can be studied and applied only when Step 3 is a determined and persistent practice. It is only when Step 3 becomes a way of life that the remaining steps can be applied and become an effective healing in our life. Without an active ongoing relationship with our Lord Jesus Christ, we cannot and probably will not succeed. Our success in the healing process is directly related to our oneness with our Lord.

LET'S DO IT - COME TO JESUS NOW!

Our human will is of little or no value in overcoming our addictions. Our past has demonstrated this fact over and over again. Finally, we have admitted our total powerlessness over our addiction. But now we are asked to submit our total self to God. YOU can only do this on your own. All by yourself, in the light of your own will, you need to willingly give yourself over to Jesus Christ. This is a process of LETTING GO - by lifting up the hands of your inner heart to Jesus saying, "Here I am Lord Jesus. I'm yours. Help me! I'm in your hands now!" This requires your willingness. Most of your past life has been given over to willingly doing those things which cause pain and struggle in your life. Now you are being asked to willingly do the one thing that can cause you to be healed and bring order and peace into your life. Trying to do this is an act of your own free will. No one can force you into it. All you need to do is to say, "YES", deep inside you to Jesus Christ and begin to move toward Him. You need to let go of your own stubborn free will and give it over to Jesus in the best way that you can. He does not ask you to do the impossible. Just do what you can - but freely give yourself over to Him. All you need to do is try. Jesus will do the rest. Have a sincere heart; don't try to fool yourself or anyone else. You just keep trying and doing it over and over again. See it happening within your spirit and it will happen. It takes time, so be patient. Remember, practice makes perfect.

VISUALIZED PRAYER

At this point, I would like to suggest a type of prayer in which you turn your will and life over to Jesus. This prayer is called visualized prayer. It simply means that you clear your mind of all outside distractions in a quiet place and close your eyes. In a comfortable position, visualize Jesus

Walking the 12 Steps with Jesus Christ

STEP 3

Step 3 Lesson 8

"I made a decision to turn my will and my life over to the care of God as I understood Him."

Action Words:
DECISION TO TURN

sitting or standing with you. See Him in the eyes of your mind. Then simply pray the Overcomer's Prayer very slowly and with much meaning. A simple conversation on your part with Jesus is all that is necessary. Speak to Him from your heart, and see Him there listening to you. Feel His love for you and see Him reach out and receive you into His arms. Hear Him whisper how much he loves you and see the love in His eyes. Give yourself to Him word by word and live each word. He will bless you and change your life. You have now entered into a lasting, personal relationship with Jesus Christ, which is available to you at anytime.

GIVE YOUR WILL AND LIFE OVER TO JESUS

It is when you try to make your will conform to God's will that you begin to use His will rightly. When you give your will over to His will, you are guaranteed success. The extent to which you fail to give your will to Him is the extent to which you will fail. The more you turn it over, the greater becomes your victory. In the past, we all have become experts at failure. Now we give ourselves over to Jesus Christ and we become successful As we give ourselves to Him. To give ourselves to Jesus Christ is, to all who do it, a wonderful revelation. Our whole trouble has been the misuse of our will power. We have tried to solve our problems with our will instead of attempting to bring our will into agreement with God's will for us. This program opens the door to God's power in our lives.

A PRAYER FOR PEACE AND DIRECTION IN TIMES OF STRESS

Once we have come into agreement with these ideas and we believe and practice them, it is really easy to begin the practice of Step 3. In all times of trouble, emotional disturbances, indecision or temptation, we can pause and ask God for peace and direction in our spirit. We can say to our God:

THE SERENITY PRAYER

God, grant me the serenity to accept the things I cannot change (the other guy);

The courage to change the things I can (me); And the wisdom to know the difference.

Living one day at a time; Enjoying one moment at a time; Accepting hardships as the pathway to peace.

Taking, as He did, this sinful world As it is, not as I would have it; Trusting that He will make all things right If I surrender to His will; That I may be reasonably happy in this life And supremely happy with Him Forever in the next.

Lord - not my will be done but Yours.

AMEN.

(Reinhold Niebuhr)

Walking the 12 Steps with Jesus Christ

Step 3 Lesson 8

"I made a decision to turn my will and my life over to the care of God as I understood Him."

Action Words: DECISION TO TURN

STEP 3

SALVATION

Salvation refers to: becoming saved, safe, sound, healed, whole, healthy, delivered, prosperous, and doing life with Jesus by accepting Him as your Savior. Accepting Jesus, turning your will and your life over to Him, is the beginning of this process. Learning to truly live as a new creation in Christ is a process that requires patience, perseverance, and continually seeking God and His truths.

UNDERSTANDING OUR NEED OF SALVATION AND HOW WE RECEIVE IT

God's Plan & Purpose: God created people to praise Him, to know Him (which is a process), to have a satisfying life, and to have peace. God is love and He created us to love Him and to love each other. God created us in a family relationship mainly to learn about His love and to live it out. (See: Genesis 1:26-27, Psalm 127:3, Psalm 139:13, Isaiah 42:5, Jeremiah 1:5, John 10:10, John 16:33, Acts 17:22-28, and Ephesians 1:4)

Our Problem: We are cutoff or separated from God by our sin, which leads to death. (Romans 3:23 & Romans 6:23) Also, if we did not experience healthy, wholesome, God-like love in our families, then we do not know what God's love is. Others have wronged us and we have wronged them. These wrongs are sins. We have missed out on the reason we were created, to experience and learn God's love and to give it away.

God's Remedy: The Cross. Jesus paid for our sins so that we don't have to remain cutoff or separated from God. We have the choice to come together with God in a love relationship. (Romans 5:6-8, 1 Peter 2:24) Here enters His unconditional love and grace. Jesus came and died on the cross and rose again so that we all might be forgiven of the wrongs/sin of our past and be made whole again. In Biblical terms, being made whole means to enter into that spiritual love relationship by coming to Jesus and receiving His forgiveness and His touch of healing. We can and will learn to love, the Jesus way, by coming to Him. (John 3:16-17, John 14:23)

Our Response: We should love Him because He first loved us. Because we love Him we should come to Him and give our lives to Him through receiving His son, Jesus Christ as our Lord and Savior. (John 1:12, 1 John 4:9-11)

1. We admit our spiritual need and we come to Him by faith, which is our simple belief in Him (Hebrews 11:1, Ephesians 2:8-9)

2. We repent—change our mindset about our sin and sinful behavior. (Acts 2:38, Acts 3:19, Acts 17:30-31) **True Repentance:** changing your views and purposes to accept the will of God in your inner self instead of rejecting it; changing your mind for the better and sincerely changing your ways; agreeing with God about sin—that it hurts you, is not good for you, is not God's best for you, and that you have offended God and need to be saved from it.

3. We confess Jesus is Lord. (Romans 10:8-11, 1 Timothy 6:11-12, 1 John 4:15)

4. We are baptized. (Acts 2:38, Matthew 3:16, Matthew 28:19, Mark 16:16, Romans 6:3-9, Galatians 3:22-28, 1 Peter 3:18-21)

Accepting Christ as your Savior is the beginning of the process of being made safe, sound, and whole through Him. (John 3:17) Learning to truly live as a new creation in Christ is a process requiring perseverance and continually seeking God and His truths.

Prayer: Dear Lord Jesus, I admit that I am a sinner and I need Your forgiveness. I believe that You are the Christ, the son of the Living God. I believe that You came and You died for my sins. I repent of my sins and I want to turn away from them. I invite You to come into my heart and my life. I accept You as my personal Lord and Savior and I want to trust and follow You. In Jesus' name I pray, Amen.

Walking the 12 Steps with Jesus Christ

MEDITATIONS

Step 3 Lesson 9

"I made a decision to turn my will and my life over to the care of God as I understood Him."

Scripture: MEDITATIONS

DAY ONE - Study Matthew 11:28-30

When we have any problem, particularly an addiction problem, we find ourselves burdened down with guilt, shame, bitterness, fear, and discouragement. These emotions have piled up inside of us since they first happened long ago back in our childhood. The huge load of all these emotions heaped upon us has caused great weight upon our shoulders and tears us down at times. We are tired of trying to make it on our own. It seems as though we can never win regardless of how hard we try. Our problem has simply been that we are trying to do it alone. As we allow God's healing love and presence to flow into our lives, we begin to experience a peacefulness and strength that we never knew before. We begin to feel whole again and can experience peaceful rest.

But, as we read this scripture, we find that Jesus tells us - "Take My yoke and put it on you, and learn from Me". It seems that, just when we begin to find rest, Jesus tells us to get up and get going. Why? For a moment, we need to go back to the time of Jesus and ask ourselves, "Just what is this yoke that Jesus is talking about?" In the time of Jesus, a farmer would yoke a cow or ox with another such animal so that the younger one could learn to pull the plow properly. By yoking two animals together, side-by-side, the total load moved much easier and effectively. Jesus uses this example to tell us that we no longer need to pull the load of our lives alone. Rather, Jesus will take the other end of the yoke over His shoulder and help us carry the load of life. He will "plow" through life with us and we will learn from Him just as the older animal showed the younger one how to plow. As we walk with Jesus, the burden and weight of our problems will move much easier with His help. And in verse 30, Jesus tells us that the yoke that He gives to us will be easy and the burden will be light. Just as in the poem "Footprints in the Sand", when there was only one set of footprints, Jesus was carrying us. Will you give yourself to Jesus and let Him help you carry your load?

Will you allow Him to carry you when the load becomes too unbearable for you to carry? It's only in coming to Him that you will receive His help and His rest and learn how to carry your load in the future more effectively with His help. Come to Him now and receive Jesus!

DAY TWO - Study Matthew 16:21-26

The process of overcoming our addiction has several important principles. We must give up (declare our powerlessness) in order to win. Jesus says, "For whoever wants to save his own life will lose it: but whoever loses his life for My sake will find it." (Verse 25).

To give up and let go of our human will is a difficult task. Sometimes, we are tempted to question our Lord and ask, "Why do I have to give up to win? Haven't You made some kind of mistake, Lord?" The disciples did not understand that statement and Peter questioned the Lord. Jesus corrects Peter rather strongly as He says, "These thoughts of yours don't come from God, but from man." Peter loved Jesus very much and did not want to see any harm done to Jesus, much less that He be crucified. But Jesus knew that He needed to "give up to win" and He did just that. Three days later He came into glorified resurrected new life.

Jesus gave His life to the Father as a sacrifice for our sins. True healing and spiritual growth requires that we also give up our will and life to the Father to be healed. Jesus assures us that if we lose our life for His sake, we will save our life. That's the promise of Jesus. And so we must turn our complete will and life over to Jesus just as He turned His life over to the Father for our sake. It is in dying to our old self and being born again to new life that we overcome our addictions and sins. Now it's your turn, friend. Won't you do that today?

Walking the 12 Steps with Jesus Christ

Step 3 Lesson 9

"I made a decision to turn my will and my life over to the care of God as I understood Him."

Scripture : MEDITATIONS

MEDITATIONS

DAY THREE - Study Ephesians 2:8-10

Just what does the opening verse of today's reading mean when it says, "For it is by God's grace that you have been saved through faith?" For some of us struggling with our addiction, it may mean that, but for the grace of God, we may never have reached an emotional, spiritual or physical "bottom". If it were not for the grace of God, we would not have reached that bottom and had the opportunity to begin that upward journey of recovery and healing. We may never have had the opportunity to find ourselves and begin that new life of recovery.

This statement - "For it is by God's grace" also means that we are receiving the free gift of God's grace to accomplish this miracle of healing and recovery from our addiction. The key word here is FREE. There is nothing that you or I can do to earn this free gift except to ask for it and receive it. By ourselves, we once thought that we could overcome our problem by our own strength and will power. Now we have come to realize that we are not only unable to heal our own problem and must turn to God, but we must also ask for and receive this free gift of healing that He has to offer us. He is a compassionate and patient Father who calls to His children and waits for us to come to Him. In addition, He forgives us ON THE SPOT for anything and everything that we have done wrong and fills us with His healing love. How great and remarkable is the love of our Father for us through Christ Jesus.

This reading clearly shows us that we must surrender our total self - all of our pride and human imperfections - to the mercy and healing of Jesus Christ. When we surrender our self and our human ego to Him, He fills us with a "life of good deeds which He has already prepared for us to do". (Verse 10) Our wonderful Father has prepared for us, ahead of time, a life of goodness and joy. What a wonderful Father we all have! Let us come to Him through Jesus Christ - His Son and our Brother! We no longer have to struggle to do it ourselves; rather, our Father has already prepared the way for us through Jesus Christ. Our only calling is to receive that new life and walk in it.

Are you prepared to do that? Don't miss the wonderful new life that awaits you when you give yourself to Jesus Christ. The reward is yours for the asking and receiving - FREE!

DAY FOUR - Study Psalm 3:5-6

In the beginning of this Psalm, David cries out the doubts of all of us when he says, "God will not help him." (Verse 2) It seems as if David is lost in despair and God will not come to his aid.

How often have you and I hit "bottom" and wondered if God even knew we existed. "Where is my God?" we cried out. "Doesn't He hear me or care about me? I'm lonely, sick and hurting. Lord God, where are you?" Finally, we begin to realize that we have hit bottom and that our addiction has got us pinned down. It seems as though we cannot live with our addiction or live without it. In our despair and confusion, we cry out the verses in today's reading.

And now we have come to Step 3 in our spiritual journey. Like David in our reading today, we must throw open our sick and starving hearts to receive the merciful and loving eternal presence of God - Jesus Christ. As David came to God so many years ago in his time of dire need, so must you and I. David wanted to be freed from his "thousands" of enemies and so do you and I want to be freed from our enemy - our addiction. Let us come with confidence to the Lord God and "lie down and sleep" for our Lord Jesus Christ will "protect me".

Jesus Christ is waiting for you right now. Will you come to Him as David did? Only you can decide to do that.

Walking the 12 Steps with Jesus Christ

MEDITATIONS

Step 3 Lesson 9

"I made a decision to turn my will and my life over to the care of God as I understood Him."

Scripture :
MEDITATIONS

DAY FIVE - Study Psalm 23

In both the Old and New Testaments, our Lord uses the example of shepherd and his sheep. In John 10:14, Jesus calls Himself the "Good Shepherd" who gives His life for His sheep. David lived in the time of sheep and shepherds and knew all about their relationship. Truly David understood what it meant for the shepherd to lay down his life for the sheep. And so David uses this beautiful loving relationship to describe God's love for us. We can receive the same love, restoration, healing, protection and abundance in our own life as David did in his. David's "Good Shepherd" is also our "Good Shepherd." All that we need to do is to come to the "Good Shepherd" - Jesus Christ - and turn our life over to Him. We need to become His sheep. As we give up our old self in this process, He fills us with His peace and healing restoration.

When we turn our life over to the "Good Shepherd" - Jesus - nothing else on earth can match the happiness and joy that we receive. Not only is Jesus the "Good Shepherd", He is also totally wise and totally powerful. He is the fullness of life (see John 10:10). No longer do you and I have to fight the devil by our own power. We now have the mighty power of the "Good Shepherd" within us. We need no longer fear the evil attacks of our addiction and sin. The "Good Shepherd" promises us His protection and victory. Even during the hardest times of our lives, we have victory in Jesus.

The "Good Shepherd" - Jesus - can do the same for you as He did for David. Are you ready to ask Him into your life? Only you can answer that question and do it.

DAY SIX - Study Psalm 91:1-4

As we choose to trust our God as our Savior and we release our will and life over to Him, "He will keep you safe from all hidden dangers and from all deadly diseases." (Verse 3) In verse 2, we declare our need for God: "You are my defender and protector. You are my God; in you I trust." In these verses, we feel the love and protection of our God continually enfolding and supporting us. As long as we continue to keep "plugged in" to our God, we can and will overcome. However, we humans like to play "head games". When things are tough, we call on God. But when things turn around and get better, WE begin to get back into the spot light; and we push God back out of our lives. Our relationship with God should be a permanent home rather than a temporary refuge. Verse 4 tells us, "He will cover you with His wings; you will be safe in His care; His faithfulness will protect and defend you." If you and I stay "under the cover of His wings", then HE will protect and defend us. If we do not, we are "fair game" for the devil and his bag of tricks.

In order to remain "under the cover of His wings", we need to communicate with Him. We cannot know the peace and serenity of our God unless we communicate with Him. To do this, regular study of His Word, the Bible, and praying to Him is essential. As we begin to place ourselves under "His Wings" by prayer and Bible study, we will be delivered from the misery and trap of our addictions and sins. Bad habits will begin to disappear along with our old way of negative "stinkin thinkin". We will become a new person in Christ Jesus!

DAY SEVEN - Study Proverbs 3:5-6

In the past, those of us who have been addicted have relied upon our own reason and intellect. We did what WE thought was right and stubbornly hung with that reasoning. This kind of thinking and acting has gotten us where we are today. How many times have we tried and tried to use our thinking and our reasoning to overcome our addiction? How many times have we been confused and unable to sort through the many and varied emotions which keep coming to us from the hurts of the past? Too many times have we told ourselves, "I can handle it"! And how many times have we blown it? All too many times! We can and must admit our powerlessness (Step 1) and our spiritual bankruptcy.

Walking the 12 Steps with Jesus Christ

Step 3 Lesson 9

"I made a decision to turn my will and my life over to the care of God as I understood Him."

Scripture:
MEDITATIONS

MEDITATIONS

When we decide to turn our will and life over to the care of God, we are involved in total surrender. We must go about the business of deflating that big "ego/pride balloon". Our pride and our arrogant intelligence have "got to go". And so, in this step we begin to learn to lean not on OUR OWN UNDERSTANDING but ON THE GOD OF OUR UNDERSTANDING. The Holy Word clearly tells us, in this reading, that we are to forsake our own will and lean on God. When you "remember the Lord in everything you do, He will show you the right way" (Verse 6). His way becomes our way and our victory. When you give up YOUR WAY to HIS WAY, you will have taken the most important step of your life to a complete recovery and a full and abundant life in Jesus Christ.

A problem understood is half solved.
— *Author unknown*

When we surrender to our Higher Power, the journey to recovery begins.
— *Anonymous*

The faults that bother us in others usually bother us in ourselves..
— *Anonymous*

SCRIPTURE STUDY:

The following scriptures relate to Step 3. Look them up and study them carefully as in the past. Try to understand how the Lord is calling you to give you will and life over to Him:

- ☐ Psalm 4:8
- ☐ John 8:1-11
- ☐ Psalm 9:9-10
- ☐ John 12:26
- ☐ Psalm 17:6-8
- ☐ John 17:3
- ☐ Psalm 28:6-9
- ☐ Acts 2:21
- ☐ Psalm 31:19-20
- ☐ Romans 3:21-24
- ☐ Psalm 56:3-4
- ☐ Romans 4:20-25
- ☐ Proverbs 14:26-27
- ☐ Romans 5:1
- ☐ Matthew 6:31-34
- ☐ Romans 5:8-11
- ☐ Matthew 10:37-39
- ☐ Romans 8:1
- ☐ Luke 9:57-62
- ☐ Romans 10:9-13
- ☐ Luke 11:2-4
- ☐ 2 Corinthians 1:3-5
- ☐ Luke 24:46-47
- ☐ Ephesians 1:3-14
- ☐ John 1:12-13
- ☐ Hebrews 4:1-2
- ☐ John 5:24
- ☐ 1 Peter 1:3-5
- ☐ John 6:35-40
- ☐ 1 Peter 2:24-25

Walking the 12 Steps with Jesus Christ

STEP 4

Step 4 Lesson 10

"I made a searching and fearless moral inventory of myself seeking to identify the wrongs of my past life."

Action Word: SEARCHING

WE BEGIN TO IDENTIFY THE PROBLEM

In this lesson, we begin the discovery and healing stage of the program. In this step, we will begin to look back into our early life to identify the wrongs that we collected and now cause us to hurt inside in our spirit. This step is the most involved step of the entire recovery program. It requires a good bit of study and "soul searching" and this will take time - lots of time. So take all the time that you need to do a good thorough job of it.

You may experience some deep emotions while doing this step. This is very normal. Please allow all the hurts and wrongs of the past to come out. To experience deep emotions will help to identify those wrongs that have, and continue to, hurt you deep inside of your spirit. Please let them come out.

THE MEANING OF THE FOUR KEY WORDS

First, let us consider the meaning of each of the four key words in this step:

SEARCHING - In making our inventory, we need to search our past completely to identify the wrongs that have caused us so much pain in our inner self. This searching requires a good bit of thought and takes much time. But search completely we must. At first, we may think that an event of the past is not important. But later, we may discover that the event in question, put together with all the other hurtful events of the past, causes one big hurt in our life today. It is important to list all events that caused pain regardless of their magnitude. Later on, we will try to put these events together to establish trends in our life. This will tell us a great deal about why we hurt and how to correct and heal this hurt. So be complete in searching your past. Please include everything.

FEARLESS - It is also very important that we bring out those things that we may be afraid to face up to. Taking this inventory may cause some additional pain at first. But such additional pain is necessary to bring out the cause of the overall hurt and bring it to Jesus to get it healed. So don't be afraid. Jesus will walk with you in your journey of discovery. In John 14:27, Jesus says, "Peace is what I leave with you; it is My own peace that I give to you. I do not give it as the world does. Do not be worried and upset; do not be afraid." Jesus tells us that there is nothing to fear.

MORAL - When we speak of a moral inventory, we are simply referring to the matters in our past life that deal with the person inside of our spirit. If the event affects our inner being and causes pain, it needs to be included in our moral inventory.

INVENTORY - An inventory is nothing more than a list or account of what happened in the past. It is a story in short form. It should be written as we go so that we will not allow the facts to slip back into the subconscious mind again. In this way, it will be before us as we go on to the next few steps of this program.

THE WRONGS OF THE PAST- What are they?

Before we go on with this step, let's just stop for a moment and ask ourselves, "Just what are these wrongs that I am looking for? How will I recognize them?"

The AA program uses several different terms for the wrongs in our life - shortcomings, abuses, and defects of character. The Bible calls these wrongs sin. In order to simplify the terminology in all this, I am using one word to cover them all - WRONGS.

Wrongs can stem from relationships in our past life that hurt us in some way or that hurt someone else in our relationship. Wrongs are not right; they are negative hurtful events that happen in the process of living. We recognize wrongs by the inner pain and discomfort they cause us in our spirit. When we feel something is "bugging" us inside and can't seem to put our finger on it, chances are very good that we are hurting from a wrongful event in our past.

Others can inflict wrongs upon us. We can also inflict wrongs upon others. So wrongs can go both ways and quite often they do in the same event. A wrong, simply put, says, "I don't love you at the moment and I am going to let you know about it by the unloving demonstration that I am placing upon you. "I don't care about you and want to hurt you."

THE CYCLE OF LIFE - A look back in the past

Before we begin our search for the wrongs of the past, it is necessary to "back up" so to speak and take an overall look at our lives as a whole. In the remainder of this lesson, I will attempt to demonstrate to you in a simple fashion the reasons why you came into this world, why God created you, what is your purpose in walking in this life, and how the wrongs we collect as we grow up come to play in the overall picture of our life.

Step 4 Lesson 10

"I made a searching and fearless moral inventory of myself seeking to identify the wrongs of my past life."

Action Word : SEARCHING

STEP 4

In Figure 4-1 you will find a chart entitled "The Cycle of Life". This chart will help you to understand your total self better and give you some insights into the wrongs of the past and as to how they happened. This chart is a time line that takes you back to your conception, then birth and then the significant events in your life to the present time. In the pages that follow, I will explain and develop this chart one part at a time.

Fig. 10-1

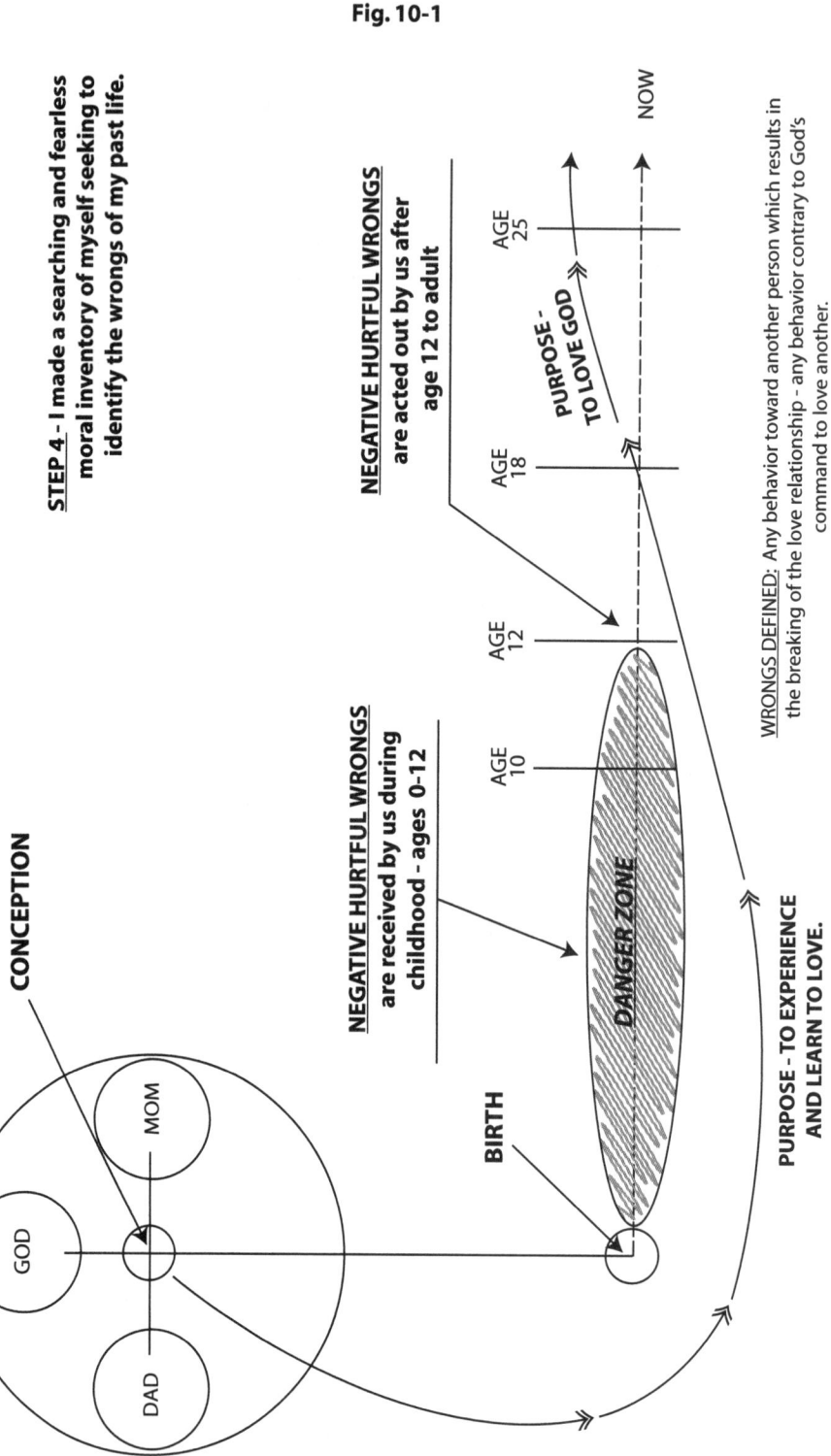

Christian 12 Step Ministry, Inc — 46 — *Walking the 12 Steps with Jesus Christ*

STEP 4

Step 4 Lesson 10

"I made a searching and fearless moral inventory of myself seeking to identify the wrongs of my past life."

Action Word: SEARCHING

WHO CREATED ME AND WHY AM I HERE?

We begin by turning to 1 John 4:7-10 - "Dear friends, let us love one another, because love comes from God. Whoever loves is a child of God and knows God. Whoever does not love does not know God for GOD IS LOVE. And God showed His love for us by sending His only Son into the world, so that we might have life through Him. This is what love is: "it is not that we have loved God, but that He loved us and sent His Son to be the means by which our sins are forgiven."

From this verse of scripture, and many others, we learn that GOD IS LOVE. The very make up of God is love. In John 15:13 we are given the Biblical meaning of love, "The greatest love you can have for your friends, is to give your life for them." I am certain that most of you who study this guide can easily recall that the world teaches us that "love is having sex". This statement is totally inaccurate in a Biblical sense. The Bible declares that love is not getting something but rather giving your life for another. A simpler saying from the past says "Love is not love until it is given away. - no strings attached." The point of all this is that God, who is love, created you and me out of love and in love for us. See the following scriptures for insight:

Ephesians 1:4 - "Even before the world was made, God had already chosen us to be His through our union with Christ, so that we would be holy and without fault before Him." Also study Ephesians 1:4-14.

Psalm 139:13 - "You created every part of me; you put me together in my mother's womb." Verse 15 - "When my bones were being formed, carefully put together in my mother's womb, when I was growing there in secret, You knew that I was there - You saw me before I was born".

Psalm 104:29 - "When You (God) turn away, they (men) are afraid, when You take away Your breath, they die and go back to the dust from which they came."

Isaiah 42:5 - "God created the heavens and stretched them out, He fashioned the earth and all that lives there; He gave life and breath to all its people."

Genesis 1:26-27 - "Then God said, and now We will make human beings, they will be like Us and resemble Us. So God created human beings, making them to be like Him. He created them male and female. Blessed them and said, "Have many children so that your descendants will live all over the earth and bring it under control."

Acts 17:22-28 - See verses 24-25 - "God who made the world and everything in it, is Lord of heaven and earth and does not live in temples made by human hands. Nor does He need anything that we can supply by working for Him, since it is He Himself who gives life and breath and everything else to everyone."

Psalm 127:3 - "Children are a gift from the Lord, they are a real blessing."

From the above scriptures, we draw the following conclusions:

1. God is love.
2. God's measure of love is to give one's life for another.
3. God loves us so much that He sustains us with His breath of life.
4. God created us out of His love for us and made us to be a reflection of His love to Himself and others.
5. God creates us to live out His love for us together in a family unit - father, mother and child.
6. In the end, at death, God calls us back to Himself to spend the rest of our eternity together with Him.

Step 4 Lesson 10

"I made a searching and fearless moral inventory of myself seeking to identify the wrongs of my past life."

Action Word:
SEARCHING

The following drawing (Fig. 4-2) is a visual picture of what God did for us by creating us and placing us in a family:

Fig. 10-2

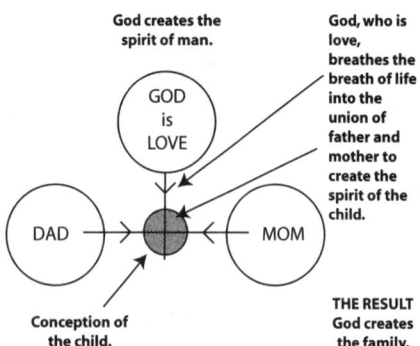

In the above illustration, we see that God is love and He created us to love Him and to love each other. God created us in a family relationship for one reason mainly, to learn love and to live it out. Therefore, our family was and is the basic school in which we experience and learn to love God's way.

PHASES OF DEVELOPMENT

As we go through life, we reach certain points along the way where we mark our development. These are described below:

Ages 0 to 12

This is the very sensitive and impressionable formative stage of our life. During this time, we soak up everything that happens, good or bad, and we begin to establish our behavioral patterns in life. We are constantly asking, "Who am I, what do I believe and how should I act?" Children are great imitators which tells us that they will act out exactly what they see, learn and experience in their family life. The example of family, including mother father and siblings, is very important during this time.

Peer pressure also begins to take hold as they learn to relate to other children outside of their family. This is a very important time indeed.

If you will refer back to the chart on page 46, you will notice the danger zone during the period from birth to age 12. It is during this time that the child is most open to soaking up the wrongs and hurts that he may have received. It is this period of time during which seventy percent or more of the damage is done in the young person. The influence that this child receives from those close to him will make a permanent mark on his inner person, his spirit, for the rest of his life.

Ages 12 to 18

Teens now come into puberty and starting to act out strongly what they have learned in the first 12 years of their life. If they observed addictive, violent or abusive behavior in their family, with close friends, or in the media they may begin to act out the same behavior that they witnessed. This is why we have young people who are alcoholics. They are acting out the alcoholic behavior they learned while in their family unit. It is during this time that young teens may begin to act out sexually in the same way that they observed and experienced sexual behavior in the first 12 years of life from family, the media and peers. It is during this time that behavioral habits are established firmly in the life of young people. This is the time that they may experiment with the poor habits that they may acquire. There is a strong tendency for these habits to become compulsive and highly addictive. This is a very difficult time for young people.

Ages 18 to 25

A young person reaches mental and physiological maturity at or near age 25. Prior to that time, however, the process has been a very difficult struggle. Persons in this age range have times of severe confusion and sometimes a deep sense of being lost in finding their way in life. This can be a very trying time in a person's life. Parental love, kindness and understanding are vital to that person during this time.

Finally, the young person reaches the age of maturity and is completely responsible for their behavior. Any compulsive habits that they have picked up during their early life are now strongly fixed in their lives. It is at this time that they may find themselves addicted to a habit or substance or both and it is then that they may be willing to deal with their problem. It is then that God can speak to them to come to Him for healing. Healing can come to them completely at this time. All that is needed is a strong willingness to do so and desire to come to Jesus for healing.

GOD'S GREATEST COMMANDMENT - TO LOVE

Previously in this lesson, I discussed the meaning of love and how it relates to the wrongs that we collect during life. Let us now take a look at the family relationship and how God's plan fits within the family.

STEP 4

The Lord gave us all a Dad and Mom that He picked out for us. We had nothing whatsoever to do with that choice. This was not an accident in God's eyes. He could have created His children in a different way than the way He selected. He could have spoken us into existence as fully-grown human beings much the same way as He spoke the universe and all that is in it into existence in Genesis chapter one. But that was not God's plan. Rather, He chose us to be physically born to a mother and father. Remember - His plan is love. In order to love, a lover and a beloved are needed. It requires two persons or more to have a love relationship. In God's original plan, He is the lover and we are His beloved. He is the giver of love and life; we are the receivers. In Matthew 22:36-40, God states it this way, "Teacher" he asked, "which is the greatest commandment in the Law?" Jesus answered, "'Love the Lord your God with all your heart, with all your soul, and with all your mind.' This is the greatest and the most important commandment. The second most important commandment is like it: 'Love your neighbor as you love yourself.' The whole Law of Moses and the teachings of the prophets depend on these two commandments." Then in Luke 10:25-37, these two commandments are reinstated by Jesus and Jesus goes further to explain the meaning of "neighbor" in the parable of the Good Samaritan.

THE LOVE RELATIONSHIP

So it follows, from the teachings of Jesus, that love is the greatest commandment that we have received. We are to love God and to love each other as God has loved us and as we love ourselves. This relationship of love is what I call the LOVE RELATIONSHIP! As a child of God, we are placed into a family to experience and learn about this love relationship. When we grow into adulthood, we naturally become interested in the opposite sex. The reason God created us that way was to give us the opportunity to give away the love that we learned in our earlier years. If, however, we did not experience healthy, wholesome, God-like love in our early years, then we do not know what God's love is. Therefore, as an adult, we will be unable to participate in that love relationship in a healthy normal way since we never experienced much of that earlier in our lives. We have missed out on the very reason we were created by Almighty God, to experience and learn God's love and to give it away. It appears then, that any behavior that we received as a child that was contrary to God's love is a wrong and hurts us inside. These broken love relationships are the wrongs and hurts we collect as a young person. They continue to accumulate in our subconscious "baggage" deep inside and hurt later in life during our teen years and early adulthood. Because we did not receive a good God-like healthy love relationship in our early life, we don't know how to love later in life and these scars hurt as a result.

DAD AND MOM - What's their purpose?

The Lord gave us one father and one mother for a very specific reason. He selected these two people to bear us up as their child. He gave Dad and Mom the privilege of causing each of us to be born to them and the responsibility to teach us the true meaning of love God's way. When a parent fails in this task or ignores this task, the child is seriously hurt inside. God created us to live in a healthy loving family relationship for the first 18 years of our life and then to find our "rib", or mate and to create another family in which the children will be able to experience that love over again from their parents. See Genesis 2:18 and Genesis 2:21-24. God joins man to woman and they "become one" in the eyes of God. In verse 24, God tells us, "That is why a man leaves his father and mother and is united with his wife, and they become one."Our inner spiritual desire in life from birth to death is to be in love with God and with each other in that special relationship of man and wife called marriage. This is how God creates and carries on His whole wonderful plan of love for mankind.

Once again, the definition of a wrong - "Any behavior toward another person which results in the breaking of the love relationship. Any behavior contrary to God's command to love one another. This is what causes us to hurt inside and is exactly what we are trying to discover and identify in our past life in taking this inventory. Once we discover these wrongs, we can bring them to the Lord Jesus for healing that takes place in Steps 5, 6 and 7.

IT SEEMS I MISSED THE LOVE BOAT - What now?

At this point, you may wonder, "It seems that I grew up in such a way that I missed the boat as far as God's love in my life is concerned. Will I ever be able to correct that situation? Will I ever be able to love God and others as Jesus commands me to do?"

There is hope. Jesus came and died on the cross of Calvary and rose again on that first Resurrection day that you and all of us might be forgiven of the wrongs of our past and be made whole again. Being made whole in Biblical terms means to enter into that spiritual love relationship by coming to Jesus and receiving His forgiveness and His touch of healing. As grown men and women, we can and will learn to love, the Jesus way, by coming to Him. It is never too late. John 14:23 - Jesus answered

---

Step 4 Lesson 10

"I made a searching and fearless moral inventory of myself seeking to identify the wrongs of my past life."

Action Word :
SEARCHING

Step 4 Lesson 10

"I made a searching and fearless moral inventory of myself seeking to identify the wrongs of my past life."

Action Word: SEARCHING

STEP 4

him, "Whoever loves Me will obey My teaching. My Father will love him, and my Father and I will come to him and live with him." This coming of the Father and Jesus into us in Godly love is called the Baptism of the Holy Spirit. As we yield our lives over to Jesus, we receive the Holy Spirit. And so dear friend, God in the person of Jesus Christ, stands ready, willing and able to love you and heal you. Begin to give Him your hurts now. We will learn how to do that more completely in the lessons that follow.

FOOTPRINTS IN THE SAND

One night a man had a dream.
He dreamed he was walking along
the beach with the Lord.
Across the sky flashed scenes from his life.
For each scene, he noticed two sets of
footprints in the sand; one belonging to him,
and the other to the Lord.

When the last scene of his life
flashed before him, he looked back
at the footprints in the sand.
He noticed that many times along the path of
his life there was only one set of footprints.
He also noticed that it happened at the very
lowest and saddest times of his life.

This really bothered him and he questioned
the Lord about it.
"Lord, you said that once I decided to follow
You, You'd walk with me all the way.
But I have noticed that during the most
troublesome times in my life, there is only one
set of footprints. I don't understand why
when I needed You most You would
leave me."

The Lord replied,
"My precious, precious child, I love you
and I would never leave you.
During your times of trial and suffering,
when you see only one set of footprints,
it was then that I carried you."

-Author unknown

STEP 4

Step 4 Lesson 11

"I made a searching and fearless moral inventory of myself seeking to identify the wrongs of my past life."

Action Word: FEARLESS

In Step 3, we turned our will and life over to the care of God - Jesus Christ - as we understood Him. Now we take the next Healing Step on the left side; and, the Growth/Strength on the right side of the Road Map of this study guide. First, we will make a searching and fearless moral inventory of ourselves (Healing Step 4), and then we will study the elements of a good, prayerful conversation with our God, Jesus Christ (Growth/Strength Step 4).

LET'S CONCENTRATE ON THE PROBLEM

In the previous lesson, we discussed the purpose and meaning of life and the importance of a good healthy love filled relationship with God and others. Now we go back to our problem and concentrate on the cause - the wrongs in our life.

Our past has been filled with addictive behavior. Something is driving us to cover up our past hurts by drinking, drugging, or the use of some other habit. We desperately need a healing and a new direction in life. We have gone down the wrong road in the past. But now, we have started on a new road; we have come to accept Jesus as the answer and that new direction in life.

In order to find and to understand this new direction in Jesus, we need to take a good, hard look at where we have been in our past life. In the process of looking back at those things that have troubled us, we identify the problems of the past; and, we bring them out into the open so that we can give them to Jesus to be healed.

So, a personal inventory is essential to understanding this new direction of spiritual growth in our lives. We must turn the old, bad habits into new, good habits. In asking ourselves who we want to become in Christ Jesus, we need to examine what aspects of our character we need to keep and emphasize and what aspects of our character we should modify or eliminate. We will process six areas of our lives, which will help us to determine what we should keep and what needs to go.

A. WE TELL OUR STORY

First and foremost, we need to "tell our story". This can be done by making a written journal, which is nothing more than a story of a certain part of our life. The purpose of writing this story: First, we put it down where we can see it with our own eyes. We can read it over and study it by ourselves. Second, we can, if we desire, share it with another in recovery or privately with one person who is really close to us.

To illustrate this, let's take a look at the story of the "Woman at the well". In John 4, Jesus meets the Samaritan woman. She was amazed and taken back that Jesus would have anything at all to do with her. In the time of Jesus, Jewish men had nothing whatever to do with Samaritans, especially women. Then Jesus told her that she had five husbands and that she was then living with a man who was not her husband. Next, we see the tremendous compassion and love that Jesus has. He accepts the Samaritan woman just where she is. In verse 14, Jesus fills her with life giving water and cleanses her spirit. He was fully aware of all that she had done in her life but, in spite of all that, He loved her unconditionally. This was a life changing experience for this woman.

Following this encounter, the woman heads for town where she promptly tells all the towns people about Jesus. In addition to accepting her right where she was and forgiving her, Jesus used her to bring the good news to her peers in town. Just think, Jesus used a prostitute to spread the Good News.

As in the story of the Samaritan woman, we also need to look at our past life with Jesus so that we can be healed as she was. Preparing our story allows us to assess the major events of our life. Writing down and identifying the wrongs in our past journey through life helps us to evaluate and study honestly our present situation and correct it.

The second part in our inventory is discovering the root causes of our addictions.

B. WE DISCOVER THE CAUSE

In most cases, this means going back into our childhood to take a good look at ourselves and where we have been. We may ask, "What needs were not met back then? What difficult, harmful, or negative influences did we absorb during that time in our lives? How did we receive the wounds in our spirit which we carry in the present day?" Within the family of origin, there are six basic types of problem areas that may have affected us in childhood. Chances are very good that these problem areas have caused us severe hurt inside and have generated or caused a later adult addictive habit. These problems are described below:

1. **Active abuse** - Very often our parents had some problem with which they were unable to deal. This problem probably caused them much pain and frustration. Many times parents direct this pain and frustration toward their children in destructive, uncontrolled behavior. Any form of direct physical, verbal, mental, psychological, or sexual abuse can be classified as active abuse. Active abuse happens when any form of destructive behavior is vented toward another, which causes hurt inside. This

Step 4 Lesson 11

"I made a searching and fearless moral inventory of myself seeking to identify the wrongs of my past life."

Action Word: FEARLESS

STEP 4

abuse may be directed toward you by another, or may be directed by you toward another person. The question: Did anyone, not just your parents, treat you in any way that was hurtful to you physically, verbally, mentally, emotionally, or sexually? If your answer is yes - then you received active abuse.

2. **Passive abuse** - This form of abuse occurs when a child does not receive the attention or care that he is rightfully due. Every child needs 15 to 18 years of nurturing, loving care from two sane, sober and caring parents. A child requires time, affirmation, support, attention, discipline, and loving affection. When a child is denied these elements of healthy growth, his parents/caregivers have passively abused him. He has been denied the love relationship that is the very source of life that he needs to grow into a mature, responsible adult. The question: Did your parents love you and give you the attention, affirmation, discipline, and guidance that you needed during your early life? If your answer is no - then you received passive abuse.

3. **Child is forced to be a parent** - When one or both parents in the family are in some way emotionally, mentally, or physically disabled, a young child may begin to assume or take over that parent's role and responsibilities. Maybe the child winds up taking care of a sick or alcoholic parent instead of the parent taking care of the child. For example: If seven-year-old Mary's mother is an alcoholic, Mary may begin getting herself up and ready for school, fix her own breakfast and meals, and get her Mom out of bed in the afternoon to keep peace with her Dad. Mary is now becoming a mother to her own mother. The question: Did you have to take over any or all of the responsibilities of one or both of your parents because they could or would no longer do that job? If your answer is yes, your parent has emotionally used you.

4. **Parent infects the child** - When a parent refuses to deal with a serious problem or defect in their own lives and this problem continues to affect the child and the family, the child may pick up the parent's problematic habit. An example would be a father who is an alcoholic and refuses to deal with his problem. By his behavior, he may pass this problem over to his son or daughter. The question: Did one or both of your parents fail to deal with and correct a problem in their own life that affected you and which you now carry in your life? If the answer is yes - you have been the victim of your parent's infectious sickness. You have caught your parent's problem.

5. **Negative messages to the child** - These are spoken or experienced messages that destroy or tear down the self-worth of the child and become part of the child's personality. Examples of spoken negative messages are: "You'll never amount to anything." "Can't you ever do anything right?" "Don't you realize how unhappy you have made me?" "You're nothing but a rotten kid." An unspoken, experienced message of neglect would be a father who spends all of his free time watching TV or is out with the "guys" and never plays or spends quality time with his child. The question: Did your parents accept you as their loved one, as part of them, and spend quality time with you? Did they give you compliments when you tried to do your best? Were they patient with you when you fell down in your life? If the answer is no, then you have received this type of abuse.

6. **Buried/hidden feelings or needs** - Many members of spiritually sick families deny or bury their true feelings and needs. After a while, these needs will begin to surface and may do so in some very damaging behavior. The person eventually brings out the feeling or need and finds it impossible to handle. In doing so, they inflict their behavior on the other members of the family. Example: A child who is constantly scolded and sent to his room without being able to talk to the parent about his problem because the parent has a problem deep inside and will not listen to the child.

The child will bury these feelings deep down inside until some day, maybe much later in life, these feelings will come out to haunt him. The question: Do you have some feelings or resentments deep down inside you regarding your family or others that hurt and have never really been healed? If your answer is yes, you have this type of spiritual problem.

As we learn and discover what was damaging or missing in our early life, it is important not to blame our parents or others involved. Instead, we make a genuine effort to understand what has happened and what is "bugging" us and causing us to act the way we are today. Our purpose is to understand and get to the underlying cause of our addictive behavior today. Why are we doing the things that cause our life to be out of control? Why are we using the escape mechanism of our addiction to try to run from these problems? These are the questions. We are not attempting to blame anyone, including ourselves, for that behavior. Rather, we seek to uncover and understand the cause of the hurt deep down inside which causes us to act the way we do today.

Walking the 12 Steps with Jesus Christ

STEP 4

Step 4 Lesson 11

"I made a searching and fearless moral inventory of myself seeking to identify the wrongs of my past life."

Action Word : FEARLESS

C. WE CONFRONT AND ASSESS THE FULL EXTENT OF OUR ADDICTION

Next, we confront and assess the full extent of our addictive behavior. There are reasons why we are acting the way we do. This step will help us to assess and uncover the root causes. We begin by looking at the primary or basic causes of our behavior - the big obvious problems. In this process, we may also discover other areas of our life that also affect our behavior that we may not have considered before. These are called secondary causes. We should make a written inventory identifying all of our addictive symptoms and behaviors that have come to us through our past life. As we search ourselves in our 4th Step inventory, we must be certain to identify all of the possible addictions or behaviors that have brought us to the present day. Our goal is to discover all of our problem areas and to treat the entire person. We do not want to "band aid" the issue with a partial solution; rather, we are out to correct the entire "ME". Some examples of areas which may be somewhat hidden are as follows:

1. Alcohol or drugs, possibly prescription drugs.
2. Work, achievement, or success.
3. Money addictions: overspending, gambling, hoarding, credit card spending.
4. Control addictions: seeking to control others in personal, family, business, or sexual relationships.
5. Food addictions: overeating or starvation.
6. Sexual addictions: any form of sexual involvement outside of marriage including masturbation, sexual fantasy, and pornography.
7. Approval dependency: the need to please others to gain their approval and admiration.
8. Rescuing addiction: the need to save others regardless of the cost.
9. Dependency addiction: being involved with those we know will hurt us in the end.
10. Physical illness: over concern about the physical wellness and health of our body.
11. Excessive exercise and physical conditioning: also includes excessive concern about weight loss, including addiction to steroids or weight control medications.
12. Grooming addiction: over concern about cosmetics, clothing, and cosmetic surgery.
13. Intellectual addiction: over concern about book learning and excessive intellectualizing.
14. Religious addiction: preoccupation with the form, rules, and regulations of religious practices. Over concern with the legalism of religion. The inability to live a balanced, spiritual life.
15. Perfectionism: obsession with being perfect in all things. The inability to admit making a mistake. A "never wrong" person.
16. Cleanliness addiction: The "Mr. Clean" person who is always concerned with cleanness at all cost.
17. Organizational addiction: The person who has to have everything in perfect order in life and who has a panic attack when anything is out of order.
18. Materialism addiction: the person whose "god" is the material things of life. He values things much more than people.

The above list is only a partial description of those things that can control us and cause addictive behavior. We may have something that has gotten way out of control that is not on this list. Be sure to put that down on your inventory.

D. WE LOOK BACK AT OUR HISTORY

Now, we need to take a look back at our relationship history with the people who have played an important part in our lives - parents, teachers, brothers, sisters, friends, close school mates, co-workers, romantic interests, etc. We need to identify in our inventory all the ways that we have hurt them and ourselves by practicing our adult addictions or dependencies. This is the first step along the way that helps us toward ridding our lives of resentments and guilt.

It is very important here to begin to bring these things out of our lives to be forgiven. It makes no difference who was at fault. The mere fact that a hurt was given to someone, maybe even you, is all that matters. Hurts are hurts and they tear us up inside ourselves regardless if they come to us from another or are directed by us toward another. The Bible does not say that we must forgive only the one who was at fault. Forgiveness has nothing to do with fault; it has everything to do with hurt and pain. So we are to forgive every situation in which there was hurt and pain, where there was a broken "Love relationship" - regardless of fault.

Resentments, anger, and bitterness, which arise out of fear and insecurity, may lie behind much of the hurt we have inflicted on others and on ourselves. As part of this inventory, we must first acknowledge and bring out our resentments and then identify the fears and insecurities that underlie them. The question: "Why am I 'on the outs' with that person? Why do I resent (or can't stand) that person? What is it that separates us?" After we have

Step 4 Lesson 11

"I made a searching and fearless moral inventory of myself seeking to identify the wrongs of my past life."

Action Word: FEARLESS

STEP 4

identified the break with that person, we must try to recognize what happened in our spirit to cause these bad feelings against that person. Why do I feel the way I do about them? Only in this manner can we deal effectively with these resentments that will otherwise rot and stink inside of us like an emotional cancer.

E. WE ADDRESS OUR GUILTY FEELINGS

Most addictions are usually driven by deep guilt and possibly shame. In order to understand this problem, we need to look at just what guilt and shame really are.

As a preface to my remarks, I wish to state that there is a great deal of confusion about the meaning of these two words, guilt as opposed to shame. In many addiction treatment circles, these two words are used interchangeably and appear to have the same or similar meaning. This is incorrect, in my view. It is important to understand the very distinct difference between these two conditions. Guilt is a very necessary and healthy emotion; while shame can, and sometimes does become a very destructive and negative emotion that can lead to very serious consequences. We must remember that emotions are OK. Emotions are merely God's way of telling us what is going on inside of our spiritual being. It is what we do with these emotions that can be constructive or destructive in our life.

Guilt - Guilt merely tells us that we have made a mistake. One of the ways that we human beings learn is to make mistakes. Some people think that mistakes are terribly devastating and disastrous. This is an over-reaction. Mistakes are signposts that tell us that we have gotten off the correct path in our life. They merely tell us that correction is needed. If we continue to make the same mistake over and over again, we are ignoring the signal and are refusing to correct the cause of the mistake. This can and many times does, cause great pain in our lives.

Shame - Shame, on the other hand, does not state that we have made a mistake but that we ARE a mistake. When we "buy" the idea that we are a mistake, we have given into one of the most powerful tools of the devil, the father of lies. In John 10:10, Jesus states, "The thief (devil) comes only in order to steal, kill and destroy." The devil's game is to kill us and to steal from us the glorious eternal life given to us by our Father God, through Jesus Christ, by the power of the Holy Spirit. Shame is an attempt, by the devil, to get you to believe that you ARE a mistake, that you can't do anything right, that you are a total misfit and therefore have no constructive use in this world. That is the lie of the devil and those who buy into it will surely die and could be lost for eternity. Quickly summed up:

Guilt - says I made a mistake that can be corrected.

Shame - says I am a mistake - that I am no good - and that cannot be corrected.

Now that we understand the difference between these two emotions, let us turn to some further explanation of the various kinds of guilt and shame:

1. **False guilt or carried blame** - This is undeserved blame that we have taken upon ourselves for people or situations over which we may have had no control. We must realize that the only person I am responsible for is "ME". When I blame myself because my father was the "town drunk", I am taking on blame for something over which I had no control. When I think to myself, "I'm no good! I'm worthless!", I am thinking thoughts of shame which are total lies of the devil. This type of thinking is totally wrong and should be immediately rooted out of our hearts and minds. IT IS A LIE! Adult children of spiritually sick families often carry enormous amounts of false guilt and carried blame for their parents' misbehavior. The question: "Am I experiencing feelings of shame for something someone else did over which I had no control?" If your answer is yes, you have been carrying false guilt and blame which has turned into shame. Now is the time to get rid of it. Push it out of your mind and spirit; declare it the LIE that it truly is and release it from your mind and spirit.

2. **Authentic guilt** - As adults and sinners, we have probably hurt many people in many different ways during our life. We have caused this hurt through our speech, our attitude, through neglect, through the wrongful actions we have committed, and through the actions we should have taken, but refused to do so. If this is your case, and it more than likely is, then you have authentic guilt. You have every right and are obliged to feel guilty for your actions or lack thereof.

In the previous two sections, I looked at my guilt to determine if the hurt caused was due to someone else's actions or by my actions. If it was due to someone else's actions, it is false guilt and carried blame and should be removed entirely from my thinking and inner spirit. I should ask myself, "Did I do this; am I the responsible one?" If the answer is yes or even a partial yes, then I have a case of authentic guilt. I am the guilty one, partially or otherwise. If I did it, I need to stand up and be re-

STEP 4

Step 4 Lesson 11

"I made a searching and fearless moral inventory of myself seeking to identify the wrongs of my past life."

Action Word: FEARLESS

sponsible for my actions. In this area of authentic guilt, it is very necessary to seek and ask forgiveness whenever possible from the injured person.

Authentic guilt is generally a healthy emotion. It simply reminds us that we have made a mistake, we need to correct the behavior behind the mistake, and we need to ask forgiveness for our actions and need to learn from that experience. Correction of our behavior is most important. Without an attitude of correcting our mistake, the mistake has no value to us and will happen again and again until we deal with it constructively. It is very important at this point to adopt a healthy and positive attitude toward this event and to learn from it. We are all on the road to recovery from our addiction and therefore we need to change the only person we can change - "ME".

3. **Shame** - When we adopt an attitude of self-condemnation and depression over our mistakes, we are buying the lie of the devil. We are telling ourselves that, because of our inability to deal with our problems and habits and our continued failing in our attempt to recover from our addictions, we are "no good" and that we are a "washout". This attitude and method of thinking is a lie and is very destructive to any possibility of recovery. Such thinking leads to self-condemnation, which eventually can lead to destruction of life itself in suicide. It causes hopelessness and self-destruction and is very, very dangerous. If you have had thoughts of this kind in the past, rebuke them immediately from your mind. Get into your Bible and read what God says about you. You are a good person because He made you. You may have messed up in following His way of life, but you are able to follow His way again beginning today. Beware of shame and do not give in to it!

F. WE LOOK FOR THE GOOD IN OURSELVES

In the next part of our inventory, we need to look for the good in us and in our relationships. We ask ourselves a series of questions, which will help us to identify the good in ourselves:

1. What are some of the good traditions, the happy memories that I remember from my parents and my family and my early life?

2. What good habits and skills have I learned in my growing up years?

3. What are the skills, talents, and gifts that God has given me today? What do I do well in my life? What am I good at?

4. What are my goals in life? What do I want to accomplish in the rest of my life?

5. What constructive ways have I learned as a result of my addiction? What positive ways have I learned to cope with my habits? How can I learn more about these ways and build on them? How can I become a better me?

I urge you now to take some serious time to complete this inventory as soon as possible. The very heart of this program is to identify both the hurts and wrongs in our lives as well as the right and good things. The object is to deal with and heal the hurts as much as possible and to build on the good points that are within each of us.

In completing our inventory, we have taken a good look at ourselves from the inside out in the following areas:

A. We told our story.

B. We discovered the causes.

C. We confronted and assessed the full extent of our addiction.

D. We looked back at our history.

E. We addressed our guilty feelings.

F. We looked for the good in us.

During the days ahead, I urge you to reread this lesson several times and think about your past life. You should begin to write down some of the things that you are being questioned about in these lessons. The more complete and honest with yourself you can be, the quicker and more complete will be your healing and recovery. I urge you to pray to the Lord Jesus for help. Ask Jesus to help you in looking into yourself. Please read Matthew 11:28-30 several times. Jesus wants you to come to Him so that He can help you. He asks you to learn from Him. He will help you carry your burden and give you rest and healing from your struggle.

Walking the 12 Steps with Jesus Christ

Step 4 Lesson 12

"I made a searching and fearless moral inventory of myself seeking to identify the wrongs of my past life."

**Action Word:
SEARCHING**

STEP 4

WHAT BROUGHT US TO THIS POINT IN LIFE?

When God created you and me, He created us for a distinct purpose. Without a purpose in life, we would not be complete human beings. If we, as human beings, did not work at our purpose in life, we would not survive in this world. We have a basic need to harvest food, construct houses for shelter, have children, and to love and care for one another. If we did not work at these things, society would fall apart. So these desires that we have for material and emotional security, for a loving partner (spouse), for companionship, etc. are perfectly right and in God's plan for us. This is the way we act out the love we have for God and for each other.

Yet, these purposes in our lives can sometimes get out of control and run away with us. At times, they can become powerfully blinding over us. They can dominate us and completely run our lives. Our desires for material things and emotional security and our desire for an important place in our society can completely take control of our lives. Therefore, when we allow these good and natural desires to get the best of us, we can find ourselves in deep and great trouble. This is another cause of addiction or dependent behavior and this situation hits us all, at one time or another. Nearly every serious emotional or spiritual problem can be traced back to some event or relationship in our early lives that hurts us and winds up controlling our behavior. When that happens, we have become addicted persons. Our wonderful, natural instincts which God gave us have become bent out of shape and turned us into a total nightmare pulling us down into the "pits of Hell" itself.

In Step 4, we make a painstaking effort to discover the nature of the problem that controls us - that causes us to be powerless in certain areas of our lives (remember Step 1?). We are trying to find out exactly how, when, and where our natural instincts and desires to be in a loving relationship have gotten out of control. We want to look squarely at the unhappiness that this has caused others and ourselves. We want to take a good long look at the CAUSE of the problem as well as the SOLUTION.

By looking into our past life, we can discover just exactly what "bugs" us down deep in the depths of our hearts and we can begin to move toward the solution and healing of the problem. Unless we are willing to do this, we cannot get to the center of the problem and there will be little chance for a solution and recovery. Unless we are willing to take a good look at "ME", we will not be able to deal with the drugs, alcohol, sexual, or violent misbehavior in our lives along with the other things which control us and tear us down. Without a searching and honest moral inventory, most of us have found that the Jesus Christ faith which really works in our daily living will always be out of our reach. So this step is absolutely essential to our recovery. We must take and do it very seriously, for it is the key to our ultimate healing and recovery.

Before we tackle the problem in detail, let's have a closer look at the nature of the basic problem. Just what is it? Simple examples like the following help us to understand the answer to that question - What is it?

Let's suppose that a person has a huge and uncontrollable sexual appetite and he places that desire above everything in his life. This huge urge within him can destroy his chances for material or emotional security as well as "black ball" him with his friends and family. His relationship with his girlfriend or wife will be shattered because he cannot control his urge. He will be totally pre-occupied with the getting of sex.

Let's suppose that a person has a huge and uncontrollable desire for money or material wealth (things). He wants to get all of the money he can get as quickly as possible, no matter how or what he has to do to get it. He wants to hoard it, steal for it, kill for it, fight for it, sell his wife and children for it, deal drugs for it, or sell him-self for it, etc. The lust for money has him completely out of control.

Man's thirst for security is not always expressed in terms of money or material wealth (things). Sometimes such a person will become completely dependent upon a stronger person for guidance and protection. In depending on another person, this addict becomes a "blood sucker" to his stronger friend, living off of him and depending on him for everything in his world. The dependent person never grows up. He will become depressed, disillusioned, and totally helpless. In time, his protector will leave or die and the dependent one will fall apart - alone and afraid.

STEP 4

Step 4 Lesson 12

"I made a searching and fearless moral inventory of myself seeking to identify the wrongs of my past life."

Action Word: SEARCHING

BEWARE OF NATURAL INSTINCTS

In short, whenever we allow ourselves to let our natural instincts, our physical bodies, run wild and out of control, there can be no peace in our lives - just misery. In the Bible, this is referred to as allowing the lusts of the flesh (our bodies) to take control of our spirit and run our lives. Paul warns us that we must not let ourselves be run by our bodies, but rather we must be controlled by our spirit in communion with God's Holy Spirit that lives within us.

Allowing ourselves to be controlled by our natural, bodily instincts are not the only problem. When this happens, we not only mess up our own lives and behavior, we also proceed to affect the lives of those around us - especially those really close to us. When we allow our instincts to run wild, this can produce a minor problem with others; or it can create a revolution that can tear apart other lives by the hundreds or thousands. In this way, we are set up in conflict not only with ourselves but with lots of others around us as well. In short, our sickness in spirit spreads to infect others.

When we allow our natural bodily instincts to run wild by our destructive drinking or drugging, we create all kinds of horror. We drink or drug to drown our feelings of fear, insecurity, frustration and depression. We get drunk or "high" to escape the guilt of our passions or sexual misbehavior only to find that this drinking or drugging creates more sexual misbehavior. Instead of our problems getting better, the end result is they get worse. We get drunk to experience power or to hide our problems. We hide behind our addiction because we can't stand to look at the problem deep within ourselves. As long as we continue on this insane rollercoaster, we are denying our problem and we are projecting that problem, through drugs, alcohol, etc., to others in our lives. There are just as many excuses for not taking a searching and fearless moral inventory as there are people. This program shows us clearly that there is NO EXCUSE for not taking that inventory. It is only in taking that inventory that we can come to recognize the problem, bring it out into the open, and be healed through the grace and power of Jesus Christ, the Great Physician.

OUR SPONSOR/PRAYER PARTNER

It is at this point in the program that we need a sponsor or a prayer partner as we call him. It is in preparing for and during the inventory taking process that the Prayer Partner can begin to pray with us and help us to search ourselves in truth regarding our past.

Our Prayer Partner can help us to see that our case is not strange or different from all others, that we are not some kind of "freak" or "oddball". He can help us to see that our problem is not larger or worse than those of anyone else around us in the program. The Prayer Partner can and should share with the recovering addict his own experiences by talking freely and easily about the wrongs of his past which caused him to fall into his addiction. He should feel free to share his past experiences. The result - both parties learn and grow from the sharing. This should be a time of deep trust and sharing between the Prayer Partner and the recovering addict. The Prayer Partner should help his friend by pointing out not only the wrongs in his life but also the good points of character within him. This process will encourage both people. They will see the good as well as the not so good in each other and begin to build on the good and deal with the not so good. This will encourage the recovering addict to talk more openly and fearlessly about his past wrongs and a more complete inventory taking will result.

The Prayer Partner of those who feel they need no inventory sometimes has quite another problem. This is because some people are driven by pride of self. They are unable to see the past wrongs that have built up over the years that cause them to act in insane behavior. The problem is helping them discover a crack in the wall of their stubborn pride through which the light of reason can shine. It is the task of the Prayer Partner to help this person find an opening in the wall of self-pride that he has built around himself. It is through this opening that he can examine fearlessly and honestly the wrongs of his past. That wall of pride must be broken in some way to get to the problem. As long as the wall remains in tact with no opening, the problem cannot be dealt with. It is the task of the Prayer Partner to work to break down that wall and get to the problem deep within the recovering addict. Of course, this requires the help and cooperation of the recovering addict. Without that cooperation, that task is impossible.

BREAKING DOWN THE WALL OF SELF-PRIDE

The first step in this process is to show the recovering addict that the majority of those addicted suffer from severe self-pride, self-justification, and egotism during their times of drunkenness. These recovering persons need to be shown clearly that self-pride was the maker of excuses for all sorts of crazy, wild, and damaging conduct. For those with self-pride, hang-ups become the inventors of all kinds of temporary insanity driven by wild excuses. "We had to do our thing because times were hard or times were good. We had to do our thing because we were smothered with love or we did not get any love at all. We had to do our thing because at work there were great successes or dismal

Step 4 Lesson 12

"I made a searching and fearless moral inventory of myself seeking to identify the wrongs of my past life."

Action Word:
SEARCHING

failures. We had to do our thing because our team won the football game or lost the football game". And so the list goes on and on into insanity; excuses, excuses, and more excuses for our addictive behavior.

We try to reason that "conditions" around us drove us to do our thing. We reasoned that we tried to control those conditions and found out that when we could not do so, we went off to practice our addiction. It never occurred to us that we needed to change OURSELVES to deal with the problems, whatever they may be. Rather, we tried desperately to change the conditions outside of us instead. We failed to recognize that the problem was deep within us, rather than without.

As we break down our pride, we begin to realize that something needs to be done about our resentments, self-pity, and gigantic ego. We had to see that every time we play the "big shot", we turned people against us. We needed to see that when we harbored grudges and planned revenge for such defeats, we were really beating ourselves with the club of anger - the anger we had intended to use on others. We learned that if we were seriously disturbed, our FIRST need was to quiet that disturbance regardless of who or what we thought caused it. The method that we use to accomplish this quieting is called prayer. We are being tempted and the Bible teaches that we need to deal with this temptation immediately when it comes upon us. The Bible teaches that we need to bind or kick out this temptation in the mighty name of JESUS CHRIST. This temptation is the work of the devil and requires immediate prayer. Prayer is the companion to Step 4 in our program and will be discussed next in our program.

In the lessons to come, we will continue to deal with our erratic emotions and feelings and we will begin to see how these emotions can victimize us and control us over long periods of time. For the moment, however, we need to look at our self-pride and ego and begin to deal with it the Jesus Christ way. Bring out the wrongs caused by that prideful ego and get them on our inventory in black and white. Then, and only then, will we be able to effectively change our lives.

Miracles are prayers answered.
-Author unknown

"Great works are performed not by strength but by perseverance."
- Samuel Johnson

"We don't see things as they are. We see them as we are."
- Anais Nin

"Before you can inspire with emotion, you must be swamped with it yourself. Before you can move their tears, your own must flow. To convince them, you must yourself believe."
- Winston Churchill

"The door of success swings on the hinges of obstacles."
- Denis Waitley

SCRIPTURE STUDY:

The following scriptures are directly related to Step 4. Look up each scripture, study it, and write down how this scripture applies to this step.

The question: "How does this scripture show me that I must bring out the wrongs of the past?"

- ☐ Psalm 66:18
- ☐ Proverbs 30:11-12
- ☐ Psalm 73:21-22
- ☐ Matthew 5:27-32
- ☐ Psalm 90:8
- ☐ Luke 11:33-36
- ☐ Proverbs 10:17
- ☐ Luke 12:15
- ☐ Proverbs 13:13
- ☐ Luke 16:14-15
- ☐ Proverbs 14:14-15
- ☐ Luke 17:3-6
- ☐ Proverbs 15:11
- ☐ Romans 7:15
- ☐ Proverbs 15:31-33
- ☐ 1 Corinthians 3:1-3
- ☐ Proverbs 19:19
- ☐ 1 Corinthians 7:3-6
- ☐ Proverbs 20:1
- ☐ 1 Corinthians 15:34
- ☐ Proverbs 20:19-20
- ☐ 2 Corinthians 6:14-7:1
- ☐ Proverbs 21:9
- ☐ 2 Corinthians 10:12
- ☐ Proverbs 22:24-25
- ☐ 2 Corinthians 13:5
- ☐ Proverbs 23:27
- ☐ Galatians 5:19-21
- ☐ Proverbs 23:29-35
- ☐ Ephesians 5:3-7
- ☐ Proverbs 25:28
- ☐ Ephesians 5:22-33
- ☐ Proverbs 26:20-22
- ☐ Ephesians 6:1-4
- ☐ Proverbs 29:1
- ☐ 1 Timothy 5:8
- ☐ Proverbs 29:11
- ☐ James 2:2-8
- ☐ Proverbs 29:20-23

MEDITATIONS

Step 4 Lesson 13

"I made a searching and fearless moral inventory of myself seeking to identify the wrongs of my past life."

Scripture:
MEDITATIONS

DAY ONE - Study Matthew 23:23-28

Our modern understanding of addiction suggests that all addictions and compulsions are based on a sense of guilt and/or shame. It really makes little difference where our feelings of guilt come from. Maybe they are from an early family situation that we witnessed and experienced, or are the result of our recent behavior. The fact remains, that we must clear away and clean up these guilty, shameful feelings in order to be healed. The Bible tells us that this cleansing must take place from the inside out. Our 12 step recovery program tells us that these feelings connected with our crazy behavior must be addressed by taking a "searching and fearless moral inventory" of ourselves. In order to be healed, we must find out what "bugs us" inside.

Our effectiveness in this inventory process requires that we find the sources of both our false and our authentic guilt. (See lesson 11 - for a description of false and authentic guilt. Beware of shame. It is terribly dangerous). We could be carrying some false guilt about a childhood experience of sexual abuse or the impact of drunkenness or drugs that were used by our parents. Maybe we are carrying some authentic feelings of guilt about the damage we have caused others through the practice of our addictive behavior.

This particular study today deals with the cleansing of our insides - in our inner being, our spirit. Jesus tells us very plainly that we are to cleanse the inside of ourselves so that the outside will be clean. Step 4 of this program is a special opportunity to bring out the garbage in the darkness of our past lives into the cleansing light of God's Holy Spirit. We can begin again with a clean slate.

I pray, dear friend, that you will come to Jesus. He will help you bring out the garbage in your life that so desperately needs to be cleansed from your spirit. Begin now and stick with it until you are completely satisfied that the process is complete. God bless you!

DAY TWO - Study Luke 12:1-7

In the first verse of this study, Jesus warns His disciples against the sin of hypocrisy in which we pretend to be something or someone we are not. To us who are addicted, this means that we speak one thing with our mouths but we act entirely different in our lives; we say one thing and do another. Step 4 encourages us to look at our lives carefully and to fearlessly accept the truth of our past. We need to take a good look at who we really are rather than what we SAY we really are.

As we look into ourselves for this answer, let's keep in mind the following guidelines:

1. Jesus already knows everything about us anyway (See verses 2 and 3). There is nothing to fear and nothing to hide from Him. Trying to hide our problem is denial and DENIAL is the attitude which keeps us hooked in our addictive behavior. If we hide our problem, we refuse to bring it out. If we refuse to bring it out, it cannot be healed and we will continue to have the problem.

2. We must take a good look at our fears in order to move beyond them. Otherwise, we will be so hung up emotionally that we will not be able to deal with the most important issue in our lives, our relationship with Jesus (See verses 4 and 5).

3. Jesus cares about us very deeply, more than we care about ourselves (see verse 6 and 7). Our Fourth Step inventory process becomes a special opportunity to feel that personal healing touch of Jesus. As we experience that healing touch, we will receive the tremendous grace and help in His acceptance and forgiveness of us just where we are. We will feel whole and clean again.

Now that we have put our trust in Jesus, He is present with us to help in the process of uncovering our real selves. We need not fear, and we do not have to pretend or play games with Him. Our real self is the person that Jesus loves and desires to touch.

Walking the 12 Steps with Jesus Christ

59 Christian 12 Step Ministry, Inc

Step 4 Lesson 13

"I made a searching and fearless moral inventory of myself seeking to identify the wrongs of my past life."

Scripture: MEDITATIONS

MEDITATIONS

DAY THREE - Study Romans 13:11-14

The time has come for you to "WAKE UP FROM YOUR SLEEP". Those of us who have walked around in the past in our drunkenness know without fail that we were dead to our real life. We lived in a stupor state, out of control in our behavior. Now the Word of God tells us to WAKE UP!!! Life is passing us by and the sooner we wake up to our real self, the more we will receive the fullness of life that Jesus promises us (See John 10:10). Just think about it; when you and I wake up, the night is over. We now can see where we are going; we now walk in the light and have some good direction. We are no longer half asleep in our drunkenness; rather we are now sober, in control of our lives. When we live in the light of day, we must give up those sinful habits of ours; orgies, drunkenness, immorality, indecency, fighting, or jealously. We are called to take up the weapons of Jesus Christ and stop paying attention to our sinful nature with all of its crazy desires.

How do we do this? Step 4 is the beginning of this process. In Step 4, we take a good look at the wrongs and hurtful experiences we have had in the past that have been driving our addiction. We identify the wrongs and soon we will admit them openly and ask Jesus to remove them. This is the sure path to our spiritual healing. Covering them over with drugs, alcohol, sexual misbehavior, etc. will only make the sickness of our spirit worse. We need to become aware of those things in our past that have hurt us, bringing them out and giving them to Jesus for healing.

The Lord Jesus is now shaking us and calling us to awaken from our drunken nightmare. The dark night of this spiritual and emotional prison is over. The door leading out into the bright light of day is at hand. Instead of denying or excusing our past, we choose to bring it out to Jesus to be healed.

Pray, dear friend, that you will gather your strength and open the door of your inside prison and come into the light of Jesus. Say "yes" to Him, you'll be glad you did.

DAY FOUR - Study 1 Corinthians 4:19-20

To deny our problems and our hurts is to prevent the fullness of a 4th Step inventory. Our hearts may be bursting with pain and hurt in certain areas that need to be healed. To be "puffed up" with words and to hide our hurts will also change the nature of the problem we are trying to heal. We will be "playing games" with the problem instead of looking at the problem for just what it is.

We can fool ourselves with those "puffed up" words and thoughts. This results in a "snow job" on us. The adult child of a workaholic may be covering up the pain of an absent father. The abuser of prescription drugs may cover up his growing addiction because the "doctor ordered it". The relationship addict or sex addict may cover up countless violations of others by saying that these things are done "in the name of love".

This program warns us that recovery is within the reach of all except those who refuse to be honest with themselves. The Kingdom of God in Jesus Christ is available to all those who come to Jesus in honesty with a sincere heart and confess their sins. This scripture tells us unmistakably that there is POWER in His Kingdom. This power will result in our complete healing if we plug into and use it correctly.

Pray, dear friend, that you will be honest with yourself and with Jesus in your 4th Step inventory. Your healing will result. Believe it and claim it.

DAY FIVE - Study Galatians 6:3-5

One of the strange conditions of the recovering addicted person is that low self-esteem often results in an over concern with self or a feeling of self-importance. When I have a problem with who I am, I tend to think on that concept all during my waking day. It occupies my mind and I act out of that frustration. When I take an honest self-inventory of who I am, it serves to put everything inside back into proper balance.

What is the balance we are seeking? On the one hand, the Bible asks that we do not pretend to be something that we are not. It asks that we deflate our false ego and pride. We need to let all the air out of our great big balloon called "Pride". On the other hand, the Bible also urges that we humbly take credit for and rejoice in our goodness and our accomplishments.

MEDITATIONS

Step 4 Lesson 13

"I made a searching and fearless moral inventory of myself seeking to identify the wrongs of my past life."

Scripture:
MEDITATIONS

The balanced insight into self, gained through the doing of a Step 4 inventory, is important for two reasons. First, it releases us from the extremes of either an inflated ego or the condemnation of self. Second, our new concept of self-honesty and self-examination lifts us away from that destroying dependence and approval of others. We begin to learn to stand on our own two feet depending ONLY ON JESUS for our strength and healing. Only then can we learn to move toward a healthy, new sense of responsibility as each of us begins to "carry his own load". (Verse 5) Our lives will become balanced instead of lop-sided and out of control. We will have acquired a new sense of responsibility - a responsibility for who we really are.

Pray, dear friend, that you will be successful in taking a full and complete inventory of your moral self - that which is inside of you that makes you "tick".

DAY SIX - Study Proverbs 5:3-6

This reading seems to concern itself with adultery alone. Yet we can all learn a lesson from the type of behavior described here.

When we first begin to lean toward out-of-control, compulsive behavior; we do so because it is pleasant. We like what sex or our addictive behavior will do for us. We are overtaken by this pleasure and we totally ignore whether this behavior is proper or good. We find our new compulsive behavior to be an escape from the reality of our life crisis. Unfortunately, in the end, our behavior causes us to become very bitter and filled with guilt. The end result can wind up in rape, death or some other very serious consequence. Only long after we fall into our addictive behavior can we see how destructive this has become to ourselves and to those around us. We have become a threat to ourselves and to those who are closest to us.

How very important it is for us to seriously "think on this path of life" which we have chosen to walk. This is just what each of us is attempting to do in Step 4. We realize that many of our ways and reasons for doing things have been unstable and "off the wall".

But now, we determine that with the help of Jesus Christ, we will begin making an honest personal inventory. What we have done in the past, and put on paper, will help us to see ourselves just as we really are. This will help us to courageously seek out and identify our weaknesses. As we do this, we know, deep down in our hearts, that Jesus is with us to give us His wisdom, forgiveness, and unconditional love as we advance through this healing process.

DAY SEVEN - Study Proverbs 16:2-3

A pilot, in flying his aircraft, may very well become confused in a thick dark cloud or rainstorm. In order to keep him straight up and flying into the horizon, each airplane is equipped with an instrument called an artificial horizon indicator. When the pilot runs into this visual problem, he relies on this instrument to guide him safely through the dark clouds or heavy fog.

This illustration clearly shows us that our minds can become very mixed up during the storms of life. We can, very easily, get off the right track and begin to fly upside down or in the wrong direction. You see, our Jesus is the instrument that keeps us on course when the storm clouds come into our lives. By keeping ourselves in touch with Jesus, we can know what path is best for each of us as we go through the storm. Trying to run our own lives without Jesus is like trying to fly a plane through a black cloud bank with no horizon indicator.

As we open our lives, completely and honestly, to God's presence and begin to accept His direction, we have taken a giant step toward recovery and healing. Through Him, we can find our way through the storm back into the sunshine. Let's keep our eyes on Him!

Walking the 12 Steps with Jesus Christ

Step 4 Lesson 14

"I made a searching and fearless moral inventory of myself seeking to identify the wrongs of my past life."

Action Word : MORAL

STEP 4

OUR ERRATIC EMOTIONS

In lesson 12, we took a look at some of the "head games" we played with excuses for not taking our moral inventory. Now, we continue to deal with some of the erratic emotions that get in our way to keep us from taking this inventory and the ways in which we have hurt others in our life.

Let us understand fully - we did not get into our problem over night and we will not kick the problem over night in most cases. Years, sometimes many years of problems have caused us to get where we are today. Let us be patient but determined in dealing with this old and very painful problem of our addiction. It will take time to dig out and identify the problem, then to apply God's healing touch; and finally to learn to live without our old self as a new creation brought about by the saving power of Jesus Christ. We are on the road to finding our true inner self. It is most important that we stick to this process of healing and keep working at it. It will work as we give ourselves over to its mighty healing power, the power of God's Holy Spirit. Our Lord Jesus Christ is our faithful healer. He promises to heal us when we come to Him.

ADMITTING OUR MISTAKES

In the past, we were very quick to recognize the faults of others. We were unable to recognize and deal with the faults in ourselves. No one likes to admit a mistake or some difficult, painful, and humiliating part of their life. Sometimes, we can hardly bring ourselves to look at the "dark side" of our self. In order to begin this process and stick with it, we must eliminate the word "BLAME" from our mind. Blame has nothing whatever to do with solving our problem. Jesus never said a thing about forgiving only the guilty. Instead, He said that forgiveness was for ALL OF US. The Bible tells us "everyone has sinned and is far away from God's saving presence." (Romans 3:23) Therefore, we are all guilty and we must ALL forgive. We must seek forgiveness from God and from those around us. But we don't stop there. WE MUST ALSO FORGIVE OURSELVES - ME!!! This requires great willingness to change and to heal our past. We must begin right now, for Jesus is calling us into the fullness of life. (John 10:10) "I have come that you might have life - life in all its fullness." Jesus said. If you want the fullness, the joy, love and peace of a full life, you must begin NOW. Once you begin this journey and get past the first few "hard spots", you will begin to feel the relief and joy of the healing process. The more you work at it, the more you will find Jesus as your ultimate Healer and the more you will find the joy of being "ME", the me that Jesus created. The more you are willing to admit to God, to yourself, and to another human being the exact nature of your wrongs, the cleaner you will feel and the more in touch you will be with Jesus and yourself. This will clean up your behavior and your life. You will become the YOU that God created.

HOW DO I MAKE THIS CHANGE?

"How do I come to find the person that God intended me to become?", you may ask yourself. This is a process of submitting ourselves to God and learning. The Bible is the source of this learning and experience. Jesus said - "I am THE way, THE truth, and THE life." (John 14:6) We find Jesus and learn about Jesus in the Bible, hence the reason for Growth/Strength Step 5 found in lesson 19.

We human beings are never quite alike in our spiritual and mental makeup. Each of us, when we make our inventory, will need to determine what the wrongs of our past have been. In the AA program, these types of wrongs are called "defects of character". Once I begin to identify the trends in my life which are caused by the past wrongs that I suffered, I will begin to learn more about "ME" and I can begin to remove or change these defects to reflect the true me that God created me to become. I can begin to deal with these defects and correct them by the grace of Jesus Christ. I can begin to walk on the right path with confidence that, at last, I am on the right track.

THE SEVEN "DEADLY SINS"

In previous lessons, I have discussed the wrongs that other people have done to us - hurting us inside in our spirit.

Now, I will discuss the wrongs that we do to others that hurt them as well as ourselves.

The vast majority of our own wrongs or sins were started long ago in our lives. Again, we may try to play head games and call these - defects of character, immorality, maladjustments, problems etc. The Word of God calls them sin and sin is wrong. Let's take a look at the definition of sin.

Sin is a form of thinking that results in behavior that separates us from our relationship with God and each other AND will eventually cause us to end up in spiritual and possibly physical death. In John 10:10, we read, "The thief (the devil) comes only in order to steal, kill and destroy." Sin is the tool of the devil of lies and his intentions are quite clear.

In making our inventory, we need to be brutally honest with ourselves. We need to examine ourselves in the area of these seven deadly sins (see Proverbs 6:16-19):

STEP 4

Step 4 Lesson 14

"I made a searching and fearless moral inventory of myself seeking to identify the wrongs of my past life."

Action Word : MORAL

1. **PRIDE**—Pride isolates us from others. This sinful attitude makes "ME" the most important person in my life over God and anyone else. This sin can completely blind us from living righteously through Jesus Christ. It is the basic breeder of all difficulties in our relationships with God, ourselves, and others. We constantly seek to justify ourselves, making demands on others and ourselves that cannot be met without getting into disobedient behavior. We get into addictive behavior and then our pride seeks to justify that behavior. Can you see how pride infects our thinking and becomes a vicious cycle of destruction in our life? The fear that we are not as good as we ought to be lies beneath pride. Again, we will do anything in our power to justify ourselves in all that we do. We compete by trying to place ourselves above our competition. We seek to prove our excellence. (Durrance)

2. **GREED**—Greed is a self-centeredness that wants more of whatever it wants. Greedy thinking makes us believe that everything can belong to us and we will get it at all costs. Greed is an appetite of the flesh to possess whatever we can see or touch. The motive of greed is to satisfy that appetite of "I want" and the fear beneath greed is that we will not have enough and we want to get more and more and more. (Durrance)

3. **LUST**—Lust is a compulsion to possess someone or something and it may be driven by the desire for power. Lust is the acting out of pride and greed. We birth the idea that we want someone or something and we go about getting it. Lust applies to all forms of greedy behavior, not just to sexual misbehavior. However, it is the most serious in sexual acting out. Under lust, we will find the fear that we will not be able to control the world in which we live. Therefore, we want to seize control now—whether by possessing a person or grasping for some sort of power. (Durrance)

4. **ANGER**—Anger produces unforgiveness and resentment. It is usually triggered by an unmet expectation. Either something did not happen that we did expect, or something did happen that we did not expect. An angry attitude says, "I'll fight you for what I want and I don't care what happens or who I hurt." It starts with being prideful, then greedy, then lustful, and ends with uncontrollable rage and violence. In the advanced stages of anger, it is a sign of a person who is totally out of control. Anger is an emotion that we all experience. We must be very mindful of how we handle our anger in our relationships with God, ourselves, and others. Anger needs to be vented in nondestructive ways. Violent and uncontrollable anger is sinful and wrong. The fear that others are not meeting our expectations lies beneath anger. Therefore, we will be out of control. (Durrance)

5. **GLUTTONY**—Gluttony is the over-indulgence in any of the body's desire. Gluttony causes a person to act out his pride, greed, lust, and anger by "eating" himself to death. He drowns his problems and his life in food, substances, or any unbalanced behavior patterns. This is particularly destructive with food and substances because the body is harmed and possibly destroyed. It is as much a form of self-destruction as is alcoholism, drug addiction, and smoking. It is the fear that we will not have enough food or enough of whatever it is that we want that lies beneath gluttony. We "eat" all that we can to make sure that we do not starve. (Durrance)

6. **ENVY**—Envy also isolates us by setting us over or against others who have something that we want, but do not have. Envy stirs up dissatisfaction with who we are and what we have. An envious person becomes terribly jealous of what others have in their possession or status in life. An envious person tends to want to "get even" with others by stealing or cheating. Other methods of "getting even" include gossiping or any other form of tearing down or destroying another person's reputation. The fear beneath envy is that someone else has more than we have or something that we really want to make our lives as full as theirs seem to be. (Durrance)

7. **SLOTH**—Sloth is mostly considered pure laziness. However, it also includes the dis-order that causes us to neglect things we shouldn't. Slothful people try to live off of others. The person who is suffering acts out by using others for what they want. They think, "I'm here and you owe me a living and the good things of life. I'm going to sit here and let you take care of my needs and I will not do anything in return." This type of person thrives on their laziness; it has become their drug of choice. This is the way they act out their rebellion in life. Beneath sloth is the fear that we cannot do something well enough, therefore, we put off starting. (Durrance)

It is important to note that unforgiveness and resentment are two great sins that are deadly, but not counted in the seven. Unforgiveness seems to be the fear that something is not fair. Resentment seems to be the fear that if we forgive, we will only be hurt again by the one we need to forgive. Remember, forgiveness does not mean to excuse and forget. Forgiveness means to accept people as they are instead of as we think they ought to be.

Step 4 Lesson 14

"I made a searching and fearless moral inventory of myself seeking to identify the wrongs of my past life."

Action Word : MORAL

STEP 4

FEAR - THE UNDERLYING CAUSE

All of the above deadly sins are generated and driven by a sense of fear and insecurity. We are a broken people and something is very much missing in our lives. This causes us to become very much afraid deep down inside our spirit and creates a terrible sickness within. Once overtaken by fear, we generate more sickness of the spirit and the problem becomes worse and worse. This fear and insecurity stirs up our insides and causes us to experience terrible hurt. In our desperation, we seek to find ways to put out the fire of our desperate hurts; we become addicted to some substance or behavior. We eventually fall and find ourselves totally helpless over our problem, pinned to the ground by our inner sickness. We try to cover up the root of the problem with our pride followed by many of its six other companions.

The terrible fear that comes from our pride causes us:

1. To desire to steal the possessions of others.
2. To lust for sex and power over others and ourselves.
3. To become angry when we "can't have our own way".
4. To become envious when others succeed and we fail.
5. To eat, drink, and grab for everything that we want.
6. To become overly concerned that we will never have enough.
7. To cause us genuine alarm at the thought of having to work - to become terribly lazy and dependent upon others.

These fears become the termites that chew up the house that we live in. The more we feed them, the stronger they will become and the sooner our house will crumble.

The purpose of the searching and fearless moral inventory is to identify all of the areas of our life to which the many messages of the cross need to be brought. We need to know specifically what to give to Jesus to redeem and heal. He will give us beauty for ashes. He will dispel our fears. Our fears will no longer control us. We will conquer our fears through the power of Christ at work in us.

SOME QUESTIONS TO GUIDE US ALONG THE WAY

The Step 4 process is a new method of living, which will go on for the rest of our lives. We no longer will allow our inner self to become "junked up" with the wrongs of the past or the present. In Step 10, which follows later, we will adopt a new method of taking inventory each day and learn to deal with the wrongs each day - one day at a time.

But now, let us consider some thought provoking questions that will help us to consider and identify our past wrongs:

1. "What were the past wrongs which resulted because of my family ties - mother, father, sisters and brothers? Did I use this as an excuse to get drunk and act out my hurts?"

2. "What is my primary instinct for sex? Has there been any sexual abuse in my past life? Was I used by another for sexual pleasure? How do I feel about the opposite sex? When, how, and in just what instances did my selfish pursuit of the sex relationship damage other people and me? What people were hurt and how badly? What has been my own idea about my sexuality - what is its purpose? Have I experienced a 'live in' affair? Have I parented children outside of marriage? Have I been a party to an abortion? Have I been in a marriage that failed? Have I been in same sex relationships?"

3. "How did I apply myself during my school life? Did I succeed in school? What caused me to "blow it"? What was behind my inability to learn and apply myself the way I should have?"

4. "What has been my relationship to others, especially with those that I do not know very well? What holds me back from making friends? Have I made a mess of my personal image among my friends in the community? How? Do I tend to take it out on others? How? What is my relationship with most of my friends? Have I hurt someone deeply who was once my trusted friend? Why?"

5. "In the process of making a living in my occupation, how did my addiction cause me to "blow it"? What caused me to be unable to hold down a job? Did I experience fear and inferiority about my fitness for the job, which destroyed my confidence and filled me with fear? What were the causes of my fear and insecurity? Did I try to cover up these feelings of inadequacy by bluffing, cheating, lying, stealing, or failing to do my job properly? Did I complain or "con" my way through the day? What was the cause of these feelings? Did I want to play "big shot" and run the show? What caused these feelings? Was I wasteful or careless - did I have an "I don't give a darn attitude?" What caused me to feel that way? Was I a penny pincher or freeloader borrowing money and refusing to pay it back? What caused me to do that? Did I refuse to support my family paying no attention

STEP 4

Step 4 Lesson 14

"I made a searching and fearless moral inventory of myself seeking to identify the wrongs of my past life."

Action Word: MORAL

to my spouse and her needs? What caused that behavior? Did I try to cut corners financially in "quick fix" deals? Why?"

LOOKING DEEPER "UNDER THE COVER"

Now that we have touched on the "biggies", let us take a look "under the cover". Here we find the problems of emotional insecurity, which are fear, worry, anger, self-pity, guilt, and depression. These problems are the result of something deep inside our spirits that is very wrong. Somewhere along the line, we have been exposed to a personal relationship which has "set the ball rolling" in the areas mentioned. We now find ourselves with a problem, but the question is, where did it come from and how did it get here today? Let's take a look at some more questions:

1. "What sexual situations have caused me to become anxious, bitter, frustrated, or depressed?" Look at each situation carefully and see where you have wronged another. "Was I selfish or did I make unreasonable demands on others? Do I feel guilty about these wrong relationships?"

2. "Was my problem caused by the behavior of others or situations over which I had no control? Am I blaming myself for this condition? Did I lack the ability to accept conditions that I could not change? Do I feel guilty about these areas of my life because I was unable to change them? How did I handle my reaction to this problem? Am I now willing to change my attitude toward this situation? Was I either too dominating over others or was I too dependent upon others, leaning on them for every little need in my life? Whichever was my reaction, it caused me anxiety and stress and caused me to "go off the deep end" of life. Just how did this happen and why did I become out of balance in this response?"

UNDER/OVER DEPENDENCY

All of us have a basic need to be loved by God, by others and to be accepted by friends. Because of our over-dependence (our leaning on others) or our under dependence (our control of others), we developed hurt feelings and a sense of persecution. "Nobody understands me and how I feel", we cry. Then we get angry at others because we think it is always the other guy's fault and we rise up to retaliate or get even. We struggle for control in our lives but we seem to be tumbling fast and hard into the pits of hell itself. We hurt badly and find ourselves unable to relate to others especially to those closest to us. This self-centered defeatist behavior has blocked our love relationship with others around us. We feel isolated and very much alone. Step 4 helps us to take a good look inside for the cause.

SETTING UP OUR INVENTORY LIST

Now is the time to get to work on your inventory. Take several large sheets of ruled paper and find yourself a quiet place alone. Pray to Jesus for honesty and wisdom. The Inventory can be completed in the following three ways:

1. You may organize the wrongs in your life under three categories:

   ▶ wrongs you committed against God or specific things you need to make peace with Him about
   ▶ wrongs you committed towards others
   ▶ wrongs others committed towards you

2. You can simply write your life story, noting the different wrongs throughout and then deal with them one by one.

3. You may simply organize your inventory following the order of the presentation of the material in the study guide. There are many, many guiding questions throughout. For example, once you have completely read through Step 4 once or twice, you may return to pages 51-55 and then 62-69 and begin reading again—much more slowly and carefully beginning to write about the life events that come to mind as you are reading. List specific wrongs and the emotions that seem to go with them that need healing.

For any of the three ways described for completing your inventory, the following six questions should be considered about each situation or life event that you write about. These questions will help you pinpoint exactly what happened and what you experienced emotionally that needs healing.

▶ When did this happen?
▶ Where did this happen?
▶ Who was involved?
▶ What were the wrongs committed by you and by others?
▶ How do you feel about these wrongs?
▶ How have these wrongs had an impact on you?

INVENTORY

Step 4 Lesson 14

"I made a searching and fearless moral inventory of myself seeking to identify the wrongs of my past life."

Action Word:
INVENTORY

PERSONAL INVENTORY CHECK LIST

NOTE: Your personal inventory should be made up of the wrongs that happened to you in your past. These wrongs include those done by others toward you and those wrongs done by you toward others.

The following check list will help you to consider some of the situations in your life that caused hurt. This list is by no means a complete one. It is intended as a guide to get you to think about your past. Remember not to blame anyone. You are simply trying to identify the events in your past that caused you hurt in your spirit today.

WRONGS DONE BY OTHERS TO ME

A. AT CONCEPTION:
- My parents - was it real love or was it lust? Did they want and expect this pregnancy or was I an accident?
- Were drugs, alcohol, or violence involved at the time?
- Were my parents committed to each other in a married love relationship?
- Why did my parents come together? What was their motive?
- Was there rape, incest, or some other sin involved?
- What, if anything, do I remember about my conception?

B. IN THE WOMB
- Did my Mom rest and eat right while I was within her womb?
- Did my parents stroke me in love while in the womb? How was I treated at that time? Was there any violence, hatred, fighting (verbal or otherwise)? Was there any alcohol, drugs, smoking, or difficult behavior present by those around me, especially by Mom and Dad?
- Did my parents believe in God, pray, and go to church?
- Was there any witchcraft, satan worship, loud rock music or heavy metal music, prolonged and loud TV present?
- Were my parents or other family members involved in pornography or any kind of sexual sin? How?
- Was I treated in any way - physically, mentally, emotionally, spiritually, or otherwise - which made me feel unwanted?
- What, if anything, do I remember about myself before birth that brings hurt and pain to my spirit?

C. AT BIRTH
- Do I remember any darkness, pain, lack of air, or fear of any kind during the birth process?
- What do I remember about my birth? What have I since learned about my birth that makes me feel sad or hurts me inside?
- Was I a normal birth or did I need special medical assistance, breech birth, "C" section, etc? Did I have any painful complications during birth?
- Am I disabled in any way as a result of the time in the womb or birth process?

D. BIRTH TO AGE 3
- Did my Mom feed me and care for me like I was a part of her? Why not?
- Did Dad hold me, touch me, play and talk to me? How did he treat me? What do I remember about this time of my life?
- Is there any hurt or pain in my memory over anything that happened during this early stage of my life?
- Was I mistreated in any way by anyone that I can remember?
- Did I have any problems learning to potty train, walk, talk, be disciplined, obey, and handle my relationships with brothers and sisters?
- How would I describe my family relationship at this time?
- Is there any event that happened during this time that sticks in my mind?
- What did my parents, brothers, and sisters think of me at this time and how did I get along with them? What did I think of myself at this age?

"One of the greatest discoveries a man makes, one of his great surprises, is to find he can do what he was afraid he couldn't do."
- Henry Ford

"Doubt and fear are the great enemies of knowledge, and he who encourages them, who does not slay them, thwarts himself at every step."
- As A Man Thinketh

"Dedicate yourself to continuous personal improvement - you are your most precious resource."
- Brian Tracy

Walking the 12 Steps with Jesus Christ

INVENTORY

Step 4 Lesson 14

"I made a searching and fearless moral inventory of myself seeking to identify the wrongs of my past life."

Action Word :
INVENTORY

E. AGES 3 TO 10

- Was I still living at home with my parents? What was their relationship together? Their relationship with brothers and sisters? Did they really love me and care about me?
- Could I talk with my parents about my feelings? Were they there when I needed them? Did either Mom or Dad leave me?
- Was there any fighting (verbal or physical), bad language, drinking, drugging, or sexual misbehavior present at this time?
- Was there any use of heavy metal, rock music, or prolonged use of TV in my home? Was there any satan worship or witchcraft of any sort present?
- Was I ever touched or influenced in any way in my genital area by an older person? Did another person ever use me for sexual pleasure? Did any people ever expose themselves to me sexually during that time? Was I exposed to any pornography books, pictures, videotapes, DVDs, computers, etc, or sexual language?
- Did I hurt in any way that was caused by anyone close to me in my family or living in the home? Why?
- Did my parents teach me about God? Did they go to church, pray, and read the Bible to me?
- What kinds of toys do I remember using at this age? Guns, swords, whips, clubs or other toys that caused violence or pain?
- What do I remember most about this time of life? What are the good memories and also the bad? Did I fight with other kids? What was the reason for the fights? How do I feel about this now? Did anyone show me or lead me into any bad habit during this time? How?
- What did I think of school? Did I have any problems getting along with the other kids? Did I feel wanted by them - part of the "in" crowd with my friends? Did I have difficulties with other kids or teachers in authority? Was school hard for me? Why? What was my favorite subject? What was my least favorite subject? Did I enjoy learning?
- What did I think about most during this time? What did I think of myself at this time? Who did I think I was and what did I want to become?

F. AGES 10 TO 18

Communication:

- How did I get along with the kids around me? Did I have many friends? Were friends important to me? How important?
- Did I make friends easily or was it difficult? Did I feel "in" with my friends? Did they accept me or did I have to earn my way in?
- Could I talk to Mom and Dad about how I felt in school, about the opposite sex, about sex, about getting along, about my feelings and inner self, drinking, drugs, sports, money, car, my physical looks, and personal problems?
- Did my Mom and Dad express their love openly and with physical hugging and holding? Did they tell me that they loved me?

School:

- How was school in those days in general? Did learning come easily or was it difficult? What did I think of my teachers, the school in general, sports, etc? Was I able to complete my high school education? If not, how do you now feel about that?

Evil:

- Did anyone lead me into drugs, alcohol, sex, rock music, heavy metal music, satanic worship, gangs, fights, stealing, and violence? What were the circumstances of these events and who did I follow into this pattern of behavior?
- Have I experimented with wrongful and illegal behavior and why? Do I find a thrill in disobedience? What makes me like to disobey, if that is my case? What hurts of the past may have driven me into this wrongful behavior?

Work:

- What was my attitude toward work and getting a job? Did I want to work to earn some money or did I "sponge" off of others? Where did I learn my attitude toward work? Was I pushed into

Step 4 Lesson 14

"I made a searching and fearless moral inventory of myself seeking to identify the wrongs of my past life."

Action Word: INVENTORY

taking over any part or all parts of another person's job, like being a Mom or Dad because my Mom or Dad was no longer present?

The opposite sex:

▶ How do I relate to the opposite sex? What is my idea of the opposite sex and how did I learn this? Did I learn my behavior from others that may have caused my problems in sexuality? What is my idea of the purpose of sex and marriage and where did I learn this idea? Did I become controlled by my sexuality and did I use my sex in wrongful ways against others and myself? How?

Substitute parent:

▶ Was I pushed into taking the job of another person in the family? Was I forced into being a Mom or Dad in my family because that person did not do their job? How did I learn this and how did it affect me? What was my reaction?

Mom & Dad relationship:

▶ What did my Mom and Dad really think of me? How did they tell me this in every day life? Did Mom and Dad care for me in love, encouragement, by spending quality time with me, have fun with me, pray with me on a regular basis during this time? If not, why? Did we go to church together?

My self-concept:

▶ What did I think of myself during this time of my life? What kind of person was I? What good things do I remember most during this time of life? What difficult, hurtful situations do I remember during this time?

G. ABANDONMENT

Did my Mom or Dad leave me at any time in my early life? Did they show me that they did not care for me or want me in their life? Was I forced to live on my own or in the care of a stepparent? How did I feel about all of this? Did I become the ball that was kicked back and forth between my parents? What do I remember about all of this and how did this situation affect me? Do I now have a desire to find my parents?

Abandonment can be one of the most hurtful experiences that a person can be exposed to especially early in life. When parents, either or both, give up on the child and leave that child, the child has lost the primary person given to him by God to teach him the true meaning of love. The child becomes lost in a sea of other human beings and never feels wanted or secure again. His sense of belonging to a family unit has been destroyed. Even when adopted into another family, the child feels like a misfit in that family. The child generally becomes very insecure and hurts very deeply inside.

When this situation happens, a great deal of patience is needed with the person suffering. As that person matures, they will learn and experience love through the power of the Holy Spirit moving in other human beings around them. Abandonment generally takes a long period of time in which to be healed. So open up to Jesus, dear friend, and He will heal you from the hurts of your past. Your ultimate source of love is Jesus. Come to HIM and be healed!

Now is the time to work your searching and fearless moral inventory required by Step 4. Please begin now and continue until you feel that there is nothing more hurting you inside. God bless you!

SEX - WHEN IS IT AN ADDICTION?

No study of the AA Step 4 would be complete without discussing sexual addiction. In the 25 plus years of my work with those locked up in prisons and jails, I have discovered that sexual addiction is a monumental problem in our society today. Yet sadly, most young people do not recognize sexual addiction and do not even know when a person is sexually addicted.

In order to understand when the gift of sex becomes an addiction, it is important to understand clearly the true meaning of love according to the Holy Word of God - the Bible. Please refer back to lesson 10, for the discussion regarding Godly love in the paragraph entitled "Who created me and why am I here?"

INVENTORY

Step 4 Lesson 14

"I made a searching and fearless moral inventory of myself seeking to identify the wrongs of my past life."

Action Word: INVENTORY

In this discussion, we learned that God is love and that He created us all out of love as an expression of His love for us.

How then do we arrive at the idea that "love is sex"? This is a common idea that is very wide spread among our young people today. That concept is totally inaccurate, however. How then do we identify the connection between love and our sexuality?

Let us turn to scripture for the answer. John 3:16, "For God LOVED the world so much that he GAVE His only Son, so that everyone who believes in Him may not die but have eternal life." The two key words in this verse give us a clear answer to the true meaning of love

LOVE IS ALWAYS GIVING

Therein we find the answer to our sexuality. If love is giving, then the act of sex, in order to be an act of love, must also be giving. Very easily we can see that when sex becomes an act of getting, it becomes an addiction, as with every other form of addiction.

When the motive for our sexual desires drive us into a "taking" or "getting" mind, we act out that getting or taking mind, and we have become sexually addicted. The Bible gives us a very clear command in Deuteronomy 5:18, "Do not commit adultery." Adultery is defined in the dictionary as any sexual contact outside of the state of marriage. The Bible strictly forbids adultery since that act is one of getting rather than giving. Since it is an act of getting, it is called LUST as opposed to the act of giving which is called LOVE.

Strictly speaking - adultery is sexual contact by a married person with someone other than his/her spouse. Fornication is defined as sexual contact by an unmarried person and is strictly forbidden. The Bible encourages sexual intimacy between married people. However, that sexual intimacy must be an act of giving rather than getting. Therefore, married people give themselves to each other, not for what they can get but rather for what they can give their spouse as an expression of their love for each other. Sexual intimacy is the seal of the covenant of marriage; that seal being placed upon the couple at the time of their commitment to each other in the holy and sacred state of marriage.

When a person becomes obsessed with the power of their sexuality, and this obsession drives him to seek a sexual connect regardless of the situation, it becomes a very strong sexual addiction. Pornography is the tool of the devil, driving us into that lustful state of mind in which we seek to act out our sexual appetite with absolutely no regard to the commandment of God. This is totally a sin and is forbidden by the seventh commandment already quoted.

Any sexual acting out except with a person's own spouse is an addiction and sin. This includes sins of thought, pornography, sexual language, sexual fantasy etc. It includes sexual contact with a person of the same sex or a person of the opposite sex other than the spouse. It also includes indecent exposure, the "peeping Tom" syndrome, masturbation, sex with children under age 18 (of either sex), and rape, which is forced sex against the person of another. All sexual contact in thought, word, or action is forbidden by the seventh commandment except with a person's own spouse.

It follows then, that sexual addiction is the acting out of our sexuality in a way that desires total self-gratification. We seek the mental and physical pleasure of the sex act and nothing more. The purpose of this compulsion is the same as with alcohol, drugs, or any other kind of addiction. We are trying to escape from or cover up the terrible hurts of the past deep within us.

Many times sexual addiction can be fueled by sexual abuse at an early age. Somewhere in the past, there has been sexual abuse, which hurt the person badly, and then that person may choose to act out to others in that same way later in life. This is much the same as a person who has an alcoholic father in childhood. Later in life, he may become an alcoholic and act out in the same way his father did.

Sexual addiction is very difficult to overcome. It requires deep prayer and Bible study in order to break the compulsive desire for sexual acting out. This program will help to guide you along the way if this is your problem. Stick with it, friend; Jesus will heal you. May God bless you!

PRAYER
Growth & Strength

Step 4 Lesson 15

**Action Words:
OPENING UP
TO GOD**

PRAYER

DEALING WITH THE PRESENT

Up to this point in our study of addiction, we have dealt with our past life. We have looked back to try to understand the events which make up our past. Even though we have only studied four steps, we have come a long way in that process.

We now begin to look at the present time in our life. To those of us addicted, there are only two really important times in our life - the past and the present. We do not consider the future because it is uncertain and not currently within our grasp. Psalm 118:24 states - "This is the day of the Lord's victory; let us be happy, let us celebrate!" And so we begin to shape the person that we now want to become today. These are the Biblical steps found in the right column of the Road Map.

Our first Growth/Strength Step is prayer. Prayer is absolutely essential to the healing, growth and strength of our spirit, which has been so damaged by our past. In our human relationships, we cannot have growing and loving relationships with other people unless we communicate with them. We need to talk together and BE together in order to become bonded to others. As previously discussed that bond is Godly love. To become part of anyone's life, it is essential to open up and communicate with them. Our desire is that they become a part of our life.

It follows, that if we believe that Jesus is our Healer and Savior, then we need to take positive action to invite Him into our life and our very being. If Jesus is number ONE in our life, then we need to act that way toward Him and grow in that oneness with Him. This is the process of falling in love with Jesus.

THE ELEMENTS OF PRAYER

The essential parts of our conversation with Jesus are:

PERSONAL - Jesus is personal to us because we believe that He lives within us. The Bible tells us "The Spirit of the living God is within you". (1 Corinthians 6:19-20)

LORD - Jesus is our Lord because He is number one in our life above all other persons or things. This is obedience to the first commandment, which calls us to put God first before all others. (See Deuteronomy 5:7). We truly have Jesus on our pedestal in the very center of our life.

SAVIOR - Jesus is our Savior because He saves us from certain death (our sins). Without Him we are lost. Only He can rescue us from our sins and ourselves.

OPENING THE DOOR OF OUR HEART

Prayer is a conversation with Jesus in which I open my inner self to Him. The prayer should start off with a positive statement that Jesus Christ is my personal Lord and Savior. The prayer might go like this - "Dear Jesus, I love you and I need you. You are my personal Lord and Savior. You live within me. You are number one in my life, Lord, and You came to save me from my own sinfulness. I love You Lord and give myself to You now - my sins, the wrongs of my life and all that I am. Take me Lord and forgive me and heal me. I want to receive the gift of Your life that You promised me. I'm not worthy Lord but You said You would give it to me any way. I receive it now and thank You from the bottom of my heart. Thanks Lord. I love You and I'm Yours - AMEN!" In this way, I affirm with my lips what is in my heart - mainly that Jesus Christ is everything to ME. We all must open ourselves up to HIM.

ACCEPT JESUS INTO YOUR LIFE

The next step is to accept Jesus into your life. Making a statement like the following can do this: "Lord Jesus, come into my heart and my life. I open the doors of my heart wide to You, Lord. Please come and make Your home within me. Come into my heart as You came into the stable at Bethlehem on that first Christmas. I welcome You, Lord, right now". In Matthew 11:28-30, Jesus invites us to come to Him. He will give us rest. In John 14:15-17, Jesus gives us another Helper, the Holy Spirit, who will "remain with you and is in you."

Revelation 3:20 invites us to "open the door" to Jesus so that He can come in and have supper with us. The Bible is full of invitations for us to come to Jesus and accept Him into our lives. In the writings of Paul, he calls this being "born again". And so, this part of prayer is to accept Jesus into our hearts - to invite Him into the very center of our being.

ASK JESUS FOR OUR "NEEDS"

The third part of our prayer is to ask Jesus for what we need. The Bible tells us that our greatest need is to be ONE WITH JESUS. In John 14:18-20, Jesus tells us, "When that day comes (the coming of the Holy Spirit), you will know that I am in my Father and that you are in Me, just as I am in you." Since the Holy Spirit came on that first Pentecost, we are in Jesus and He is in us when we accept Him as our personal Lord and Savior. The most perfect prayer is to give yourself to Him so that He can become one with you and you one with Him. Your prayer may sound like this - "Lord Jesus, I give myself to you just as I am. I hold nothing back. I want to be one with you in beautiful spiritual communion. Here I am, Lord - I'm Yours and You're

PRAYER

Step 4 Lesson 15

Action Words: OPENING UP TO GOD

mine. Thank You, Lord Jesus, for coming into me. Never let me go, Lord, and help me to never let you go. You and I are one. Lord, I trust You to take care of all of my needs this day. I believe that those needs are being met right now. Thank you Jesus - AMEN!"

Some of us may have an idea that prayer is taking our shopping list to Jesus. We come before Him and ask for all sorts of stuff. There is nothing wrong with that practice except that we may have missed the point of our relationship with Jesus. He made us in love. He wants us to love Him in return along with loving our brothers and sisters (neighbors). This is the very reason He created us. Our Lord is most pleased with us when we give ourselves to Him, just as we are, in love. When we do that, He will provide us with all of our other needs as well. We won't need to bring Him our shopping list. Matthew 6:33 says - "Instead, be concerned above everything else with the Kingdom of God and with what He requires of you and He will provide you with all these other things." The Kingdom of God is our relationship with Jesus Christ. When we give ourselves to Him, our relationship becomes complete and He promises that He will give us whatever else we need. This is also a very strong profession of our faith in Him. He knows more about the real needs of our life than we do. So let us trust Him to know what is best for us personally.

PRAISE JESUS

The fourth part of our prayer life is to praise Him for the gift that He is giving to us - the gift of a new life. John 10:10 says, "I have come that you might have life, life in all its fullness." Jesus is calling us into new life in communion with Him. It's super important that we visualize this new life happening within us and to be transformed by it. Paul tells us in Romans 12:2, "Do not conform yourselves to the standards of this world, but let God transform you inwardly by a complete change of your mind." In doing this, the Word of God calls us to trust in the Lord and to not lean on our own understanding. (See Proverbs 3:5-6) When we trust in the Lord, He will give us the new life by transforming our mind and life. By praising Him, we believe in this gift and accept it into our inner person - we act upon our belief. Even though the new life may not immediately be visible to our eyes, our hearts and minds are being changed. Soon it will become very visible to those who know us best and us. It is miraculous to meet an old friend who tells us - "Gee, friend, you're not the same person. Something is different about you now." That's the power of God's Holy Spirit within us and it is GLORIOUS. We are on the road to the healing of our past. In praising Jesus, we act on that belief and go forth to walk in this new life and to thank Him. It becomes real in our actions toward our friends and us. His grace brings it to pass in our life.

LISTEN TO JESUS

The final part of our new prayer life is to spend time listening to Jesus. Most of us do all the talking to Him. It is against our nature to listen. Lack of listening is a big part of our lack of understanding and practicing the spiritual walk. Now, let us practice putting ourselves "in neutral" and listen to Jesus speak to us deep in our hearts. He will love us in HIS way when we stop and listen. So, we need to open up and "Be still and know that I am God". (Psalm 46:10 NKJV). Spend some quiet time listening to Jesus today but take care not to fall asleep. In time, you will BE pleasantly surprised at the results - a glorious friendship with Jesus. His will for you will become much more evident in your spirit and you will know just how to proceed to follow Him.

YOUR PRAYER - A SAMPLE ENDING

Your prayer might end this way, "Thank you, Jesus, for the new life that You are placing within me right now. Thank You for speaking to me in my heart. Lord, I feel your mighty presence in my life. I worship You my Jesus. Thanks for being within me and for placing your loving arms around me. I give myself to You this day and for the rest of my life." Be open to the Lord. Use simple language that you use every day as though you are talking to your best friend, because you are. There is no need to flower up your words; just be yourself. He is not impressed with fancy words or long prayers; rather, He wants a deep sincere prayer from a heart who loves Him. He knows that you are far from perfect so do not fear. Let your thoughts and words flow just the way they come from your heart.

ESTABLISH A ROUTINE - SELECT A TIME

It is most important that you make a regular daily habit out of your prayer life. It must become a regular routine for you, just like brushing your teeth or taking a shower. Set a time aside each day at the same time of the day, if possible. The best time to pray is upon rising in the morning. The Holy Word of God calls us to give the Lord the FIRST fruits of our labors. The first fruit of your time is at the beginning of your day. Of course, it is not mandatory that it be the first thing, but it must be daily and regularly. It does not need to be a very long time - rather it should be quality time, not time left over. Make the time you spend with Jesus count. Find a quiet spot in your life and sit or kneel. Do not get too comfortable so that you will fall asleep. Stay awake and concentrated on

PRAYER
Growth & Strength

Step 4 Lesson 15

Action Words:
OPENING UP TO GOD

> Intimacy with Jesus comes from spending quality time with Him.
> -Ray Geisel

> "When has what you feared ever become your reality?"
> -Rick Beneteau

> "Doubt and fear are the great enemies of knowledge, and he who encourages them, who does not slay them, thwarts himself at every step."
> - As A Man Thinketh

---

your relationship with Jesus. It is also important to pray the Sinner's Prayer before going to sleep at night. During this time, you look over the day just past. In the Sinner's Prayer, you come to Jesus – 1) Believing on Him as personal Lord and Savior; 2) Accepting Him into your heart; 3) Confessing your sins of that day to Him; and asking forgiveness; 4) Declaring your oneness with Him; and 5) Praising and thanking Him for the gift of new life that He is giving you. Your day should always close by talking to Jesus. Get in the habit of being quiet - stilling your mind and listening to Him. Pray regularly - it's good for you. It leads to spiritual growth and strength.

WALKING WITH JESUS DURING EACH DAY

As you learn to pray naturally and Jesus becomes more a part of your everyday life, you will find that during the day your thoughts will turn to Him. You will begin to see Jesus in the people you meet, the work you do, and the sounds and talk that you speak and hear. Jesus will pop into your mind over and over again. Spend a few seconds just thanking Him for everything He is doing for you each time He pops into your mind. Just remember those three little words - turn it over! Remember Step 3. Thank Jesus for receiving you and for coming into your life.

PRAYER - THE TOOL THAT DRIVES THE DEVIL OUT

No discussion on prayer would be complete without a few words on the mighty power of prayer to overcome temptation. Temptation is something that happens to every person alive from time to time depending on how much our lives have been in compulsive sinful behavior. Temptation is an opportunity for each of us to choose the way of the devil or the way of Jesus Christ. Since all of us have sinned and fall short of God's glory, we will always be tempted. It is part of our inheritance of imperfection from our first parents in Genesis 3.

Our first and most powerful line of defense against the temptation of the devil is prayer. Prayer is THE most powerful tool in our armor of faith found in Ephesians 6:18. So when the old devil comes to attack you through temptation, turn to Jesus in prayer and rebuke him. Cast him out in the mightiest name of all names - JESUS CHRIST. The word tells us that he must flee. Prayer, then, is our strongest defense against Satan. In prayer, we are guaranteed success.

PRAYER

PRAYER OPENS UP OUR SPIRITUAL LIFE

Prayer is the first and most important building block in our new spiritual life. It opens the communication line between each of us and our God. It builds closeness to Jesus and will make our spirit strong. Make it a regular and good habit. It is also very necessary for you to pray constantly while you are doing your 4th Step inventory. Jesus will help you to look back into your life to identify those hurtful wrongs that continue to cause your spiritual pain. Replace the bad habits in your life with the great and good habit of prayer. You will become the person you want to be, a man or woman of God. You will receive the gifts of God's Holy Spirit. (See Galatians 5:22) Believe in prayer and practice it. You will be the winner. Jesus assures you the victory. He died that you and I might have the fullness of life.

STEP 5

Step 5 Lesson 16

"I admitted to God, to myself, and to another human being the exact nature of my wrongs"

Action Word : ADMIT

OUR HEALING BEGINS

In Step 4, we searched for the wrongs in our past that caused us so much grief in our inner self. We did all that we could to identify them and get them down on our personal inventory sheet.

Having done that to the best of our ability, we begin the healing portion of the second stage of this program. This portion probably is the most challenging part in our recovery process, but it can also be one of the most rewarding and fulfilling in terms of breaking the loneliness and isolation of our past. Up until now, we may have felt alone and lonely in our struggle to overcome our addiction and the resulting behavior that it has caused in us. In this step, we become entirely ready to begin the process of letting go of the problems that are the cause of all this - we are ready to really put into practice those three little words - "TURN IT OVER"!

A CALL TO EMPTY OURSELVES OF OUR PAST

In order to successfully accomplish this healing step, the three part sharing it calls for must be acted out sincerely and completely within us. That is, all of what we have discovered about ourselves in our Step 4 inventory must come out from deep within our inner self. Our inventory must be freely admitted to God, to ourselves, and to another human being. This sharing, or "giving up of self", needs to take place as completely as possible, with nothing held back. Remember that the success of this cleansing process depends on our honesty and our willingness to let go. This is the basis of Healing Steps 5, 6 and 7.

The scriptural basis for completing this step is found in the Holy Bible in James 5:16 - "So then, confess your sins to one another and pray for one another, so that you will be healed. The prayer of a righteous person has a powerful effect."

TYPES OF WRONGS TO BE SHARED

The following five types of wrongs should be shared during this process of cleansing:

1. We need to openly admit ALL of our addictions.

2. We need to admit what went wrong in our original families that may have started us on the road to addiction.

3. We need to openly admit to ourselves the many generational wrongs that have been passed down from our grandparents and parents. We need to be compassionate and forgiving toward those who have gone before us and have struggled with addictive behavioral problems that may have been passed on to us.

4. We need to admit the wrongs that have occurred in all of our relationships with other people and be sincerely willing to forgive them for any damage that they may have caused us.

5. We need to admit the specific ways in which we have wronged others by the practice of our addiction and wrongful behavior.

THE IMPORTANCE OF A PRAYER PARTNER

As we begin to undertake this step, it is very important that we exercise extreme care in selecting another person to share with us. In, Lesson 12, I discussed the importance of a Prayer Partner in our process of recovery. If you have not already done so, it is extremely important for you to find a person who you can pray and share your inner life with. That person, your Prayer Partner, is needed all during the program, but especially at this time. To be able to totally complete the sharing of this step with another human being may not be possible at this time. This does not mean that it should not be done. Rather, you should wait until you find the proper person as a Prayer Partner whom you can trust, who is a good listener, who is compassionate and who is somewhat detached from your life. It is very important that this person is understanding, non-judgmental, and accepts you just where you are. Do not pick a person who is part of your daily life.

The person you pick should be someone who you know but who is not a part of your daily life and who knows all about you, your family, and friends. Rather, pick someone like a counselor, mentor, pastor, minister, or a distant friend with whom you feel comfortable sharing your life. Try to find a person who is somewhat familiar with the 12 step program of AA and who understands the process of confession. Pray to the Lord to reveal this person to you and wait until the Lord shows you that person. Be careful, however, not to keep putting this step off. This can lead to your denial again and can cause you to slide right back into that old addictive state of denial and projection all over again. As soon as you find that person, begin this process slowly but firmly.

FOUR POSITIVE RESULTS OF OUR SHARING

Four positive experiences can happen in your Healing Step 5 sharing process:

1. The guilt, which has been carried for so long, begins to melt away. We begin to feel better about letting our inside dirty feelings go. We begin to understand that authentic guilt for the past mistakes is a positive experience. We are

Step 5 Lesson 16

"I admitted to God, to myself, and to another human being the exact nature of my wrongs"

Action Word : ADMIT

STEP 5

emptying the garbage of our past, the wrongs and hurts, and that feels good. This practice of confession of our past wrongs is very old in the Christian Church. For many centuries this process has been a valuable tool in the cleansing, healing and renewal of the spirit of man. See the supplement to this lesson entitled, "Confessing is good for you" in the next column.

2. When we have fallen prey to the spiritual sickness of addiction, our inner self is full of resentment, anger, and fear. These emotions eat away at our insides and cause us a great deal of grief. This healing step gives us a wonderful opportunity to dump that grief and all the nasty emotions that come along with it. As we learn to use this step, we will learn that this is not just a one-time situation; but also, a practice that will go on the rest of our lives. As we "unload" the junk in our lives, we become stronger, cleaner inside, and greater will be our ability to resist and overcome that addiction which has controlled us for so long. Our minds will begin to think more logically and we will begin to see the face of God Himself.

3. In this process, we take a major step toward being honest with ourselves, with God, and with others. Perhaps the single greatest stumbling block to our recovery is our inability to be honest. This may be the first time in our life we have opened our deepest, darkest secrets and most private hurts and feelings to another human being. We must remember, again, that those who we confess to have had the same sort or similar experiences in their lives. To let go of our hurts, pains, and sins is to "Turn it over" to Jesus through that other person.

4. When we are compulsive addicts, slaves to a habit, we isolate or separate ourselves from those around us and from God. This isolation is a symptom of our spiritual sickness. In this sharing of ourselves with another, we break down the walls we have built around us through our addiction and related behavior. We are beginning to experience a close relationship with another person who cares and loves us, a spiritual friend. We no longer need to "go it alone". In this process we find the beginning of the end of our loneliness and isolation. We are on the road to recovery and healing.

NOTE: Please be sure to study carefully the following supplement to this lesson that follows, entitled - "Confessing is good for you". Be sure to pray fervently to the Lord and ask Him to help you to make a good confession to Him, to yourself, and to another person. May God be with you and bless you!

SUPPLEMENT - "CONFESSING IS GOOD FOR YOU!"

Confession is, says the old adage, good for the soul. Now, researchers are convinced of another benefit: Confession, the sharing of secrets, can also do wonders for the body.

According to James Pennebaker PhD., professor of psychology at Southern Methodist University in Dallas, people who are able to confide in others about unpleasant or traumatic events actually have fewer illnesses than those who keep their problems to themselves.

When we hold back talking about our problems - a relationship in trouble, the loss of someone close to us, or an act we feel sorry for - that inhibition serves as a cumulative stress on the body. Sharing thoughts and feelings, which have previously been held inside, not only reduces stress, but also actually appears to boost our immune systems.

It makes sense. Just stop for a minute and think of the feelings you get after confiding something troubling to someone. Whatever the hurt, frustration, sadness, or guilt, sharing that feeling with God and a trusted confidant, makes us realize that we are not alone in carrying our burdens. Confiding can offer insight, acceptance, forgiveness, and a relief that reaches to our very core.

An effective release may come in many forms. When most people hear the word confessing, they immediately think of the sacramental rite of confession practiced in some of the Christian churches. This is true, but confessing, in a general sense, can also mean simply the sharing of secrets from the past. When you have a heart-to-heart talk with a friend or trusted adviser, physician or teacher, you are sharing feelings. When you put your thoughts on paper, either in a letter to a friend, or in a personal journal for your eyes only, you are also sharing. Each time you share your secrets, you are, in a very real way, confessing.

HOW SHARING SECRETS AFFECTS THE BODY

Dr. Pennebaker's study looks at a variety of ways of unburdening ourselves by suggesting that there are many helpful means of "confessing" or sharing our problems. Dr. Pennebaker is not saying all who confess are experiencing healing in the same way. How people choose to share, and how and why confessing helps, is a very personal matter.

Yet, it seems worth a look at the experiences of those who observe the benefits of confessing through the sharing of secrets. These thoughts, both scientific and spiritual, are helpful in understanding how and why unburdening ourselves can help.

STEP 5

Step 5 Lesson 16

"I admitted to God, to myself, and to another human being the exact nature of my wrongs"

Action Word : ADMIT

Every day, Robert E. Decker PhD., sees patients who are suffering from the effects of frustration, guilt, sadness, and other forms of stress. As director of the Palo Alto Center for Stress-related Disorders in northern California, Dr. Decker also sees improvement in patients' health after they are able to confide troubling feelings.

To explain how this confession/improved health partnership works, Dr. Decker says we first have to understand the impact of negative emotions.

"When someone is upset," says Decker, "that usually translates into physiological tension. Negative emotions get us out of a normal state into a stress mode, affecting two coordinating systems: the endocrine system - those are your glands - and the nervous system. If guilt or negative feelings continue, along with isolation from people as a result of these feelings, there is a stage of exhaustion. That is when you are vulnerable to disease."

"Confession," explains Decker, "sets into motion a positive chain of events. Two things happen. First, an emotional discharge can be an actual physical cleansing. And second, often with an emotional release comes some kind of insight. Once confessed, a problem doesn't look so terrible. One can end up feeling lovable and connected with people again, even though recognizing that something he or she did may have been inappropriate or hurtful."

Tina learned firsthand of the healing impact of sharing when she took the courageous first step of standing in front of a small group of Overeaters Anonymous, one of many 12 step programs for overcoming addictions based on Alcoholics Anonymous.

In her early 20's, attractive and plump, Tina came to live in the United States for one year as a nanny. She brought with her a closely guarded secret. Tina was bulimic. At first she was successful in hiding her secret of overeating and purging from the family she lived with, but the extent of Tina's problem soon became apparent. With the family's encouragement and support, Tina joined Overeaters Anonymous.

Tina didn't know what to expect at the initial meeting. She was ushered into a room with a small group of people sitting around a table. At first glance, Tina looked at the obvious differences among the eight people there. Yet, she was comforted by the fact that a common thread held them together - a desire to share and work through a problem that caused each of them great suffering.

After hearing other stories as well as accepting comments from the group leader, Tina was ready. She stood, her eyes scanning the other members of the group.

"I am," said Tina, "bulimic". It was a simple statement, but a powerful first step. Tina had finally shared the problem she had worked so hard and long to hide.

Encouraged by the counselor, Tina told the group about her day. "I received a letter from my family in Switzerland this morning," she told them "I was homesick and reached for a candy bar. I knew I shouldn't eat it, but I couldn't help it. Then, of course, I felt worse. I was disappointed in myself." Everyone listened quietly. An acceptance was conveyed without words, as Tina told about a five-year pattern of overeating, purging, and overeating again.

"Suddenly, I didn't feel so alone," said Tina later, recalling her first meeting and "confession" at Over- eaters Anonymous. "I was reaching out to the group and they reached out to me. I have a 'contact' to call each day, and I'm still going to meetings. I'm not over my problem completely, but I feel better mentally and physically. I know I will make it."

John Keating, PhD., a professor of psychology at the University of Washington in Seattle, suggests why talking about our problems, even with a minimum of feedback as was the case in Tina's Overeaters Anonymous group, can be so helpful.

"People often don't have the chance to talk about very important things in their lives, things of a deep nature," explains Dr. Keating. "When people are given that chance, it's almost like stepping outside themselves and seeing themselves from someone else's viewpoint."

A group like Tina's, or any similar forum for sharing problems, can be a sort of mirror for us. Simply by talking about what is troubling us, we may gain insight into ourselves. By organizing our thoughts to tell others, we also tell ourselves what we need to know.

Keating believes confessing or sharing is critical for whatever burden we are carrying inside. He likens holding onto a negative feeling to a thorn in the side, always there to irritate.

Trying to forget about the thorn, or our problems, simply doesn't work. In our lives there are constant reminders of whatever it is we are trying to bury. The thorn must be removed, even if we feel we cannot change what has happened. Once the thorn is removed, the individual is free to heal.

Walking the 12 Steps with Jesus Christ

Christian 12 Step Ministry, Inc

Step 5 Lesson 16

"I admitted to God, to myself, and to another human being the exact nature of my wrongs"

Action Word : ADMIT

STEP 5

IDEAL CONDITIONS FOR CONFESSION

Dr. Pennebaker's research revealed two key elements that must be a part of any confession if healing is to take place; trust and objectivity. He strongly cautions that whom you share your problems with is as important as the disclosure itself.

When Tina first confided her problem with bulimia, she chose a confidant she had known for a very short time. "It seemed at first that we had a lot in common," recalls Tina, "I was eager for a close friend, and I thought sharing my deepest secret would create a bond."

Unfortunately, the choice came back to haunt her. The initial show of support from Tina's new friend soon turned sour, and Tina's "secret" was used against her in the form of jokes and ridicule. The friendship fell apart and the ill-directed confession ended up causing Tina more pain.

It may be worth holding onto a secret, in spite of the temptation to share, until we are sure our confidant is trustworthy. "This may be a strange analogy," said a friend recently when discussing the importance of trust in sharing, "but I see sharing a troublesome secret a little like the way I killed spiders. I would vacuum them up so I wouldn't risk getting too close to them. I thought this was a great system, until one day my older brother told me that the spiders would crawl out of the vacuum cleaner at night and return to my room. The thought used to terrify me! Sharing a secret with the wrong person, someone who hasn't earned my trust, leaves me with the same uncertainty. I want to know my secret is locked away safe and won't come back in any way to haunt me just like those ugly black spiders in the vacuum bags."

If we worry about our secrets or confidence coming back to hurt us, physical and mental energy is drained from us. We need to know the spiders will stay in the vacuum bag. We need to be able to trust.

Many of us have found truth in the advice, "Blood is thicker than water." We will share secrets within the protective walls of family because it is safer. Yet there are some cautions when it comes to unburdening guilt or confiding sensitive secrets, particularly where spouses and other family members are involved. "Look at the nature of the relationship before you decide to confess," says Dr. Decker. Family members can be the most supportive, health-enhancing relationships, or they can be the most destructive. The basic question is, "Will the family member use this information in a destructive way against me if I confess? For example, will they blame me, or will they accept me and forgive me, and help me in forgiving myself?"

Decker also warns against confessing under some circumstances. "Often a spouse who has been having an affair will unburden himself or herself and feel great afterwards," Decker explains. "But this is very destructive for the person hearing the confession."

To spare anyone from pain due to our confessions, other ways of extinguishing this type of personal guilt are available: the sacrament of confession, counseling, or confiding in a trusted friend, pastor, or clergy.

A good rule of thumb: If you do not feel comfortable sharing with someone, for any reason, change confidants. If you seek professional advice, your counselor does not have to be your best friend, but at the same time you should like the person in whom you are confiding.

NON-VERBAL 'CONFESSIONS'

It isn't always possible to find the right confidant, and even when we do, that person may not be available when most urgently needed.

Dr. Pennebaker suggests two non-verbal forms of confessing/sharing we can effectively accomplish by ourselves: prayer and writing. Both are solitary but effective forms of releasing feelings.

"Prayer works the same way as talking," explains Dr. Pennebaker, "and in a sense, it is a form of reconciliation."

For others, writing is also effective. Lynne, a mother of four who was struggling with family problems, financial decisions and, to her, the "mixed blessing" of turning 40, wrote letters to a trusted girlhood friend over the course of three months. It was a journal of sorts -one she knew a proven friend would eventually read.

"It was a giant release," Lynn explains. "I poured anxieties and concerns onto paper. It helped me order some of my priorities. It got me through a very tough three months because I had someone to talk to at all hours, someone I knew would understand and accept me, even with all my insecurities and flaws."

Dr. Pennebaker adds, "Writing about your deepest thoughts and feelings helps to resolve them. It is critical you write about not only what happened, but also why you feel the way you do." Be it by prayer or pen, suggests Pennebaker, we come to a new understanding of what we are feeling, a new point of view, similar to what we may experience after an opportunity to bare our soul with a trusted friend.

STEP 5

Step 5 Lesson 16

"I admitted to God, to myself, and to another human being the exact nature of my wrongs"

Action Word : ADMIT

Regardless of the method, Dr. Pennebaker cautions that we should not always expect the sharing of secrets to release all suffering immediately.

"You can confess and talk and write about whatever is making you feel miserable," explains Pennebaker, "and you may still experience pain and guilt."

Yet, in spite of those feelings, Pennebaker sees immediate improvements in health following confession. "The sooner you share your pain and suffering, the better, and the sooner it will be over."

The encouragement to share our burdens comes from many sources, on many levels and for different reasons. Yet the words of Jesus carry an especially powerful message, "Whatever you bind on earth shall be bound in heaven, and whatever you loose on earth shall be loosed in heaven." (Matthew 18:18)

When we safely loose the bonds of our burdens, when we share and confess, we open the way for healing, for rebirth, for starting again. This opportunity is not to be ignored, but rather to be embraced.

NOTE: It is my hope and prayer that, after studying this supplement, you will understand more completely how important it is for you to open up and bring out the wrongs of the past that are bothering you. It is only in doing this that we can be healed and experience the "NEW LIFE" that Jesus offers us. (See John 10:10) May the Lord Jesus Christ help you to come to HIM and a trusted friend for the release of your past wrongs. GOD BLESS YOU!

-Ray Geisel

Step 5 Lesson 17

"I admitted to God, to myself, and to another human being the exact nature of my wrongs"

Scripture: MEDITATIONS

MEDITATIONS

DAY ONE - Study Luke 15:11-24

Oh, what a wonderful heart warming story of God's forgiveness and love. This story reminds us well that we, too, can be healed as the prodigal son was healed when he confessed to his father. The friendship and love between them was healed and renewed and put back together again.

In this reading from the Holy Bible, we see so many of our addictive habits come out in the story. The son messed up everything the father had given him. He threw anyway his money, which was the gift of his father, on women and loose living - probably booze and drugs. He wanted to leave home and go out to do "his thing". As a popular song goes "I want to be ME!" Then he came to his senses when he hit "bottom" in the pigpen. He was hungry and wanted to eat what the pigs ate but he could not. Finally, he woke up, he got sober, and returned home filled with guilt and confession in his heart. He said, "Father, I have sinned against heaven and against you, I am no longer worthy to be called your son." (Verses 18-19)

And how did the father respond to all of this? First, when the son was still far off, the father saw him and ran out to him. He threw the cloak on him, put a ring on his finger and sandals on his feet. To the Jew, these things, the cloak, ring, and sandals, were signs of Jewish authority. You were not a respectable male Jew, a member of God's chosen people without these items.

Then what happened? The father responded to the son's confession. The son expected rejection and punishment from the father. Instead, he found compassion, forgiveness, acceptance, and renewed kinship. This is a beautiful look at a Godly father's love, and forgiveness, for a confessing child.

When we seek to correct our relationship with Father God, He does the same thing for us. We know that we are wrong in our sin, so we come to Him as the son did and confess. We quickly admit our wrongs to Him and our heavenly Father greets us warmly with a forgiving touch and a loving hug, just as the father in the parable greeted his son. When we confess our brokenness to our God in Jesus Christ, we can feel Him reach out to us, not to punish or whip us, but to forgive us, embrace us, and welcome us home into His everlasting family. So open up your heart to Jesus dear friend and feel His embrace. He loves you and welcomes you home.

DAY TWO - Study Acts 19:18-20

It seems that, as soon as a child begins to talk, that child is full of energy and joy, and also has the ability to tell lies. Some kids are just better at it than others, but all children, at an early age, begin to lie. As parents, we are faced with a difficult decision. "Should we take the necessary steps to correct the problem in discipline, or should we take the easy way out and forget it, hoping that it will blow away?" Such is the question confronting each parent when they meet this problem head on in their child. Of course, the proper way is to discipline the child. That is not always easy or pleasant to do, but do it we must, in love of course. Once the truth is revealed and the necessary discipline administered, we all feel better about the situation.

The believers in Ephesus found this to be true also. And it is true with us as well. Once we let our wrongs of the past come out in the confession process, we are cleansed and refreshed in our spirits. We can start all over again and try to live our lives more like Jesus. We may want to deny and hold onto our past sins, but the experience of confession tells us that this is wrong thinking. Rather, the right way, the Jesus way, is to let go of the wrongs of the past and give them to Jesus. He can and will heal us and send us the cleansing power of His Holy Spirit. Could it be that we should look at confessing our sins as more healing than painful? When we see it as the healing of our inner spirit and the process of overcoming our addiction, it will become just that. We will have come a long way on the road to recovery.

DAY THREE - Study 2 Corinthians 10:3-5

The final goal of the 12 step program and the message of Jesus is not only recovery from our addiction but the experience of a spiritual awakening, a new birth, a dying to our old self.

The Bible reminds us that "we live in the world, but we do not fight from worldly motives." (Verse 3) Although the sharing in this step may include the admitting of many sins of the flesh, soon we come to realize that our true recovery battle is not on the physical level at all; rather it is a spiritual struggle. As soon as we begin to work this step, we begin to feel better about the situation - all is out in the open, all is cleansed, and life can go on anew. We begin to take on a new life. We become "born again" in our spirit.

MEDITATIONS

Step 5 Lesson 17

"I admitted to God, to myself, and to another human being the exact nature of my wrongs"

Scripture:
MEDITATIONS

This awareness that all that troubles us in our spirit makes possible an important discovery in our walk toward recovery. In the past, we had thought that we were human beings passing through a temporary spiritual experience. As we grow in recovery, we find just the opposite is true. Instead of being physical human beings in a spiritual experience - we now find ourselves being spiritual children of a loving God and Father on a temporary human road through life. We can come to see that - "The weapons we use in our fight are not the world's weapons but God's powerful weapons, which we use to destroy strongholds (of the devil)." (Verse 4) When we begin to use God's weapons in the spiritual battles of this world, "we take every thought captive and make it obey Christ." (Verse 5) We then come into control of our lives through our spirit when it is in union with the Holy Spirit of Jesus Christ. Confession opens the door to that process. We are now on the winning side and we have the victory in Jesus Christ - AMEN!

DAY FOUR - Study Hebrews 4:12-16

The process of opening ourselves up in confession in this step is very sensitive. In doing this, we open up ourselves; we let down our defenses; we become honest with ourselves and we leave ourselves wide open and vulnerable. It may be that never before have we ever opened up ourselves, the experiences of wrongs of our past, to anyone. We may have deep feelings and regrets about those experiences; we may feel very guilty about our past. It is very difficult to disclose and talk about the "dark side" of ourselves, especially after we have taken such pains to hide all this for so very long.

Perhaps we are afraid and hesitant to "come clean" in this Healing Step 5. Maybe we fear criticism or the possibility of condemnation from God, from that other person involved, and we may even condemn ourselves. Yet this reading tells us that we have Jesus, our "High Priest", who has gone before us into the very presence of the Father-God. He is our defense attorney, our Advocate who stands before the Father in our place. It is this High Priest, Jesus, who forgives us. And when that happens, the Father also forgives us since Jesus and the Father are one. And so, the scripture today tells us to "have confidence and approach God's throne where there is grace. There we will receive mercy and find grace to help us just when we need it." (Verse 16)

The cure for this feeling of helplessness and fear is to have confidence as the scriptures tell us, and to select an understanding person with whom we can share this step, and to accept God's merciful forgiveness and peace. Seek a good, God-spirited person to help you. A pastor, compassionate counselor, or minister might be the one. Keep praying to Jesus to send you this person - and believe that He will. Let us be bold then and come to the throne of the Father's grace and there we will receive the Holy Spirit of Jesus for forgiveness and healing.

DAY FIVE - Study James 5:16

In the world in which we live, there is a strong sense of dislike for the words - ACCOUNTABILITY and RESPONSIBILITY. The world tells us to run around having a good time - as long as it doesn't hurt someone too much or we don't get caught. The whole idea is to be footloose and free and to do what we want to do when we want to do it. That's the whole concept of "freedom" in our land today. With this kind of idea in our mind, we no longer want to be accountable or responsible to and for our family, our work, our community or even ourselves for that matter. Even though our world today can't stand the word accountable - the Holy Bible has a great deal to say about it.

The Bible tells us in today's reading that we are not only accountable to God but also to other Christians. We stand before God and man to admit our past and to ask for forgiveness. The Bible tells us this should not be considered a burden, but rather a major source rightness, peace, joy and healing.

When we find the courage to open up and admit our wrongs to a fellow believer in confession, we receive new energy and uncover a new way to change our lives today and in the days to come. Our opening up actually causes us to grow in the spirit and get stronger in our spiritual walk.

No longer will I have to rough it alone. Now I have a friend in Jesus and a brother/sister in the Lord, my spiritual friend. This friend is helping me see myself as I really am; he is encouraging me and sharing his life with me and we are praying together. In so doing, I have taken a giant step in becoming accountable before my God, my spiritual friend, and myself. Even though I may slip for a moment and fall, I will always have God and my spiritual friend to stand with me and to help me get up and start again. I will no longer be alone in my struggle; rather, I can and will walk through life victoriously. I have learned and experienced the love of God and the love of my family in the Lord. I now belong to this new

Step 5 Lesson 17

"I admitted to God, to myself, and to another human being the exact nature of my wrongs"

Scripture : MEDITATIONS

MEDITATIONS

family of Christ, God's family, and I no longer feel alone. I have learned to become accountable and responsible for myself before God, others, and myself. I am in the process of becoming a new person in Christ Jesus.

DAY SIX - Study 1 John 1:8-9

In Healing Step 4, with great courage we looked into our inner self, into the dark side of our past. Maybe we faced this for the first time in our lives. And what we see as we look into the past frightens us. But we must not fear! The past must be dealt with and confessed openly before God, ourselves and another person who we trust. We have hidden this past for many years. We have run from our past chasing the "high" of our addiction to try to cover it up. But now, we must face that past. No more running, no more hiding. We are able to take this step because we know that God loves us unconditionally; "He will forgive us our sins and purify us from all our wrong doing." (Verse 9) He loves us just the way we are right now, in spite of our sins and wrongs. He already knows everything about us. He calls us to confess our wrongs to Him; because once we admit those wrongs, we are able to begin moving toward a healthier spirit. These wrongs have stood firmly in the way of our spiritual recovery. We have come clean and the healing process in our spirit can begin to happen. We have taken out the garbage of our past.

Our sins and wrongs of the past have kept us separated from experiencing the love and healing that God has for us. This separation is caused by our own choice. When we refuse to come to Him for forgiveness, we cut ourselves off from Him and all that He has and wants to give us as His children.

Our confession opens us up so that the love can once again flow from Jesus to us. His hand is open and extended toward you right now, dear friend. This great love that He has for you not only makes Him faithful to forgive you, but also faithful to cleanse you. The Bible says, "But I will wash you as clean as snow." (Isaiah 1:18) Once we are clean, we can release all those old "head games" that we have played for so very long. They were destroying us and now we can let them go and kick them out, never to play them again. We can let go of our guilt and possible shame for we know that we are God's chosen one, His son or daughter. We can walk into the fresh air of a stronger and more peaceful life walking with Jesus Christ who keeps us on the right path as long as we walk with our hand in His. We are on the right road to recovery and healing. The new life in Christ Jesus is ours!

DAY SEVEN - Study Proverbs 28:13-14

The practice of confessing our sins is nearly as old as man himself. In a simple look into the book of Proverbs, our reading for today will reveal that the Jews practiced this method of spiritual cleansing centuries before Christ. If we fail to practice the "letting go" of our wrongs, our deep emotional pain, fears, resentments, guilt, anger, and the like, will remain buried deep inside our spirit to haunt us and cause us to continue to try to put out their fire with our compulsive habits.

If we leave this cancer of our spirit unhealed, it will create unbearable misbehavior and end up killing us, both spiritually and physically. When we bury all of those difficult and hurtful problems of our past down deep inside, we will have all sorts of troubles in later years with those around us, with God, and with ourselves.

If we cling to this old spiritual cancer, we run the grave risk of refusing God's healing mercy. The words of Proverbs are very clear in this regard - "You will never succeed in life if you try to hide your sins. Confess them and give them up; then God will show mercy to you." (Verse 13) "If you are stubborn, you will be ruined." (Verse 14) Healing Step 5 is the active step of breaking our sinful bondage. Instead, we expose ourselves to God, who is the only one who can heal our sick spirit. Remember, He understands us better than we understand ourselves. He loves us so much that He died for us so that we would not be lost in our sin. (See John 3:16) So come to Him today, dear friend, you will be very happy you did!

A friend is one who knows all about you and loves you just the same.
—Anonymous

I can't - God can - I think I'll let him!
—Anonymous

Those who love Your law have perfect security, and there is nothing that can make them fall.
—Psalm 119:165

Walking the 12 Steps with Jesus Christ

STEP 5

Step 5 Lesson 18

"I admitted to God, to myself, and to another human being the exact nature of my wrongs"

Action Word : ADMIT

DEALING WITH OUR PRIDE AND EGO

In working the 12 steps, it seems that the purpose and intent of each of these steps goes directly against our natural desires, our pride and ego. We are constantly being asked to adopt attitudes and to engage in the opening up of our inner self. We want to resist and say "NO! I won't do it, I want to hang on to the old me." And now we come to this 5th step, which calls us to open up to God, to ourselves and another human being. "Boy, that's really rough!", we tell ourselves. And no doubt, it is rough on each of us. Hardly any other step is more ego deflating than this one. But do it we must. There is no step in all of the twelve that is more necessary to our long-term recovery than this one. We will get blessed relief, long-term happiness, and peace of mind when we use this step as it should be used, not just once, but rather as an ongoing relationship with Jesus, with myself, and with a spiritual friend, our Prayer Partner.

LETTING GO OF OUR "STINKIN THINKIN"

The experience of this program has taught us that we cannot live alone with our skeletons and wrongs in the closet. If we have taken a good look at ourselves in the Healing Step 4 inventory, this look has revealed many experiences we would rather not face up to or remember. We have learned that our thinking has been very wrong. We have hurt others and ourselves in this process of "stinkin thinkin". And others have hurt us also in the process of that same kind of thinking. We have come to the point where we need to let go of this stuff. We have to talk to somebody about this.

WE WANT TO SLIP OUT OF ADMITTING OUR WRONGS OF THE PAST - IT'S TOUGH BUSINESS

So intense is our fear and reluctance to do this that at first, we will try to do anything to by-pass this step. We try to search for an easier way - we try to rationalize and to play games to get out of this process of admitting our wrongs. No one likes to come up in front of others with "mud on their face". And so we want to beat this step, one way or another. We want to slip out of it at all cost. After all, "My pride is at stake here!", we tell ourselves.

WE FIGHT "BEING FORCED TO DO IT"

We play still another game by telling ourselves "I should not be forced to admit distressing or humiliating situations of the past to another person. It's none of their business. I just can't bear telling another soul. This stuff will go to the grave with me".

Yet, the experience of those who have walked this program before us shows that this is a positively destructive path to take. Experience shows that people who refuse to take this step will fail time and time again in their future struggle with themselves and their addictions. There is just no other way to accomplish this healing. It is absolutely essential that we take our sick spirit to the Spiritual Doctor - Jesus Christ. In order for us to be treated, we must tell Him the problem, hence our confession. This process requires us to verbalize our past wrongs in a positive physical act of taking them out of our inner self. This house cleaning is absolutely necessary and cannot be avoided. The Bible teaches this over and over again in both the Old and New Testaments. Confession is not a luxury but an absolute essential to recovery. If we refuse to do it, we will fail, guaranteed.

CONFESSION - GOD'S WAY TO HEALING

This practice of confessing our wrongs to God, to self, and another person is as old as man himself. It has been used from the very beginning by those wise men and women who recognized that wrongs and sin destroy the inner person. The practice of confessing is used in most religious communities throughout the entire world. But "church people" are not the only ones who use it. Psychiatrists, psychologists, and counselors point out the deep need that every human being has for the practical healing of the things that bother them deep inside. May I suggest that you go back and reread the supplement entitled "Confessing is good for you!".

The Alcoholics Anonymous program has long taught that without a fearless confessing of our wrongs to another, the alcoholic could not stay sober. If this principle applies to alcoholics, then it also applies to all of us who suffer from all other forms of addiction or codependency as well. So we conclude that we cannot be healed from our inner spiritual sickness unless we "Turn it over" to Jesus Christ, our great spiritual healer and Lord.

SOME BENEFITS FROM OUR STEP 5 PROCESS: CONNECTEDNESS AND ONENESS WITH OTHERS

What can we expect to receive from our practice of Healing Step 5? First, we can expect to find blessed relief from that terrible sense of being alone - being isolated. Almost always, we who are addicted feel terribly alone, left out, a "square peg in a round hole". The only people who seem to understand us at all are those who are also "hooked" on some form of addiction. Our behavior has caused those close to us and finally all those around us to walk away and to avoid any contact with us. They have

Step 5 Lesson 18

"I admitted to God, to myself, and to another human being the exact nature of my wrongs"

Action Word : ADMIT

STEP 5

positively cut us off and we feel alone and sick. This caused us to "hang" with our own kind. We either become very shy or we become very loud and aggressive. Either way, we ended up driving people away from us by our behavior. That's one reason we loved our addiction so much. We felt like we were on top of the situation when, in reality, we had fallen deep into the pit of drunkenness and despair. It was all one great big lie, which ended up in terrible loneliness.

Then, when we came to the 12 step program, we found for the first time, that we were among people who seemed to understand, and our new sense of belonging was tremendously exciting. We thought that we had solved our problem of feeling alone but we still suffered the old pains that were deep inside. Until we brought these old pains out and confessed them to another, there was be NO RELIEF; we still didn't belong; we are just playing another game. But now, we face Healing Step 5 and we are assured that this is the answer to the true healing of our despair. It is the beginning of a true fellowship with our fellow brothers and sisters and, most importantly, God.

In this step, we also experience the means by which we can and will be forgiven, no matter what we have thought or done. In working this step, we find that we are truly able to forgive others, no matter how deeply we felt they have wronged us. Our moral inventory, made in Healing Step 4, has convinced us that all around forgiveness is not only possible but also very desirable. Healing Step 5 makes this forgiveness and healing possible.

ANOTHER BENEFIT - HUMILITY

Another great plus we will experience from this confession process is a new found humility. This word is one that is often misunderstood by the world and us. What do we mean by humility? To those who have gone through this program, we have found a new sense of knowing just who and what we really are. We have taken a giant step, for the first time in our life, to find the "real us" by being honest with ourselves. We have found that we are far from who we could be - that our goals in life are sadly messed up. But since Step 5, our lives are becoming much clearer. We can now begin to see the picture that was so muddy and unclear in the past. We have come to believe, without question, that the first step in clearing up the muddy past was to recognize (Step 4) and admit (Step 5) the wrongs of our past. We have come to realize that no wrong can be corrected, nor defect eliminated, unless it is brought out into clear view and forgiven. This "bringing out" process produces true and genuine humility. We begin to see ourselves just as we really are, and now we can do something about correcting ourselves. Admitting the wrongs of our past to Jesus Christ and another human being affects this correction. We cannot correct them ourselves - it is only by using this process that Jesus can heal us. "I can now work on becoming the real me that Jesus created. I can feel good again deep down inside of my spirit." This is true humility.

MORE BENEFITS - HONESTY, A SINCERE SPIRIT

Now that we have started to become honest with ourselves, what can we expect to feel as a result? Our newfound honesty and openness will begin to show immediately. As we open up to our Step 4 inventory, we begin to see just how much trouble our self-centered game playing has caused. We were truly surprised and disturbed by what we found. We had spent much of our past playing "head games" and fooling ourselves into a false sense of "I'm OK - you're OK". We needed to wade through a really big pile of self-centered fear, pity, hurt feelings, guilt, and remorse for the things that we were ashamed of. In looking at the "real me", we discover a whole lot of wrongful defects that are part of us that we never knew existed. We took our inventory and quickly found that this inventory was not enough. We needed to do something with it. It was like the garbage that had collected in the trash pail in our kitchen. Somehow, we needed to get rid of it. We needed to empty the inside of us. And it was then that we found that the only way do this effectively was to discuss ourselves, holding nothing back, with our Prayer Partner, our spiritual friend. Only then did we experience the blessed relief that was so urgently needed in our life. It was in talking and sharing with him that we found the answer. We emptied ourselves and we talked - like two friends with similar problems. We listened to the other's advice and accepted comments and direction. Our Prayer Partner gave us a new perspective, a new look at our life that we had been unable to see before. We realized that now we were no longer going through life alone. Jesus and our new friend were with us all the way. We were honest with ourselves and we were now able to find the "real me".

WHY WE NEED TO GO TO ANOTHER HUMAN BEING

Yet, somehow, we still want to hold back. We say to ourselves, "Why can't I just go to God and have Him tell me what's wrong? If He created me to begin with, then He should know exactly what's wrong with me. Why can't I just go to Him and not to someone else too?"

First, just being alone with God is not as open and down to earth as being alone with another fellow

STEP 5

Step 5 Lesson 18

"I admitted to God, to myself, and to another human being the exact nature of my wrongs"

Action Word : ADMIT

human being. Since God is a spirit, we can't see Him in the physical, and so we can play "head games" with Him. After all, we're experts at this business of "snow jobs". And so we are tempted to cover up our old self again, and disclose only what we feel comfortable disclosing. Until we actually sit down and talk aloud to another person face to face about what we have so long hidden, our willingness to clean house is still mostly a game playing session. When we are honest with another person, we are finally being honest with ourselves and with the God of Jesus Christ who loves us and desires to give us life to the fullest.

Second, what comes to us while we are alone may be confused and garbled by our own past "stinkin thinkin". We want to rationalize and dream a bit. It is very difficult to be truly honest with ourselves. When we talk directly with a spiritual friend, we get the benefit of his thoughts and counsel. He will help us to see the problem the way it really is. If it is not clear, he will ask us questions until the situation becomes clear. We can then discuss the situation and pray about it together. There can be no doubt about the problem - it will be brought out clearly into the open, no longer to be hidden in the mind.

Taking matters of spiritual counsel into our own hands can be very dangerous. Many times we have heard "spiritual people" claim the guidance of God. Yet, by their actions, we clearly see that they were way out in "left field". They were doing their own thing claiming that it was God's guidance. They had "conned" themselves into thinking that a certain situation was good and holy when in fact it was sin. A good example of that is the person who tries to justify a "live-in" relationship as being OK and good for both parties. Many people try to actually talk themselves into thinking that this is OK, not only in their own eyes but also in the eyes of God.

CONSULT AN ELDER OF THE CHURCH

It is worth noting here that the Bible teaches that discernment is a gift of the Holy Spirit. (See 1 Corinthians 12:10). Discernment is the ability to clearly see the difference between the right Godly way and the wrong way. The Bible also teaches us to become part of and to consult with the elders of the church in matters of personal difficulties. (See Matthew 18:17) This has been the Biblical teaching since the time of Abraham. It follows then that if the very holy are not so sure and need to check with an Elder, the not so holy surely need to check with an Elder also. It would also seem logical that a spiritual advisor (a present day Elder) who lives a good Christian life would have a better understanding of the right way than someone who still has a lot of spiritual growing to do. Of course, the comments and advice of another may not be perfect, but such advice is maybe much more accurate than those of us who have lived such mixed up and compulsive life styles. It certainly would seem that a man of God should be closer to God than many of us who have come from such difficult pasts.

Again, it is very important to find the right person to share your life with. You should find a person who is experienced in a 12 step program if possible, one who understands the program. You should look for a person who has been successful in overcoming the addictions in their life; one who shows a good Christian life by his or her actions. You should seek to find this person as soon as possible. If you are unable to totally open up to that person at first, that's OK. Start slowly - grow in your friendship. But start you must. Do not fear. The Holy Spirit is with you. Do not hide behind your guilt or shame. Let your past come out.

HAVE COURAGE - GOD IS WITH YOU

Now we come to the real test. "Am I really willing to confide in the person I have selected to be my spiritual friend, my Prayer Partner? Do I have confidence in that person?" Even when I find that person, it sometimes takes great courage to open up to them. This certainly is a tough program. No one can say that it's for "wimps". It takes great courage and willpower to ask a person to be your confessor and then to open up in the sharing. Be bold; give it all you've got. You have nothing to lose but the miserable pains that have been killing you. Happily though, the chances are great that you will be in for a very pleasant surprise. When you finally open up and explain yourself to your confessor, the conversation should start easily and gently. Soon, you will become eager to get rid of the rotten stuff when you experience the dammed-up hurts as they begin to break through. Before long, your listener may share some experience about himself, which will place you more at ease. This will lead to a sharing session between two spiritual friends. As you let go and let God, your sense of relief will mount from minute to minute. The dammed-up emotions from years of piled up garbage will break their strangle hold on you and vanish as soon as they are exposed. You will feel a calmness take its place. Where there was pain and suffering, peace and healing will now take place. And when humility and serenity are so combined, something else of great magnitude is apt to occur. It is then that we will feel the actual presence of Jesus within ourselves. Even those who did not know God or who felt far away from God before, will feel a closeness with God that they never felt before. (NOTE: It is quite common for a person

Step 5 Lesson 18

"I admitted to God, to myself, and to another human being the exact nature of my wrongs"

Action Word : ADMIT

to break down crying during this time of sharing. This emotion should come out freely and purposefully. One of the best ways to heal the spirit is to speak the problem and cry about it. So, if you feel like having a good cry, please do so).

OUR NEW FREEDOM FROM BONDAGE

This freedom from the bondage and prison of the past will give us new peacefulness. Our terrible guilt will begin to break up and disappear. We will begin to find true peace and friendship with others. We will have prepared ourselves to take the next two steps, which will help us to finally come to Jesus for the complete healing that we so desperately need.

Remember what the Bible says about this step in James 5:16, "So then, confess your sins to one another and pray for one another, so that you will be healed. The prayer of a righteous person has a powerful effect." Now is the time to take action. Ask the Lord to direct you to the right person for your sharing.

> We are only as sick as our secrets.
>
> -Anonymous
>
> The Lord says to his people:
> I will make you well again;
> I will heal your wounds...
>
> -Jeremiah 30:12,17

SCRIPTURE STUDY:

The following scriptures are directly related to this step. Look up each scripture, read around it, study it and write down in your own words how this scripture applies to this step. The question, "What does this scripture show me about this step?"

- ☐ Leviticus 26:19
- ☐ Proverbs 30:32
- ☐ Psalm 32:3-5
- ☐ Matthew 23:12
- ☐ Psalm 38:17-18
- ☐ Luke 5:31
- ☐ Psalm 40:11-13
- ☐ Luke 15:4-7
- ☐ Psalm 41:4
- ☐ Romans 14:12-13
- ☐ Psalm 51:3-4

- ☐ 1 Corinthians. 11:27-32
- ☐ Psalm 62:8
- ☐ Ephesians 4:14-15
- ☐ Psalm 69:5
- ☐ Ephesians 4:25
- ☐ Psalm 119:66-67
- ☐ Colossians 3:9
- ☐ Proverbs 16:18
- ☐ James 4:7-8
- ☐ Proverbs 21:2

Walking the 12 Steps with Jesus Christ

BIBLE STUDY

BIBLE STUDY
Growth & Strength

Step 5 Lesson 19

Action Words :
HEARING GOD SPEAK TO US

Thus far in our 12 step program, we have seen much healing of our past problems and behavior. We have experienced how important this healing is to our complete recovery. Dealing with our past wrongs is the foundation of this program. But, that is not all that there is to our recovery process.

BUILDING A "NEW TODAY"

Over and over in the Bible, we are called to repent of our sins, fast and pray that we will overcome those habits AND receive the new life that Jesus desires to give us today. We have already seen in lesson 15 just how important our prayer life is to the continued growth and strength of our inner self, our spirit being. We are not only correcting the past but we are building a new today and preparing for the tomorrows to come. We need healing of our past, but we also need the growth and strength of spirit to stand firm today and in the future. We need to build that spiritual strength now and that is the purpose of the Growth/Strength part of the program.

In the past, we have been unable to control our lives in certain areas. The primary reason for this loss of control was the pain that came our way as a result of our childhood experiences. This pain was placed upon us by circumstances over which we had little or no control and which caused us to suffer greatly. We tried to drown out the pain by medicating it in some way until we gradually fell prey to an addictive habit, which pulled us into the pit where we hit "bottom".

CONTROLLING THE "FLESH"

There is still another reason for our fall. Please look up Galatians 5:16-26. Here we find that there is a constant struggle between our spirit being and our human nature, which we shall call "the flesh". Paul tells us that these two forces are enemies and that we cannot do what we are tempted in our flesh to do. The second reason for our fall is this - we were very strong in the flesh with all its appetites, but very weak in the spirit. You see, our spirit was created by God to control our flesh, not the reverse.

When we allow our flesh to run wild and control our spirit, we are out of control in our behavior. The only way to overcome this problem is to strengthen the spirit so that the spirit, which is within each of us, can take control of the flesh. Our spirit must become stronger than our flesh so that we can control the flesh. When we have come to the Holy Spirit of Jesus, then, Paul tells us, we will experience the fruit of the Holy Spirit of God which is - LOVE, JOY, PEACE, PATIENCE, KINDNESS, GOODNESS, FAITHFULNESS, HUMILITY, AND SELF-CONTROL. (See Galatians 5:22) You will notice that the last, but not least, of these is self-control. We all need self-control over our flesh or we will be totally out of control. Where do we get the self-control necessary to bring order into our lives? The answer is to join our spirit with the Spirit of God that is within us. We do that by breaking the Word of God in the Bible and "eating" it. This is called Bible study.

THE BIBLE - OUR SPIRITUAL FOOD

So, it is necessary that we not only need to be healed of the past, but we need to build up a strong spirit in union with God's Holy Spirit, the spirit that has our name on it and lives within us, so that we can overcome the desires of the flesh today, one day at a time. The Bible tells us that the Word of God is "the sword which the Spirit gives you". (Ephesians 6:17) It is the means by which we beat off the attacks of the devil. Jesus also refers to the Bible, the Word of God, when He said: "Human beings cannot live on bread alone, but need every word that God speaks." (Matthew 4:4).

So you can see that we will starve spiritually without the Word of God and we will be unable to fight the devil without the sword, which is that Word. Therefore, the Bible is absolutely essential to the serious Christian who desires to walk in the "footsteps of Jesus". You just cannot overcome your problems and succeed in life without the Word of God. It is your very life.

BIBLE STUDY - GOD SPEAKING TO US

In lesson 15, we learned that prayer is our deep conversation with God It is the time that we purposefully take to speak with our best friend Jesus. Now we begin to see that Bible study is the time we take to listen to the Father God through Jesus with the Holy Spirit speaking to us. Conversation between two people who love each other must go both ways. So in prayer, we speak to God and in Bible study, God speaks to us through "His Word".

Bible study is our daily food, the food for our spirit through which we gain growth and strength to over- come the tempting of the devil in our flesh and the world around us. No one would think of starving the body, then why do we starve our spirit and think nothing of it? The reasons are many but none of them is valid. Jesus tells us that if we want to live, come to Him and feast on His word and He will give us life. Listen carefully in your spirit to the words that you read in the scriptures. Let the "Word of God" speak to you. You will be amazed how many answers to life's problems you will find in His book.

> And do not make God's Holy Spirit sad; for the Spirit is God's mark of ownership on you, a guarantee that the Day will come when God will set you free. Get rid of all bitterness, passion and anger. No more shouting or insults, no more hateful feelings of any sort. Instead, be kind and tender hearted to one another, and forgive one another, as God has forgiven you through Christ.
> -Ephesians 4:30-31

BIBLE STUDY
Growth & Strength

Step 5 Lesson 19

Action Words:
HEARING GOD SPEAK TO US

(These next two sections are one man's opinion, and are to be perceived only as a guideline. There are many options for bible study.)

WHERE DO WE START STUDYING THE BIBLE?

The study of God's Holy Word should be a very important part of our daily life if we are to successfully overcome our addictions or any other problem in our life. Bible study should never be boring. The new Christian should stay in the New Testament, which begins with the gospel of Matthew and is found generally in the back one third of the book. The New Testament is the account of the life of Jesus as told by the four gospel writers - Matthew, Mark, Luke and John. It also contains Acts, which is the account of the early church and Paul's writings, which are called letters, or Epistles. All of these books speak of Jesus, his life, death and resurrection and His great act of salvation for all of us, the greatest act of love that ever existed. These books explain the ministry of Jesus and are the basis of our faith. They tell us who Jesus is, why He came into this world and what He did and taught.

STUDYING THE "OLD TESTAMENT"

The Old Testament contains the record of man's origin and development, the history of God's chosen people the Jews and prophesies of the coming of the Jewish Messiah, Jesus Christ. As we grow in our Christian walk, we should get into the Old Testament but only when the Holy Spirit prompts us in prayer. It is important for the Christian new to the study of the Bible to begin study in the New Testament portion only. However, there are two books in the Old Testament that was important also for the new Christian. These are known as the books of Psalms and Proverbs. The book of Psalms can be used very effectively in our daily prayer life. The Psalms will be found near the center of the Bible. These are 150 Psalms, which are hymns of praise, thanksgiving, forgiveness etc. King David wrote most of the psalms long before the time of Jesus. These psalms will speak to you as you read them. Mark the ones, which you find speaking to you the most and read them often. Immediately following Psalms, you will find the book of Proverbs. This book contains many of the wise sayings and teachings of the Jews of that time. These are especially good for us today because they teach us the right way in certain situations. Reading both the Psalms and Proverbs should be a part of our daily Bible study program.

WHAT TRANSLATION SHOULD I USE?

It is very important for you to use a translation of the Bible, which is easy for you to understand. There are quite a number of English translations on the market today. I recommend the Good News Bible - Today's English Version. We have found, through experience that most people relate best to that version. You may find it helpful for you to use two or three different translations. This method can be very helpful in understanding the same verse by reading that verse in several different translations. Your understanding of the particular verse will be broadened. Seek out the best translation for you and work with it.

READ AND STUDY SLOWLY

When you study the Bible, read slowly and with understanding. Each word of the Bible should be understood clearly. It is not a good idea to speed read the scriptures. There is specific meaning in each word and if you read too fast you will miss this meaning. Do not try to read a large portion of scriptures at one time. A few verses of a chapter are plenty in one sitting. Try to understand what you are reading. Go back in your mind and spirit and review the verses; let them sink into your spirit. Close the book and repeat the meaning of what you just studied in your own words. Take your time and let the Lord speak to your heart.

BIBLE STUDY GROUPS

You may also want to study the Bible with a friend or as a member of a Bible study group. This form of Bible study is very helpful because it broadens our understanding of the verses covered. Other people will see points in the verses that we do not see and we will be able to learn from them. One word of caution - Never, NEVER get involved in an argument about the Bible. The Bible speaks to each of us differently because we are all different people. If another person has a different view of the Bible than you do, just accept that as it is. If you would like to share your view, just say, "This is what God's Word says to me." In this way, you will express what you see in the Word as opposed to someone else who may see it differently. This does not mean that you should agree with them if in your spirit you do not agree with them. It simply means that you respect their opinion and will not argue over it. Such encounters require much patience. The result will be a sign of Christian growth and strength.

BIBLE STUDY

BIBLE STUDY
Growth & Strength

Step 5 Lesson 19

Action Words:
HEARING GOD SPEAK TO US

DAILY MEDITATION - STUDY AIDS

You may want to use one of the daily meditation booklets that are available today. There are also many Bible study pamphlets that are very helpful. Ask for and look for these aids. They can be found in churches, Christian bookstores, Chaplain's offices, religious libraries and many TV ministries by mail. There are also topical studies available to use to study certain subjects. We are doing a topical study of the Bible along with this course. This simply means that we are studying certain sections and passages of the Bible, which pertain to addiction. There are many different topical studies. If you are interested in a topical study, contact the Chaplain or a minister or priest. A good Christian bookstore will also be very helpful in selecting a study Bible and other helpful materials.

BECOME FAITHFUL AND REGULAR

Bible study requires a regular time each day. It needs to become a habit in your life. The Bible calls you to give your first fruits to the Lord. The first fruit of your time is the first hour of your day in the morning. It is an excellent idea to make your study time first in the day. This may require you to arise an hour or so earlier. The investment in this time with Jesus will pay great dividends in a stronger spiritual life.

You may combine your prayer time and Bible study time into one session if you wish. At any rate, one hour per day should be your goal. Start slowly. You may not be able to spend this amount of time at first. However, start somewhere and keep working at it. Keep trying; you will accomplish your goal.

YOUR TIME OF SPIRITUAL COMMUNION WITH JESUS

Remember, this time is your special time with Jesus. Find a regular time each day for your Prayer and Bible study. You may want to keep a journal to write down your thoughts each day, thoughts that the Holy Spirit has given you during your prayer time. You will surely grow and be strengthened during this time with Jesus.

This time with Jesus is essential to overcoming your addiction. Over the past 17 years, I have talked to many young men who have fallen back into their old ways and returned to jail. Each one of them has told me that they stopped praying and studying their Bible. The result, another failure and back in jail.

Therefore, it is absolutely essential for you to pray and study your Bible. God's Word needs to feed your spirit and make you strong. Without this, you will be weak in spirit and fall back into your old self.

The Lord says, "Wise men should not boast of their wisdom,
nor strong men of their strength,
nor rich men of their wealth.
If anyone wants to boast, he should boast that he knows and understands Me, Because my love is constant, and I do what is just and right. these are the things that please Me.
I, the Lord have spoken."
    -Jeremiah 9:23-24

In the beginning the Word already existed;
the Word was with God, and the Word was God.
From the very beginning the Word was with God.
Through Him God made all things;
Not one thing in all creation was made without Him.
The Word was the source of life; and this life brought light to people.
The light shines in the darkness; and the darkness has never put it out.
    -John 1:1-5

Walking the 12 Steps with Jesus Christ

Christian 12 Step Ministry, Inc

BIBLE STUDY
Growth & Strength
Step 5 Lesson 19

Action Words:
HEARING GOD SPEAK TO US

BIBLE STUDY

BIBLE STUDY BASICS

There is much that has been written about how to study the Bible. The intention in this study is to make suggestions to help you successfully begin your journey of regularly scheduled Bible Study.

1. **Decide on a time**—If you view your time spent with God as an appointment to be kept, you will be less likely to miss or skip it. Choose the time of day when you are at your best, fresh and alert. Consider the morning because your mind is not yet cluttered and tensions have not yet come upon you.

2. **Decide on a place**—The proper lighting, being uninterrupted and undisturbed are ideal. You should be comfortable and you should be able to pray or worship without disturbing others. Decide to make a place specifically for your study time and put your Bible, pen, journal, devotional book, and reading plan in that place.

3. **Decide on a time frame**—How much time can you realistically commit to each day? Start with a realistic goal that you feel you can meet. If you have never studied before, try beginning with 10 or 15 minutes and let it grow naturally.

4. **How to begin your study time**—Listening and/or singing along with your favorite worship songs can really help clear your mind and prepare yourself to hear.

5. **Plan to spend some time in prayer**—Talk to God and listen for God to speak to you. Prayer will be discussed further later in this study.

6. **What should you study?** Choosing some kind of Bible reading plan or specific Bible study guide will help you have a focused time of reading and study. If you just pick up your Bible and start reading randomly, you may have a difficult time understanding what you read or applying it to your life. It is very important to choose a Bible you can understand.

7. **Write in a journal**—Journaling your thoughts, prayers, and what you hear God tell you can provide a valuable record and establish your history with Him.

8. **Determine to be committed**—Rather than beating yourself up when you miss, just pray and ask God to help you.

9. **Be flexible and willing to make changes**—If you get stuck in a rut, go back to the first step above and consider what changes you can make to help yourself become more succcssful.

WHAT IS THE KEY TO BIBLE STUDY?
Persistence! Pray for God to give you the desire and the discipline to spend time with Him each day.

A PRAYER OF COMMITMENT
Lord, I commit myself to spending a definite amount of time with You each day, no matter the cost. I am depending on Your strength to help me.

BIBLE STUDY

BIBLICAL JOURNALING

The Bible is God's personal love letter to you. Learn to listen to what He is telling you and then respond. You can write a short note or a long letter depending on how the Spirit leads you. If you received an actual letter in the mail from God, what would it sound like? Consider these five steps to help you begin journaling.

Step 1: Read the Bible—Begin by reading a passage from the Bible or your daily devotional.

Step 2: Respond to what you just read.

- Address a letter to yourself from God. Write the date at the top of your paper or on your journal page.

- Select part of your reading that speaks to your heart and connects to what you are experiencing in your daily life right now. Write down where this is found either beside your name or in the margin of your paper.

Step 3: Make the words your own.

Write about the following items in the verse or verses you just read:

- Truths about God the Father, Jesus, and/or the Holy Spirit
- Instructions about others and your relationships with them
- Facts concerning yourself, life, and how to live it
- Commands to obey, promises to claim, examples to follow
- Sins to forsake (repent and turn from), errors to avoid, etc.

Carefully think about the words/phrases used in the part you have selected and expand their meaning.

Step 4: Apply Biblical truth to your life.

Write about the following questions:

- What do I believe God is saying to me through this exercise?
- How will I be different because of what God has shown me?
- In what areas of my life do I desire to be challenged and transformed because of the principles I've read and reflected on?

Step 5: Speak to God about what you learned.

Finish this exercise by writing a prayer to God about what you've learned in this time of devotion. Ask for His help to live faithfully each day. Pray specifically about what you have learned in the scripture passage today.

BIBLE STUDY
Growth & Strength

Step 5 Lesson 19

Action Words:
HEARING GOD SPEAK TO US

Walking the 12 Steps with Jesus Christ

Steps 6 & 7 Lesson 20

"I was entirely ready to have God remove all the wrongs of my past life"

"Humbly asked Him to remove these wrongs"

**Action Words:
READY TO REMOVE
- HUMBLY ASKED**

> Don't worry about anything, but in all your prayers ask God for what you need, always asking Him with a thankful heart. And God's peace, which is far beyond human understanding, will keep your hearts and minds safe in union with Christ Jesus."
> -Philippians 4:6-7

STEPS 6 & 7

WHERE HAVE WE BEEN SO FAR?

At this point in our walking the twelve steps with Jesus Christ, we have admitted our powerlessness over our addiction; we have opened up to search for a Power greater than ourselves to restore us to sanity; we have turned our will and life over to that Power which is Jesus Christ; we have made a searching and fearless moral inventory of our past in order to find the cause of our spiritual sickness and we have admitted those wrongs of the past to God, ourselves and to another human being. We can begin to see that we have made a sincere and solid attempt to deal with the problem of our addiction deep within us.

Now, we are preparing ourselves to become ready to remove the wrongs from the past and then we shall ask Our God, Jesus Christ to remove the hurt and pain connected with these wrongs from our past life. Our life is beginning to change drastically at this point.

QUESTION: Am I willing to let go of the past?

A serious question arises at this point, "Am I deeply willing to ask God to remove all of the wrongs of my past which have lead me into my compulsive addiction and its resulting insane behavior?" Some of us may have been forced into a 12 step recovery program by a spouse, relative, the courts or the terrible pain of our addiction and the problems it has caused. Whatever way this has come about, we now find ourselves being forced to deal with "ME". This can be very uncomfortable, but it is absolutely necessary in order to find and correct the underlying problem causing our addiction. The questions: "Am I ready to give it up? Do I really want to be free from this bondage that creates so much hell in my life? Am I willing to let go, to turn it over?" Only you can answer these questions

QUESTION: Am I ready to give up ALL my addictions - each and every last one of them?

This question becomes a very serious one to each of us. Many of us would like to get rid of the really troublesome addictions in our lives, those that are very public and out in the open. But the ones deep inside, now that seems to be a different story. We may be saying to ourselves, "Can't I just keep that little innocent smoking habit, or can't I just keep playing my little sex games? After all, that doesn't hurt anyone else?"

How easily we forget the compulsive nature of our personality. How easily we forget that the fleshly body has as its goal, the complete and total control of the person. How easily we forget the pain and suffering that our compulsions, in total, have caused us. Yet, we are tempted to convince ourselves that holding on to the "harmless" ones is OK. Friends, this is part of our "stinkin thinkin" and the resulting insanity. We cannot dabble in sinfulness and expect our Lord to heal us totally. We want to "have our cake and eat it too" and this behavior does not work.

Maybe these "little" addictions have not caught up with us yet. This makes us think that they are not problems, that "I can handle it!" Yet early in our recovery process, this is the attitude that we attacked with such vigor in Step 1. Step 1 - our addiction - we cannot "handle it" - we are out of control - powerless - our life has become unmanageable as a result. The real question at issue here is, "Am I ready to give up ALL - ALL of the wrongs of my past and the behavior connected with those wrongs, even the ones that seem to be "harmless?" You must answer that question for yourself, dear friend.

As in the case just mentioned, we may have difficulty in seeing other addiction problems and admitting them. The "biggie" problems are very obvious. However, we may have to search and deal painfully with the ones that are not so obvious and are more difficult to detect and admit.

Therefore, it is very important that we be open and sensitive to the guidance of the Holy Spirit in detecting those areas of our lives that we cannot see clearly. We must be willing to listen to, and learn from, those around us who are more familiar with the problem of addiction; those we have shared our lives with like our spiritual friend - our Prayer Partner. "Are there certain patterns of addictive behavior in my life that I cannot see too clearly? Do I find myself called to a habit that repeats itself over and over and over which I have no power to stop?" Be open to hearing answers from God and from others around you. Listen and don't hide from them.

GO BACK OVER OUR 4th STEP INVENTORY

This may be the time to look back over our Fourth step inventory for any repeating patterns of addictive behavior that may help us to detect hidden wrongs in our life. Beware of the lie of the devil that will try to tell you that overeating, smoking, sex games etc., the "harmless" habits are OK and won't hurt you. The fact remains that you can die from overeating, smoking or aids. That should be enough proof to show you that the devil is a liar and will trip you up if he can. If it is not God's will in your life, it needs to be torn out of your life drastically.

STEPS 6 & 7

Steps 6 & 7 Lesson 20

"I was entirely ready to have God remove all the wrongs of my past life"

"Humbly asked Him to remove these wrongs"

Action Words :
READY TO REMOVE - HUMBLY ASKED

CHARACTER DEFECTS - WHAT ARE THEY?

So far in our walk with Jesus Christ, we have studied only those wrongs that cause pain and hurt in our lives. In the AA program, these wrongs are called "defects of character". These defects of character are the result of the wrongs which have accumulated in our past and which shape our present personality. Since these wrongs are basically destructive, they can and will create certain defects in our character that can gradually cause us to become very difficult people to live with. We may not be able to recognize these defects "up front" because they are hidden by the past wrongs that caused them. Example: Do we go off, by ourselves, and sulk after not getting our way in a relationship with someone? Do we find ourselves losing control in a fit of violent anger when we are not able to "have our own way" in a relationship? Do we allow ourselves to get hooked into some wrongful sexual behavior simply by saying that "everybody is doing it"? Do we play a "head game" with lifting something from work that does not belong to us by telling ourselves that "the boss won't miss it" or "I have it coming to me"? These are all examples of patterns of addictive behavior. And, there are lots more too. Just put on your thinking cap and you'll be sure to come up with some that are nearly and neatly hidden.

Some other questions we might ask ourselves: "Do I have times of deep depression, fear, guilt, shame, unforgiveness, violence, restlessness, irritability or times where all I want to do is sleep, drink, eat, watch TV, have sex etc? Do I bury my mind in sexual fantasy or indulge in self-sex? How do I relate to other people? Do I allow them to manipulate my life when I allow them to use me as the "doormat"? Do I push people away from me or am I afraid or uneasy with people? Does it always seem to be the other guy's fault? Do I always seem to want to be in control of what is happening around me? Do I have problems letting others be the center of attention? Do I compete for attention in the moment? Do I use others for my own selfish advantage?"

HOW TO IDENTIFY DEFECTS OF CHARACTER

Let's take a good look at the person that is "ME". It's very important to be specific and honest in identifying these character defects. Remember, they come from the accumulated wrongs of our past. When we examine those wrongs and put them together into trends of behavior, we will be able to identify the general category of our defects. Our wrongs will show us the underlying problem that needs to be brought to Jesus. Healing and a change in our thinking need to take place in these areas to recover from their effects. Remember, we are asking Jesus to bring about in us a "NEW CREATION" - "a new person". Psalm 51:10: "Create a pure heart in me, O God, and put a new and loyal spirit in me." Even though our addictions are different in nature, their healing requires that one "special touch". That special touch comes to us from Jesus directly in prayer and from each other as His Holy Spirit uses us to minister to each other. There is no doubt that the Lord uses us to minister to each other if we are open to Him and His Word.

HOW WE ACT OUT OUR DEFECTS OF CHARACTER

Most defects of character involve some imbalance in the way we act out and experience our most basic human needs. For example: Sexuality and ambition are healthy drives unless we experience them and act them out in out-of-control compulsive behavior. Then they become an addiction to us. If we are addicted to sex or driven by ambition to the point of "workaholism", our acting out of these drives has ceased to be healthy and constructive and has turned into our enemy, which will eventually destroy us. We must begin to recognize these areas of imbalance and take steps to correct them. We must address the underlying wrongs of the past that directed us to feel and act out in the ways that we do today. When we come to pray about these two problems of sexuality and ambition, we might pray to the Lord, "Lord, teach me how to have a healthy expression of my sexuality. Show me your way in my sex life." In the area of ambition, we might pray, "Help me Lord, help me to see the balance You want me to have as I do my work in life today. Lord show me the happiness that I should have in doing my job, in my relationships with others, in my family, my spiritual and work life."

IDENTIFYING WRONGFUL TRENDS OF THE PAST

As we think and pray about these various problems in our past as shown by our out of control behavior, let us try to establish and identify patterns of behavior. Example: Have I had certain violent fits of anger in my life that started slowly and mildly then built up in time into violent rage? If this is the case, we have identified an addiction to anger and violent rage. Example: "Have I been involved with pornography during my life which has caused me to dwell on my sexual behavior with myself and others? Do I spend a large portion of my time thinking and fantasizing about sex?" Obviously, such behavior may end up in sexual addiction. So, it is very important to look for and identify the trends or patterns of behavior that may be causing you a great deal of difficulty. Look carefully and you will find them. Do not be afraid or run from

Steps 6 & 7 Lesson 20

"I was entirely ready to have God remove all the wrongs of my past life"

"Humbly asked Him to remove these wrongs"

Action Words:
READY TO REMOVE
- HUMBLY ASKED

STEPS 6 & 7

what you see. Face up to the problem and bring it to Jesus for healing. Ask your spiritual friend to help you with this.

TAKE COURAGE

In Step 6, we become ready to have God remove all of this hurtful past from us. The question is - Are we ready and willing to do it? This requires preparation, prayer and courage. The Lord Jesus will heal you if you will come to Him and give your past to Him. In lesson 23, I will discuss a method which I have used to help others give their past hurts to Jesus. It is called visualized prayer. But for now, please ask the Lord Jesus to help you to want to do it and prepare yourself to do just that.

HEALING - AN ONGOING PROCESS

Most of us will not be fully healed at once for the healing process is ongoing. We will recover gently and slowly as we yield ourselves to the mighty power of Jesus Christ. As we do this, we need to talk to our God, Jesus Christ, daily about our problem. Keep giving the wrongs to Him over and over again and believe. BELIEVE AND CLAIM YOUR HEALING with all that you are. In John 10:10, Jesus clearly states, "I have come that you (put your name in here) might have life - LIFE IN ALL ITS FULLNESS." You don't have to earn it, as a matter of fact you can't earn it. It's a free gift, so just open up and receive it.

STEP 7 - ASKING GOD TO HEAL ME

In discussing these two steps, we find that they are very closely related. In Step 6, we become WILLING to release our wrongs and defects of the past to Jesus Christ. In Step 7, we HUMBLE ourselves to actually do just that. Now, to some of us, humility is a tough word to understand and to live out. Humility simply means being the person that I really am instead of trying to be someone that I am not. Some of us may confuse this word with humiliation, which does not have the same meaning as humility and presents a very different concept. God does not want to "wipe us out" by humiliating or embarrassing us. Rather, He wants us to come to Him with love in our hearts searching for His healing. This is what happened to the lost son described in Luke 15:11-32. In this story, the younger son decided to collect his inheritance from his father and venture out into the world. He made a sinful mess of his life and, after returning to his senses, decided to come back to the father, a broken man. The reaction of the father is a powerful example of the reaction of Father God when we, His children, mess up our lives and return to Him. He welcomes us with open arms, forgives us on the spot, and calls us to celebrate with Him. For the lost son has returned and is once again part of the Father. This is a perfect example of the healing power of this step.

HUMBLE OURSELVES BEFORE THE LORD

To humble ourselves before the Lord is the process of coming to Jesus. Here are some reasons:

1. By being humble (being our real self), we can recognize the wrongs and the character defects revealed by our habits from the past. We need to stop covering them up and proceed to bring them out to be healed by the mighty saving power of Jesus Christ. The Bible teaches us that this is the ONLY way. This process may be somewhat painful at first, but complete healing and release of the pain connected with our wrongs will happen in time. We will be healed, no more pain, just peace and oneness with Jesus. Therefore, we must give in and turn it over to Jesus. This is humility.

2. By being humble, we recognize the limits of our human power. In a sense, we affirm the First Step all over again which simply says, we admit that, by ourselves, we are powerless over our addiction. We cannot overcome it on our own. We will never be healed until and unless we come to Jesus and give our wrongs to Him. It is not within our own power to heal ourselves.

3. By being humble, we can appreciate and begin to relate to the mighty power of God to change our lives. We are being called to come out of our drunken stupor and witness the mighty power of God who loves us so very much that He sent His only Son to us so that we can be saved from our sick state of spiritual being. We learn that God is the very source of our life, both physically and spiritually. In taking this step of faith, we declare that we believe that God is "ALL", that without Him we are nothing, that with Him, all things are possible including but not limited to our spiritual healing.

STEP 7 - OUR INVITATION TO JESUS

In this step, we invite God to come and live within us. This invitation is not intended to pull us down. In fact, the reverse is true. A poor self-image may be hidden by a false sense of pride. This pride can cause us to do our thing rather than turn to God for help. In contrast, a healthy self-image will free us to come out of the closet marked pride to receive God's goodness and healing and to find the right path for our life. As our self-image is being healed and restored to a proper sense of balance, we become comfortable about coming to God and

STEPS 6 & 7

Steps 6 & 7 Lesson 20

"I was entirely ready to have God remove all the wrongs of my past life"

"Humbly asked Him to remove these wrongs"

Action Words:
READY TO REMOVE
- HUMBLY ASKED

---

allowing Him to be our best friend. We begin to feel comfortable with ourselves and those around us. We have found joy and a new sense of security within ourselves.

LET GO OF OUR PRIDE

In order for us to fully experience this life-changing event, we must be humble, and we must let go of our pride. We must see that our healing has nothing at all to do with OUR material world. All the money or power in this world cannot accomplish our healing. We have already tried that and it did not work. We cannot be healed in our spirit by material or worldly things. ONLY the power of God in Jesus Christ can heal us. It is a spiritual healing by the Spirit of God. Only His Holy Spirit can accomplish this. No money or power can buy it at any price. So we must get pride off the pedestal of our life. It can no longer be our god.

HAVE FAITH IN GOD

Our humility has everything to do with our relationship to God and our FAITH in Him. Faith is the key that unlocks our humility. As long as we fail to believe completely in Jesus and His healing power, we will stay stuck on the god of our pride. Faith in God frees us from this condition. Faith is a free gift from God himself. Hebrews 11:1 states, "To have faith is to be sure of the things we hope for, to be certain of the things we cannot see. Over and over, in this chapter of the Bible, we are given examples of various people in scripture and their faith in God. We are shown how their faith moved mountains. Jesus will give us all the faith we need for the problems we face. All we need to do is to ask Him for it believing in Him and it will happen. Jesus wants to give you the gift of life, life in all of its fullness.

Although this step is the shortest and perhaps the least talked about step in our recovery process, it is the most important in terms of our actual healing. When we come to God and surrender ourselves to Him, we receive His healing touch and we become healed within. A miracle of transformation takes place. Jesus molds us and transforms us into the new healthy sons and daughters of Father God. Romans 12:2, "Do not conform yourselves to the standards of this world, but let God transform you inwardly by a complete change of your mind. Then you will be able to know the will of God, what is good and is pleasing to Him and is perfect." We truly become transformed into His children when we come to Him and receive His healing touch and grace. We are filled to the brim with the very life of God. (See Galatians 5:22)

A SAMPLE STEP 7 PRAYER

"Dear Jesus, I am now willing that You should have all of me - the good and the bad.

I ask You Lord to remove from me every single wrong in my past and its resulting character defects that stand in the way of my friendship and love for You, myself and the brothers and sisters in my life. (Mention one specific wrong that you are currently struggling with. Talk to Jesus in your own words about this wrong.) I give this wrong to You right now, dear Jesus. I also give You the rest of the wrongs on my 4th step inventory one by one. Take the pain and hurt of these wrongs from me Lord and fill me with Your grace and healing.

I see You touching me and healing me right now. Thank You, Jesus. Lord, give me Your strength as I continue my day. I want to live my life according to Your will. I receive Your presence and healing in my life right now, dear Jesus. I thank You for coming to me and healing me. May I live Your new life in me now and always. AMEN!"

I am not responsible for my feelings, only for what I do with them.
—Dr. Ceophus Martin

I tell you, there will be more joy in heaven over one sinner who repents, than over ninety-nine respectable people who do not need to repent.
—Luke 15:7

What God knows about us is more important than what others think about us.
—Author unknown

Worry is futile, but faith is faithful and God's blessings are merciful!
—Author unknown

Steps 6 & 7 Lesson 21

"I was entirely ready to have God remove all the wrongs of my past life"

"Humbly asked Him to remove these wrongs"

Action Word:
MEDITATIONS

MEDITATIONS

DAY ONE - Study Romans 6:11-12

The recovery process is a repeated dying to self over and over again and a series of rebirths. We must die time and again to our old addictions and bad habits. This death is continually followed by a birth to a new life that is spiritually filled with the love of God in Jesus Christ.

In Healing Step 6, we ask God to remove the wrongs of our past and any defects of character that they may have caused. This process requires that we die to our old ways of living and acting out our lives. We must die to a false sense of our possessive and jealous relationships with others. We must die to our self-centered attention to money and material things, power, lust or authority. We must die to our dependency on the painkillers that we used in the form of chemicals, food or other mind-bending attitudes and behaviors that cover up our spiritual hurts and needs.

It is only when we completely die to our old self that the Holy Spirit of Jesus can enter into our spirit to cleanse and heal us. We seek to be completely cleaned out inside by God's Holy Spirit and to become one with Him. We will not stop along the road but we will drive on until we have become fully healed, joyful sons and daughters of God our Father!

DAY TWO - Study Ephesians 4:17-24

The process of letting go of old dependencies and habits is easier to talk about than to accomplish. Individually, each one of us must resolve to do it. We must dump our load of garbage from the past no matter how much it hurts.

Paul is quite clear as he states in verses 22-24, "So get rid of your old self, which made you live as you used to - the old self that was being destroyed by its deceitful desires. Your hearts and minds must be made completely new, and you must put on the new self, which is created in God's likeness and reveals itself in the true life that is upright and holy." Paul encourages the early Christians and us to make up our minds once and for all to let go of our old dirty compulsive self. He calls us to put on a new self, made in the likeness of God himself. The only way to put on this "new self" is to come to Jesus, give yourself to Him and be healed. Why not do this now! The new life in Christ is WONDERFUL!

DAY THREE - Study Colossians 3:5-10

As we travel the road of life, our greatest challenge in our relationships with one another is to achieve a proper balance in our basic need for love, security and affirmation by others and ourselves. As we fell prey to our addictions, we became very mixed up and confused in our search for these basic needs in our lives.

It seems that, in our struggle to find this balance in our basic needs, we either fall far short of filling these needs or we can't seem to get enough of them. Somehow, we are never able to find that happy medium which will bring us a sense of balance and in control behavior.

When we improperly try to fulfill these basic needs of love, security and affirmation, we wind up in great pain and frustration. We become people who are empty and lacking and we have a huge appetite inside which seems impossible to fill. And so, we try to fill ourselves with our addiction. In the heart of our problem, we discover that there is never enough of the drugs, alcohol, sex etc. to drown our pain and to satisfy our needs. The problem is that we are looking in the wrong place and at the wrong solution. We lack the presence of God in our lives - we lack His healing and righteous guidance. In place of God, we set up our own false gods of money, drugs, alcohol, sex or some other false idol to run our lives. The Bible warns us to PUT TO DEATH these false gods. And so we come to God, give Him these false gods and ask Him to remove them from our life so that we may be able to experience true love, security and affirmation. In Jesus, we find the way, the truth and the life, our own precious life.

Walking the 12 Steps with Jesus Christ

MEDITATIONS

Steps 6 & 7 Lesson 21

"I was entirely ready to have God remove all the wrongs of my past life"

"Humbly asked Him to remove these wrongs"

Action Word :
MEDITATIONS

DAY FOUR - Study 1 Peter 1:13-16

This reading encourages us to "have your minds ready for action". (Verse 13) Paul calls us into action. Enough of dwelling on the problem - it's now time to do something positive about it. Step 6 is that action point. We have looked at our past long enough. Now is the time to begin to "clean it up".

Paul also calls us to be filled with hope in the Lord. This hope is the blessing we expect "when Jesus Christ is revealed." (Verse 13) There is an excitement in Paul's letter at this point, and so are we getting excited. We are getting ready for a great event in our life. We are ready for action and filled with hope. Jesus is about to come to each of us. We are about to be transformed into a "New Creation".

Finally, Paul calls us to holiness. That's a strange word for us in the 21st century. It certainly is not a popular word among most people today. We think being "holy" means that we shave our heads and enter some religious place for prayer and fasting for the rest of our life with no more "fun". That is not the meaning of holy. To be holy, in every day terms, means that we do the best that we can to walk with Jesus. Jesus calls us to walk with Him. Luke 9:23: "If anyone wants to come with me, he must forget himself, take up his cross every day, and follow me." To be holy is to do just that. When we walk with Jesus, we have found the righteous life, we become happy in Him. We no longer struggle in the dark of our addiction and sin. We have found the light and we walk in it. Are you ready to do the same? I pray that you are.

DAY FIVE - Study 1 John 4:18

When we reach this step, we are like a patient in the hospital awaiting surgery. We dread the thought of the pain and misery we must go through in order to correct our physical problem. We know that it will hurt and that there will be discomfort involved. But, we must do it in order to accomplish correction of the problem.

Our spiritual life is no different. When we are addicted, we suffer from a spiritual sickness and this problem requires spiritual surgery. We need this surgery to restore us to whole, healthy, spiritual people. The thought of this surgery is frightening, but our reading today tells us not to fear. Jesus is love and there is no fear in Jesus. The reading tells us that "fear has to do with punishment". (Verse 1) Jesus is not punishment; rather, He is forgiveness and love. Love is the opposite of fear. Therefore, there is no fear in Jesus, who is love.

It is very important at this point to understand that fear is the tool of the devil. The devil is the master of deception and confusion. Jesus is the God of order and healing. So, we must not fear letting go of the old habits. Let us rebuke the fear of the devil in the mighty name of Jesus Christ!

So cast out the fear in your spirit and come to Jesus who is your healing, dear friend. You will be very glad that you did.

DAY SIX - Study Revelation 3:19-20

As we go through the process of dying to our old self, we may want to mourn the "old me" with it's old habits, compulsive behavior, addiction and resulting sin. We may feel badly about letting go of the old me, for in doing that, we are saying good-bye to the past. But was that old self really a "friend" after all? It was that "old friend" in us that caused all of the pain and suffering that is present today and has been present in us for so very long.

Instead of mourning over the loss of an "old friend", let's look forward to a "new friend" who awaits us on the other side of the door in verse 20. Jesus stands patiently at the door of our hearts waiting and wanting to come into the very center of our lives - down deep inside where it counts. He is our new life. In order

Steps 6 & 7 Lesson **21**

"I was entirely ready to have God remove all the wrongs of my past life"

"Humbly asked Him to remove these wrongs"

Action Word:
MEDITATIONS

MEDITATIONS

to let Him into our heart, we need to lay down our old destructive habits. We want to open the door to a new way of life, a communion with Him, where He is part of us and we are part of Him.

How can we know this new relationship with Jesus? When we open the door to Jesus, we will experience the fruit of His Holy Spirit. (See Galatians 5:22) The anger-filled person will put on new self-control and patience. The desperately obsessive person will begin to take hold of a new balanced life within. He will become self-controlled and kind. All of what we seek from the Holy Spirit of Jesus, in the reading from Galatians, is ours in just the right amounts from God, just for the asking. He knows exactly what we need and how much of each. We have opened the door to His grace and His Spirit. A transformation has taken place; we are no longer the old person we once were. Instead we are a "NEW CREATION" in Jesus Christ.

DAY SEVEN - Study Psalm 119:28-40

Psalm 119 is called the Psalm of Wisdom. In this prayer, the Psalmist speaks to the Lord from his heart. He has turned to the Lord and he prays for strength, obedience, understanding and wisdom. This is truly the prayer of a person who desires to follow the Lord in his total life.

Could this also be our prayer as we reach out to the Lord for healing in Steps 6 and 7? We cry out to the Lord as we search for the right way in life. And the beautiful part is that He answers us. He is the way, the truth and the life.

Can we pause right now and ask the Lord to "keep us from going the wrong way, and in Your goodness teach us Your law"? (Verse 29) Are we willing to place our total life into the care of God, Jesus Christ? When we do this, we take our "eye" off of our problems and the past and put our eye on the God of Jesus Christ where it belongs. When we keep our eye on God, the problem is no longer impossible because we know that with God, all things are possible. (Matthew 19:26) Jesus will do anything that is good in our lives simply by yielding to Him and asking Him. We have unlocked the door to our hearts. Jesus is now free to come in and complete the saving of our lives. When we can focus this mind of ours completely on God's power to accomplish what is necessary in our lives, we will find a total readiness to "turn it over" to Jesus. We will let go of the prison of addiction and walk out into the glorious light of Jesus Christ. We will truly be free, "If the Son sets you free, then you will be really free". (John 8:36) Are you ready to become "free in Jesus"? I pray your answer will be "yes" and that you will open that door right now!

STEPS 6 & 7

Steps 6 & 7 Lesson 22

"I was entirely ready to have God remove all the wrongs of my past life"

"Humbly asked Him to remove these wrongs"

Action Words:
READY TO REMOVE
- HUMBLY ASKED

WHAT ARE MY CHANCES OF SUCCESS?

As we approach our actual stepping out to Jesus in the next lesson, let us consider the effectiveness of Steps 6 and 7. We may ask ourselves, "Just how successful has this business of these two steps actually been? How do I know that this works?"

The AA program alone is an unshakable example of the work that God is doing in the lives of millions of people around the world as you sit and read these words. God will remove our wrongs and defects of character when we humbly and sincerely come to Him and ask Him. All over the world, there are millions of people, just like you and me, who have been healed of their addictions. God has removed their defects of character and they are now walking in complete sobriety, healed from that which once drove them insane.

CHEMICAL ADDICTION - A path to self-destruction

There is a strange happening as we use chemical substances to alter our minds. We seem to be insanely bent on self-destruction, out to destroy our bodies with the addictive substances we put into them. Our bodies take a terrible beating as a result of this situation. Finally, in desperation and helplessness, we come to a point physically and spiritually when we can go no farther. It is then that the mighty grace of Jesus can enter us and we can be healed. Then the powerful God given instinct to preserve life and to LIVE AGAIN can operate fully with the grace of God that we have received. We begin to realize what Jesus wants to give us, LIFE INSTEAD OF DEATH. You see, God did not give us an instinct to die; the devil sold us that. It is when we listen to the devil and act on his prompting that we set out to kill ourselves. Instead, God gave us an instinct to live. He also gives us the grace (support) for that life. If He can keep you going physically, He can keep you going in the fullness of life in your spirit also. All you have to do is ask Him for that fullness of life. These two healing steps do just that.

ASK JESUS FOR HIS HEALING

We must ask God for this right way, this healing path to life. He will not cleanse us of our past if we do not come to Him. Neither will we be cleansed of our past until we ask Him - there is just no other way. We not only need to ask Him but we also must release ourselves and give Him the permission to enter within us. In the past 25 years of working with men in the prisons and jails, I have seen many men who have prayed to the Lord over and over for the healing of their past but never received that healing. Why you may ask? I believe the answer is a very simple one, so simple at times that we do not even recognize it. When we ask God to heal us, WE MUST ALSO YIELD OURSELVES TO HIM SO THAT HE CAN HEAL US - HIS WAY! Yet, there seems to be something in most of us that prevents us from letting go of our past completely. We want healing, but we want it OUR WAY.

Remember, our addiction problem is a spiritual sickness. We need healing in our spirit and the only One to heal us is our spiritual doctor, Jesus. We must take positive strong steps toward Jesus if we are to be healed. These steps must be motivated by our faith in Jesus and His process of healing us. Once we show our willingness and honestly release ourselves to Him, He will take care of the healing we so desperately need. He asks only that we try. He does not ask us to do the impossible. Remember Matthew 11:28, "Come to me, all of you who are tired from carrying heavy loads, and I WILL GIVE YOU REST!" He will give you rest when you come to HIM.

BE PATIENT AND DETERMINED

Now it is time to declare with confidence, "I am entirely ready to have God remove all the wrongs and defects of my character." Firmly, we state - "I'm ready Lord, come take this stuff away from me." This is not just a one-time event and it's done. Rather, it is an ongoing attitude that we practice day by day for the rest of our lives. Even after we ask God to lift this miserable past out of our lives, we may still struggle with the same thing again. Sometimes, we may struggle more intensely than before. You may ask, "Why is that? I thought that I was done with this stuff." The Bible teaches us that the devil is a very strong spirit. He will continue to tempt you in these areas because he knows that this is your weak spot and he does not want to let go of you. You see, when we play the devil's game for so long, the devil claims us as his. When we go to break this bondage, the devil fights to keep control. But we have the victory; "I have the strength to face all conditions by the power that Christ gives me." (Philippians 4:13) So, we must claim the victory in Jesus over and over again. In this way, the bondage of the devil will be broken and we will be healed. This may not happen all at once, so be patient. It will happen. JESUS guarantees it.

There is also the question of faith in this matter of healing. Paul says in Hebrews 11:1, "To have faith is to BE SURE of the things we hope for, to BE CERTAIN of the things we cannot see." Faith in Jesus requires that we walk in His way even when everything and everyone seems to indicate

Steps 6 & 7   Lesson 22

"I was entirely ready to have God remove all the wrongs of my past life"

"Humbly asked Him to remove these wrongs"

Action Words :
READY TO REMOVE
- HUMBLY ASKED

Teach me Your ways, O Lord; make them known to me. Teach me to live according to Your truth, for You are my God, who saves me.
I always trust in You.
-Psalm 25:4-5

"We felt that the death sentence had been passed on us. But this happened so that we should rely, not on ourselves, but only on God, who raises the dead. From such terrible dangers of death He saved us, and will save us; and we have placed our hope in Him that He will save us again."
-2 Corinthians 1:9-10

---

the opposite. When we walk with Jesus, we are guaranteed the victory in time. We are SURE and CERTAIN in Jesus, so keep trying.

GET READY - BE READY - STAY READY

These steps call us to be READY. That's a difficult request. Even if we want to, most of us still have doubts; we want to keep on with our old way even if that way has caused us so much pain and suffering. So, for most of us, all we can do is give it our "best shot". All we can do is TRY to the best of our ability and trust the Lord for the rest. Some of us may be able to let go of most of our wrongs but may want to hang onto one or two "oldies". We tell ourselves, "Well, this isn't so bad after all. I think I'll keep this one." Such is the pull of the devil. Remember, friend, his job is to steal, kill and destroy us. See John 10:10, if you have any questions about the devil's plan of attack against us. In the same verse however, Jesus calls us to come to Him for the fullness of life, HIS LIFE.

There are all sorts of extremes of thinking in this matter. We are tempted over and over by our old "stinkin thinkin", our old "head games". Letting them go requires brutal honesty and courage. Remember, you will be healed only to the extent that you are honest with yourself and God and "TURN THEM OVER"! So, quit the "stinkin thinkin" and the "head games" and come clean! Please!

Maybe a quick trip back to our 4th step inventory will help us to redefine the wrongs of the past again and help to bring them out into the open. Check your inventory and talk to God about it, friend. Remember, we are not just looking for the "biggies" but also all the little wrongs that caused us to get sick in the spirit. Now is the time to get it all. Jesus promises us fullness of life but we have to give our total self to Him. We are not striving to just "squeak by" but rather we desire total healing.

PERFECTION - OUR GOAL

You may ask, "How can I accept the whole result of these two steps? Because, that is perfection!" This sounds like a hard question, but practically speaking it is not. Only in Step 1, where we made the one hundred percent admission that we were powerless over our addiction, can we practice absolute perfection. The remaining steps of the program state perfect ideals - goals that we are shooting for. These are goals toward which we look ahead and measure our progress. We are on the road to perfection - we have not arrived there yet. Rather, we are still on our journey. If we look at these two steps in this light, our success becomes more possible. The urgent thing that we should do right now, is to make a beginning.

This whole process requires us to keep our eyes on a "GOAL". In football, the team that gets the highest score wins the game—this is the team's goal. This goal takes place moment-by-moment, play-by-play throughout the game. Our lives are like that game of football. We must keep our eyes on the goal. That goal will be reached in God's fullness of time. The secret to winning is, - "NEVER QUIT - KEEP YOUR EYES ON THE GOAL AND GO FOR IT!"

NEVER SAY - "NO - NEVER!"

Remember that the object of these two steps is to get ready to let go of the wrongs of the past and then to do just that. The moment we say "No never!" our minds close up tight against God and we shut Him out. We close ourselves off from His grace and healing and we run back into our former prison. Delay is dangerous, rebellion, "I won't!" is fatal and will kill you. At this point, we must abandon ourselves and move toward God and His healing grace.

IT'S TIME TO DO IT

The final part of this process of healing is to DO IT. In order to have the right frame of mind, we need to ask ourselves, "Right now, this moment, who is on the pedestal of my life?" I have talked about this concept many times during this program. In order to be successful in these two steps, or the entire program for that matter, we must have Jesus Christ in the center of our life on that pedestal. If we have "ME" on that pedestal, then we are right back where we started. When we have God on our pedestal from the bottom of our hearts, we are humble people and God will recognize and answer our prayer and come into our life.

The Bible says, "Anyone who is joined to Christ is a new being; the old is gone, the new has come." (2 Corinthians 5:17) Do you want to be healed? Then place yourself IN CHRIST. The scripture tells us that then we become a new creation. The old part of us will be gone and a new creation in Christ will have come in its place. That's being "born again", that's humility. That's our NEW LIFE!

Now is the time to take action. In the lesson that follows, I will describe a process or way of ac-

STEPS 6 & 7

Steps 6 & 7 Lesson 22

"I was entirely ready to have God remove all the wrongs of my past life"

"Humbly asked Him to remove these wrongs"

Action Words:
READY TO REMOVE
- HUMBLY ASKED

complishing these two steps within you. I suggest that you study this lesson very carefully, then pray and ask the Lord Jesus for your healing.

SCRIPTURE STUDY:

The following scriptures are provided with respect to Healing Step 6. Please study each scripture and ask yourself: How does this scripture speak to me regarding my willingness to yield my wrongs and character defects to God?

- ☐ Matthew 3:8
- ☐ James 1:5-6
- ☐ Matthew 5:3
- ☐ James 1:21
- ☐ Matthew 7:24-27
- ☐ 1 Peter 2:1-2
- ☐ Romans 6:1-4
- ☐ 1 John 2:28-3:3
- ☐ Romans 12:2
- ☐ Psalm 4:4-5
- ☐ 1 Corinthians 15:57
- ☐ Psalm 16:7-11
- ☐ 2 Corinthians 5:17
- ☐ Psalm 19:12-13
- ☐ 2 Corinthians 7:9-10
- ☐ Psalm 32:9-11
- ☐ Galatians 5:16-17
- ☐ Psalm 94:12-13
- ☐ Ephesians 5:8-10
- ☐ Psalm 119:10-12
- ☐ Philippians 4:13
- ☐ Psalm 139:23-24
- ☐ 1 Thessalonians 4:3-8
- ☐ Psalm 141:3-4
- ☐ Titus 2:11-14
- ☐ Proverbs 3:11-12
- ☐ Hebrews 6:11-12
- ☐ Proverbs 13:18
- ☐ Hebrews 12:1-2
- ☐ Proverbs 17:10

JESUS

Jesus is my Savior's name,
from glory is where He came.

When He died on the cross,
Satan new that he was lost.

When I asked Jesus to cleanse me,
Satan knew he had to flee.

All because Jesus died for me,
from my sins He set me free.

With my Savior is where I long to be,
because Jesus first loved me.

And His Kingdom one day I'll see,
that's where I'll spend eternity.

When He comes back for me,
on that day - where will you choose to be?

-Mark Elliott, Nov. 5, 1992

Walking the 12 Steps with Jesus Christ

Steps 6 & 7 Lesson 23

"I was entirely ready to have God remove all the wrongs of my past life"

"Humbly asked Him to remove these wrongs"

Action Words:
READY TO REMOVE
- HUMBLY ASKED

The Almighty God, the Lord, speaks:
"Let the giving of thanks be your sacrifice to God, and give the Almighty all that you promised. Call to Me when trouble comes; I will save you, and you will praise Me."
    -Psalm 50: 1, 14-15

"We felt that the death sentence had been passed on us. But this happened so that we should rely, not on ourselves, but only on God, who raises the dead. From such terrible dangers of death He saved us, and will save us; and we have placed our hope in Him that He will save us again."
    -2 Corinthians 1:9-10

"But His answer was: My grace is all you need, for My power is greatest when you are weak."
    -2 Corinthians 12:9

Healing Steps 6 and 7 are, in my view, the most important steps in the entire 12 step program. As we prepare to actually turn to the Lord Jesus in these steps, I believe that it is necessary for us to stop for a few moments and to study the workings of our spirit since it is our spirit that we will be giving to Jesus. In this lesson, I will try to give you the benefit of the learning and experience that has come to me, by God's grace, over the many years that I have been involved in this work.

EXAMPLE - THE "ICEBERG"

In discussing the thinking process, I will use two mental pictures or images. The first image is that of an iceberg. In the drawing following, you will notice the triangle with a wavy line drawn through the top part. This is my version of an iceberg. Shape does not matter at this point. Scientists tell us that the vast majority of an iceberg floats below the surface of the water, while only a small portion floats above the water line. In my drawing, the triangle represents the iceberg floating; the wavy line represents the waterline.

THE CONSCIOUS vs. THE SUB-CONSCIOUS MIND

For the moment, we will call this picture "our mind". We know that our minds are made up of two distinct parts. The smaller, upper part of our mind is the conscious mind or the present. This is represented by the part of the iceberg that is above the water. In this part of our mind we function in the now - this 24 hours. The larger part of our mind is the subconscious which houses our memory—our past. This part is represented by the part of the iceberg that floats under the water line. In this part of our mind, we store all of the events of our past, both good and bad, regardless of whether or not we can remember the event at the moment. It is in this subconscious past that we store all of the 4th step wrongs from our past. These events have affected us, formed our personality and developed the character that we now possess, including those defects and shortcomings to which the AA program refers. It is this subconscious mind that needs a good house cleaning. Several years ago, one young man in a class of mine referred to this part of the mind as "The Gut Box".

You may ask, "How did these events of our past (both good and bad) get into my subconscious mind?" As we travel through each day, we accumulate the events of that day in our conscious mind, represented by the small part of the iceberg sticking out above the water line. Each day, we may experience both good (positive) and loving relationships and also hurtful (negative) and harmful relationships with those we meet. At the end of each day, when we lay our head on the pillow to finish the day, an imaginary trap door opens between our conscious and subconscious mind. All that is in the "today" of the conscious is dumped into the subconscious mind. Tomorrow, when we awake, the slate of the conscious mind is clean. We begin a new day of conscious experiences that will, at sleep time, be deposited into the subconscious memory within our mind. Tomorrow, when we awake, the experiences of today will no longer be in the conscious today—they will be in our memory or sub-conscious.

The following drawing will illustrate all of this:

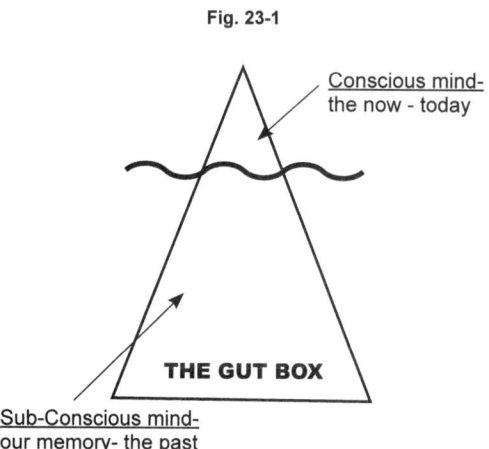

Fig. 23-1

So, you can readily see that what we experience today becomes our past tomorrow. As we go through life, we accumulate many difficult wrongs in our subconscious mind. These wrongs we may have received from others; or they may be wrongs that we ourselves have done to others. Either way, they have caused hurt and pain and they destroy our spirit. It is these wrongs, caught down in our subconscious mind, our gut box, that we want to give to Jesus for healing.

In Healing Step 4, when taking our searching and fearless moral inventory, we identified these wrongs and put them down on paper. Now in Healing Step 7, we want to humbly give them to Jesus and ask Him to remove the pain and hurt connected with them.

In the preceding illustration of the iceberg, I have showed you the difference between the conscious (present) mind and the subconscious (past) mind. I ask that you keep this information firmly planted in your thinking as we now turn to a method that can be used to remove the hurt and pain of the wrongs from the subconscious mind.

STEPS 6 & 7

Steps 6 & 7   Lesson 23

"I was entirely ready to have God remove all the wrongs of my past life"

"Humbly asked Him to remove these wrongs"

Action Words:
READY TO REMOVE
- HUMBLY ASKED

EXAMPLE - THE "AUTO ENGINE"

Our next image will be that of an auto engine. I will continue to use the same drawing as above but simply add a circle over the top tip of the triangle. I will call the triangle an auto engine and the circle at the top an oil filter.

We know that there is oil in the crankcase of an auto engine and the purpose of this oil is to lubricate (make the engine run smoothly), increase the engine life, keep the engine clean and reduce the friction of wear and tear. Whenever the engine is running, the oil pump circulates the oil from the crankcase through the oil filter and back into the engine. The purpose of the oil filter is to keep the engine oil clean so that it can do what is intended as I have described. No careful person would ever consider running an engine without keeping the oil and filter clean. Every responsible person knows the tremendous value in the proper care of your auto engine, which is the life of the vehicle. The greater the care, the better it will serve and the longer and better it will run.

The function of the oil filter is to receive the dirty oil from the engine via the oil pump, filter the impurities out of the oil, and return the clean oil back to the engine again giving it new life. This is the design and purpose of the oil filter.

Now, let's visualize the auto engine as being our spirit. This spirit is what God put there when He made us and this spirit is intended to make our life run smoothly each day. It is the center of our inner being - the part that makes us "tick". We all know that hurtful situations do happen in our lives. These hurtful situations we call wrongs. How do we get rid of these hurtful wrongs? Let's compare this with the auto engine example. Let's visualize the circle at the top of the triangle as the "filter" of Jesus Christ. Simply by taking the wrongs out of our spiritual "engine", and sending them through the "filter", Jesus Christ, we can be cleansed and purified, as was the oil in the auto engine when it was pumped through the oil filter. See the illustration in Fig. 23-2 that follows.

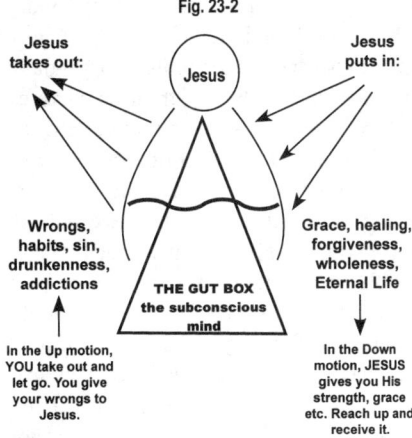

Fig. 23-2

THE SPIRITUAL CLEANSING PROCESS

This is the process of cleansing and healing that we seek to accomplish in our spirit. As the auto engine runs, the filter does its job of keeping the oil clean. As our spiritual engine runs, so does the filter Jesus Christ in removing the hurts and wrongs of our past. He fills us with His grace and healing. In order for this to happen, however, we must give the hurts and wrongs of our past to Him for healing as the oil pump needs to pump the dirty oil through the filter to be cleaned and sent back into the engine. When we do this on a daily basis, we will experience a spiritual person that "runs smoothly", is cleansed of our impurities and is kept clean to live a long healthy life. Our God who is Jesus Christ accomplishes this for us. We become healthy again to live the fullness of His life within us.

As you reflect on these two images, which I have given, you will see how important it is for all of us to "keep the oil clean". The oil is our inner spirit. Only Jesus can accomplish this for us. We have to give ourselves to Him and ask Him to remove the pain and hurt of our past wrongs and help us to correct the defects of character that have come about as a result. His healing makes us new and fresh again and gives us new life.

VISUALIZED PRAYER

In order to accomplish this healing, I suggest that you use a type of prayer that I call visualized prayer. This type of prayer is by no means the only way to accomplish this giving of self to Jesus. It is merely one way, a way that I have successfully used many times and I strongly recommend to you. Please feel free to try this. Remember, it takes time to accomplish this healing, so be patient. We need to do this over and over again and, in so doing, we break down the old self, we die to the "old me" so that Jesus can create a "new me". Please feel free to do this anyway you wish, BUT PLEASE DO IT.

Steps 6 & 7 Lesson 23

"I was entirely ready to have God remove all the wrongs of my past life"

"Humbly asked Him to remove these wrongs"

Action Words:
READY TO REMOVE
- HUMBLY ASKED

Jesus gave His all for me - How can I give Him less from me?
-Author unknown

Joy is the by-product of confessing and trusting Jesus Christ!
-Author unknown

When you hang onto self, you lose;
When you yield to God, you gain Eternal life.
-Author unknown

Answer me Lord, I have lost all hope. Don't hide Yourself from me, or I will be among those who go down to the world of the dead. Remind me each morning of Your constant love, for I put my trust in You. My prayers go up to You; show me the way I should go.
-Psalm 143:7-8

STEPS 6 & 7

Visualized prayer is a form of mental imagery in which we use mental pictures to help us see clearly in our minds what is happening in our thoughts and spirit. Most human beings think in pictures. That is how we learned when we were infants and that type of learning continues throughout our lives. In using this form of prayer, we simply get comfortable, not too comfortable where we fall asleep. It might be a good idea to have your inventory and the Bible on your lap. As you relax and get comfortable, try to clear your mind of all the thoughts and concerns of the day. Quiet is very important, so find a place where no one will be likely to disturb you. You may want to ask your spiritual friend to pray with you and be with you at this time. It is very important to understand that we can and must do everything possible to release our wrongs ONE AT A TIME to our Lord Jesus Christ. Therefore, it is perfectly acceptable to speak out loud or to cry. In some cases, where there is extreme anger and rage involved in these past wrongs, you may want to vent this anger in a loud manner. It is acceptable to do whatever is necessary to bring release to the bottled up emotions and feelings inside of you as long as you do not lose control of yourself or become violent. This will only defeat the healing process.

Your next step is to close your eyes and visualize Jesus with you. See Him in human form standing or sitting next to you. You are talking to Him as you would your best and closest friend. Tell Him how you feel. Ask Him to help you to unload the past and heal you. Remember to take one wrong at a time. Be specific about each situation. Do NOT try to cover all wrongs all at once in a general prayer.

Finally, see yourself reaching down deep inside of your spirit into your gut box. As you do this, see yourself taking each hurt one at a time out of your subconscious mind and handing it to Jesus. You may want to take your two hands and reach down as though you were reaching inside of yourself. Grab hold of the hurt and hold that hurtful wrong tightly in your closed fist. Now lift your closed hands, hurt and all, high up in the air and give it to Jesus. As you do this, see it happening in your mind's eye. Give it to Jesus who is there reaching out to you to receive it from you. Ask Him to take it from you. Ask Him to forgive you and to help you seek forgiveness from others you have hurt. Ask Him to help you to forgive yourself and to let go of the hurt and pain involved with these memories. See Jesus reaching out and taking the pain from you. See Him placing His arms around you and healing you with His comforting touch.

It is VERY IMPORTANT that you consider only one wrong at a time during this process. Be specific about each problem when talking to Jesus. Don't just ask Jesus to forgive you in a general way but deal with the specific situations and people involved. As you do this, you may want to bring into your mind the person/s who were involved in the hurt that you are asking Jesus to remove. See Jesus along with those people and yourself as He goes about placing His hand of forgiveness and healing on each one involved. Be patient with this process. You may have to work through a good bit of resentment of others in order for this to happen. Ask Jesus to help you to let go of those resentments in this process. Jesus can and will work miracles of healing if you will try it and use this method regularly. As you work this method out, you will see Jesus touch you in your spirit and you will receive the "in-filling" of His grace and the peaceful presence of His Holy Spirit within you. You are now in the process of healing inside.

HEALING OF MEMORIES

Healing of Memories takes place in a variety of ways and can be an effective tool to heal a person of their past so they are free to live in the present.

Every person's history is recorded in their memory. Recorded memories include life events as they were perceived by the five senses along with the emotions the person was experiencing at that time. Our entire life script is within us, powerfully influencing our reactions to things outside of us such as people, places, or things. Present day experiences are processed through past perceptions which are sometimes not completely accurate.

Therefore, how do we change the recorded memories of difficult and sometimes traumatic life events? We cannot go back and change the outcome of the events we have recorded. However, with the power of Christ, we can go back and change our perception of those events. We cannot go back and change what the senses perceived, but we can go back and change the emotional content of the record we hold of our past. (Durrance)

In Step 2 we learned that God is omnipresent—present everywhere at the same time. As life happens, we forget this very important characteristic of God. Therefore, humbly asking God to remove our wrongs may include inviting Jesus into some specific experience to show us where He was and what He was doing or to simply minister to us in the way that He knows is best for us. We simply ask Him to bring His presence into that situation to heal our perception of it.

See the sample prayer on page 105 for Healing a Memory.

STEPS 6 & 7

Steps 6 & 7 Lesson 23

"I was entirely ready to have God remove all the wrongs of my past life"

"Humbly asked Him to remove these wrongs"

Action Words:
READY TO REMOVE
- HUMBLY ASKED

SOUL TIES

A Soul Tie is a strong emotional bond that connects you with other people, places, or things of any kind.

Soul Ties between people are formed by spending time together. The more time spent together the stronger a Soul Tie will be. Soul Ties are formed through vows such as, "I will never stop loving you," "I will always love you," "We will be together forever," and "Until death do us part." Soul Ties are also formed through commitments and promises we make with each other and physical intimacy or sex. (Savelle Foy, 2010, 2012)

Sex is a physical action that bonds us with the one that we have sex with—making us one flesh. God's purpose for sex is to unite a man and a woman to create a strong core for a family. Sex with more than one person adulterates us—it adds additional bonds to us that we weren't intended to have. See Genesis 2:21-24, Matthew 19:5, 1 Corinthians 6:13-18, and 1 Corinthians 7:1-5. (Durrance)

Soul Ties with places or things are formed by the kinds of feelings and memories we associate with them or what they mean to us. For example, a straw may be associated with sipping a beverage or snorting cocaine. A romantic song can remind us of a beautiful time during our marriage or it can remind us of an adulterous relationship we ran to for comfort during a very distressing time.

Godly Soul Ties respect and honor your relationship with God. They are rooted in the foundation of Christ and God's unconditional love. In godly Soul Ties, God's power is increased. God wants us to have healthy relationships that build us up, provide wisdom, and give wise counsel. God will strategically bring good relationships into our lives whenever we ask Him.

Ungodly Soul Ties do not respect and honor your relationship with God. They are rooted in your soul, more specifically the areas of your mind, will, and emotions that are not yielded to the Holy Spirit. In ungodly Soul Ties your enemy, the devil's power is increased.

Adulterous affairs and sexual relationships before marriage involve ungodly Soul Ties. Controlling and obsessive relationships involve ungodly Soul Ties. Verbally, emotionally, physically, or sexually abusive relationships also involve ungodly Soul Ties. Whenever we give someone more authority over us than God, we have formed an ungodly Soul Tie.

Signs that may indicate ungodly Soul Ties include: finding yourself tormented by thoughts of someone, excessively wondering about someone, constantly checking on someone, rehearsing or reliving times with someone, and excessively grieving a broken relationship with someone. Feeling very confused, miserable, or tormented in a relationship may also indicate ungodly Soul Ties. If a relationship has become characterized by disobedience of any kind, an ungodly Soul Tie is involved. (Savelle Foy, 2010, 2012)

The good news is that once we become aware of ungodly Soul Ties they can be broken through the power of Christ. Humbly asking God to remove our wrongs definitely includes breaking ungodly Soul Ties. See the sample Soul Tie Breaking Prayer on page 104 and use it as often as you feel the need. The power of Christ will prevail.

Steps 6 & 7 Lesson 23

"I was entirely ready to have God remove all the wrongs of my past life"

"Humbly asked Him to remove these wrongs"

Action Words:
READY TO REMOVE
- HUMBLY ASKED

STEPS 6 & 7

SOUL TIE BREAKING PRAYER

First, pray some kind of prayer of repentance to God.

Repentance: changing your views and purposes to accept the will of God in your inner self instead of rejecting it; changing your mind for the better and sincerely changing your ways; agreeing with God about sin—that it hurts you, is not good for you, is not God's best for you, and that you have offended God and need to be saved from it.

Breaking Ungodly Soul Ties w/People—See sample prayer below.

"In the name of Jesus, I break any and all ungodly Soul Ties between me and _____ that may be rooted in pride, judgment, greed, lust, anger, gluttony, envy, sloth, bitterness, rejection, fear, insecurity, unforgiveness, etc.

(You can insert any other root that the Holy Spirit may be revealing to you.)

Jesus, please bring the parts of my spirit and soul that are remaining with _____ back to me that I may be healthy and whole—please return the parts of _____'s spirit and soul back to him/her that he/she may be healthy and whole. Jesus, please fill these places with your Holy Spirit that the fruit of your Spirit may take root and grow into its fullness that I/we may never be the same. In Jesus' name we pray, Amen."

(You may continue in prayer however you feel the Spirit leading you.)

Pray asking Jesus to rebuild any Soul Ties that He desires on the foundation of Him, His work on the cross, and His unconditional love.

Breaking Ungodly Soul Ties w/Places or Things—See sample prayer above adjusting as needed.

EXERCISE FOR CONFESSING SIN TO GOD—if desired

- ▶ Approach God through praise and thanksgiving—Read Psalm 111:1-6
- ▶ Read all of Psalm 139
- ▶ Write out a prayer of confession & repentance for the things that the Spirit brings to your mind.
- ▶ Read all of Psalm 51
- ▶ Write out an additional prayer of confession & repentance for things that come to mind.
- ▶ Write out 1 John 1:9 across your written prayers of confession & repentance: "But if we confess our sins to Him, He is faithful and just to forgive us our sins and to cleanse us from all wickedness."
- ▶ Destroy your confession in some way
- ▶ Complete this exercise through praise and thanksgiving—Read Psalm 111:7-10

Walking the 12 Steps with Jesus Christ

STEPS 6 & 7

Steps 6 & 7 Lesson 23

"I was entirely ready to have God remove all the wrongs of my past life"

"Humbly asked Him to remove these wrongs"

Action Words:
READY TO REMOVE
- HUMBLY ASKED

HEALING MEMORIES

This is a suggested healing prayer exercise that is completely left to the discretion of the individual. Please practice only what you feel comfortable with.

1. Select any memory from a life event that you wish to invite the Lord into.
2. Close your eyes and picture that time exactly how it was. Can you see where you were, who was there, and what was going on?
3. Picture the details of this event, hear what was being said or done.

Now, ask Jesus to come into this life event and show you where He was and what He was doing. Ask Jesus to minister to you in this event.

4. "Lord, Jesus, I believe you are not bound by time or space. You have always been with me. You are present everywhere at the same time, but I have not always been aware of Your presence. Jesus, please come to me now in this wounded, painful place. Show me where You were when I experienced this pain and love me through it. Please comfort me according to Your will."

Give yourself some time to notice how or where Jesus comes into the event and what He does. If you cannot see Him, can you sense His presence with you in any way?

5. Close with prayer—"Thank you, Lord, for coming into this wounded, painful place, which I have covered with anger, fear, pride, and sadness and which I have protected from ever being hurt again. Lord, by the power of your Holy Spirit at work right now, please enable me to be willing to release forgiveness to those who hurt me. Thank you that when I am willing, You are able. Lord, I forgive _____ for hurting me this way. Lord, I forgive myself for how I felt and how I reacted, what I said, or what I did because I didn't know what to feel or how to act or what to say or what to do. I didn't know how to help myself, but You are my Help and my Deliverer. (Psalm 40:17) Lord, I forgive You for allowing this to happen to me. By faith, I receive your peace, your grace, your mercy, and your love all given to me for my healing. Holy Spirit, I ask you right now to be rooted in this place and to grow in Your fullness within me that I may never be the same. In the name of Jesus I pray, Amen."—You may continue in prayer as your feel led.

Note: Many have asked why we need to forgive the Lord. Sometimes we blame Him for things that have happened in our life, we forget that we can be hurt by the free will of others. This prayer exercise can be seen as giving the Lord the opportunity to change our perception of the event. This has been extremely helpful to many.

Please only practice what you feel comfortable with.

Steps 6 & 7 Lesson 23

"I was entirely ready to have God remove all the wrongs of my past life"

"Humbly asked Him to remove these wrongs"

Action Words:
READY TO REMOVE
- HUMBLY ASKED

STEPS 6 & 7

HEALING PRAYER FOR ABANDONMENT

We are not abandoned. God has always pursued us out of His love because He greatly desires that we be in a relationship with Him. We become adopted into God's family through our belief and faith in Jesus Christ and the power of His death on the cross.

Healing Prayer

You, O God, are a father of the fatherless, a judge and protector of widows. You have now placed me in a family, Your body, Your church, for all of the times that I have felt and still feel lonely, deserted, or ruined. (Psalm 68:5-6)

You are the helper to the fatherless, and whether I truly may have been forgotten and abandoned by my mother and/or my father or if I only perceive and feel that I was forgotten and abandoned by my mother and/or my father, (Psalm 10:14, Psalm 27:10) I now trust that You are able to now take me up, and adopt me as Your very own, You offer me adoption through my belief in, my trust in, and my reliance on Your Son Jesus. (John 1:12, Ephesians 1:5, Ephesians 2:19)

I thank You, God, that You have given me the opportunity to be led by Your Spirit and to be Your child. Help me believe, trust, and feel how dearly You love me. Thank you, God, that the Spirit I receive from You is not a spirit of slavery that puts and keeps me in bondage to fear—no! You have given me the spirit of adoption to receive—by which I may cry Father! Father! (Romans 8:14-16, Galatians 4:4-6)

Show me, help me to remember all those whom you have placed in and throughout my life to help and to care for me when I was in pain, sorrow, or need (James 1:27)—even if it seemed they were there by "chance" and just for an instant, for I now know that there is no chance with You because Your eyes are in every place, and I have never been hidden from Your sight because You fill the heavens and the earth. (Psalm 139:1-12, Jeremiah 23:23-24, Proverbs 15:3, Hebrews 4:13)

You tell me in Your word that You will not in any way fail me, nor give me up, nor leave me without support, You will not, You will not, You will not in any degree leave me helpless nor forget me nor let me down—You will not relax Your hold on me. (Hebrews 13:5)

Therefore, I desire that my mind, my will, and my emotions be transformed now, by the power of Your Spirit comforting and encouraging me. I desire to confidently and boldly believe and to from now on confess that You are my helper (Psalm 121 all); I will no longer be afraid and I now choose to be more willing than ever to forgive all those whom I have felt abandoned by that I may truly be set free.

We agree together and pray all these things in the Name of Jesus, Amen!

Walking the 12 Steps with Jesus Christ

MEDITATIONS

Steps 6 & 7 Lesson 24

"I was entirely ready to have God remove all the wrongs of my past life"

"Humbly asked Him to remove these wrongs"

Action Word:
MEDITATIONS

DAY ONE - Study Matthew 18:4

Childhood is a very special time. Children are so pure and simple. At first, they are unstained by the world around them. They respond with honesty and openness. Unfortunately, this childlike attitude also leaves them open to abuse by others around them. Often those abuses come from their own family members. When Jesus tells us, in this reading, that we must become as a little child in order to enter into the Kingdom of Heaven, some of us may find this very difficult to grasp and put into practice. In fact, some of those abuses we received, as little children, may be the cause of the hurtful wrongs that resulted in present day defects of character deep within us. Our addiction became our way of covering all this up. Therefore, it takes both humility and lots of courage for us in that situation to take this step of trust toward Jesus.

Yet, if we will enter into this walk of faith, coming humbly before Jesus as His child, He is faithful to remove our wrongs and resulting defects. It is at this point in our life that Jesus builds the Kingdom of Heaven within us. We become a "New Creation" in Christ Jesus. The old self with its hurts and abuses has died.

DAY TWO - Study Acts 3:19-20

In Healing Step 7, we experience the powerful forgiveness and healing of Jesus, which causes us to experience the miracle of "New Creation". In verse 19, we are urged to repent, to turn to God, and He will forgive us. We have been traveling in the wrong direction in life. This scripture calls us to - STOP - take a good look at where we are going; turn to God and receive His forgiveness. As we do, we begin to walk in the right direction instead of our old, wrong direction.

In the Overcomer's Prayer, we find the opening words - "Lord Jesus Christ, I abandon myself to you, just as I am, the good, the bad and the indifferent." This is exactly what this reading calls us to do. And what is the result? Verse 20 tells us, "If you do, times of spiritual strength will come from the Lord and He will send Jesus, who is the Messiah He has already chosen for you." When we abandon ourselves to Jesus, He will come to us. It is important here to understand the meaning of the word Messiah. Messiah means the anointed (chosen) one of God the Father. So this verse tells us that when we repent, turn to God for forgiveness, He (God) will send us Jesus who will give us times of spiritual strength. Step 7 embodies God's mysterious power to rebuild our character and leads us toward the miracle of a "New Creation" and the healing of our past wrongs and defects. We have experienced a rebirth into new life.

If we step out and come to Him with a sincere heart, Jesus will fill us with His strength and new spirit, the Holy Spirit.

DAY THREE - Study Hebrews 12:5-11

This reading uses the words: correct, rebuke, and punish. These words may seem harsh toward us coming from a God who loves us. But, as we study this reading and reflect on it, we find that the reward of this correction by our Lord is, "the peaceful reward of a righteous life." (Verse 11) These passages call us to a life of humility and submission toward our God in our lives as believers.

It seems that these early Hebrew Christians had trouble obeying the ways of their God and doing the work that He gave them. Hebrews reminds us that our God is a holy God (verse 10) and that if we obey Him, we will reap the peaceful reward of a righteous life (verse 11). As a son submits to the discipline and punishment (when necessary) of a loving earthly father, so we are to be disciplined by our God who is our heavenly Father. This discipline is not given to us to hurt us, but rather to show the righteous life of the Father. Discipline should be looked upon as the Father guiding us in the right path of life.

Apparently, these early Hebrew Christians were having trouble yielding and obeying the ways that God had chosen to work in their lives. The writer of Hebrews reminds them that God is a wise and loving Father.

Walking the 12 Steps with Jesus Christ

107 Christian 12 Step Ministry, Inc

Steps 6 & 7 Lesson 24

"I was entirely ready to have God remove all the wrongs of my past life"

"Humbly asked Him to remove these wrongs"

Action Word:
MEDITATIONS

MEDITATIONS

And as a son should humble himself to accept his father's discipline, so we believers should also be willing and humble to place ourselves under the loving hand of our Heavenly Father's infinitely wise discipline Even though we may feel sad at the time we are disciplined, verse 11 tells us that we will reap the reward of a peaceful, righteous life. Not just in this world, but more importantly in the eternal life to come.

Dear friends, let us willingly submit to the loving discipline of our Father God so that Jesus will dwell in our hearts and lives. AMEN!

DAY FOUR - Study 1 Peter 5:6-7

In our experience of Healing Step 7, when we humbly ask God to remove our wrongs and their resulting defects of character, we may find ourselves in some confused thinking. This step calls us to be humble and yet, the experience of our addictive behavior has many times caused us disgrace, embarrassment, shame, and untold guilt. We seem to have been dragged down into the "pits" of hell itself, into more difficult situations. We may ask ourselves - "Is this what God wants for me? Is this being humble, to be dragged into the pits and the mud of life?"

Of course, the answer to that question is a resounding "NO"! God does not want to drag us down still further and tear us apart. Instead, He wants us to come to Him and submit to His leadership and guidance in our lives as little children come to their daddy with a problem. He will then lift us up and fill our innermost hunger for love and affirmation. Healing Step 7 is a humble, down to earth, no nonsense way of letting go of the hurts inside of us. When we come to Jesus, He restores our inner being to the way it was when He created it. He takes the pieces and puts them back together in a perfect way doing something that is impossible for us to do for ourselves. When we cast our burdens and difficulties into His care, it is only then that we can be healed and made whole again.

DAY FIVE - 1 John 5:14-15

In our reading today, we discover how open and loving God is. We can see Him right here and now listening to the innermost thoughts and feelings deep inside. When we come to Him sincerely and according to His will, the door is always wide open. Jesus has office hours 24 hours a day, seven days a week and an appointment is not necessary. As a matter of fact, we don't even have to move a muscle to talk to Him because His presence is within us. All we have to do to be with Him and talk to Him is to turn our thoughts inside of ourselves. And when we do, He will give us whatever we need. When we hurt, He will calm and soothe our fears and pain. When we feel down and beaten, He will lift us up and put us back together again. When we feel hopeless, He will show us the way through the storms of life. When we feel dirty with sin inside, He will wash us "white as snow".

Yes, Jesus is much kinder and greater to us than we can possibly imagine. He is our all - all our needs. But we cannot experience Him without coming to Him. That is what Step 7 is all about. So come to Him, dear friend, and let Him make you whole again. You will be happy that you did. Psalm 37:4 says—"Seek your happiness in the Lord, and He will give you your heart's desire." So, stop trying to trust in yourself and your own power. Come to Jesus and trust in Him. He will give you your heart's desire.

DAY SIX - Study Psalm 32-6-8

What a wonderful promise today in the reading from the Psalms of King David. David trusted in the Lord and so he calls to us to come to the Lord in our times of need. When a "great flood of trouble comes rushing in", David calls us to come to the Lord and trust Him. Just as the God of David rescued him from

Walking the 12 Steps with Jesus Christ

MEDITATIONS

Steps 6 & 7   Lesson 24

"I was entirely ready to have God remove all the wrongs of my past life"

"Humbly asked Him to remove these wrongs"

his troubles, so will our God Jesus rescue us from ours. When we come to our Lord with humility, being our true self, He will repair the mess of our past and bring us to the fullness of life.

In verse 8, the Lord says, "I will teach you the way you should go; I will instruct you and advise you." Verse 10 says, "The wicked will have to suffer, but those who trust in the Lord are protected by His constant love." How strange it is that, when you and I persist in following our wicked ways, we will suffer. But when we come to Jesus and trust in Him, we are protected by His constant love.

In verse 7 we read, "You (Lord) are my hiding place; You will save me from trouble." Can we take Jesus at His word? Are we willing to come to Him and "hide ourselves" in Him? If we do, we will be saved from trouble. He will protect us and show us the right way through life. We are not just a statistic or number to our Lord; rather we are His children, as if we were the only one. He cares about each one of us individually just as if we were the only person who ever did or will live. Only the God of Jesus can do that. He knows you personally and so intimately that He knows "the number of hairs on your head." He will deliver you and heal you of your old habits. Won't you come to Him and try to love Him just a little bit in return? He's waiting for you, so please come now!!!

Scripture: MEDITATIONS

DAY SEVEN - Study Psalm 37:23-24

In today's reading, the Psalmist declares, "The Lord guides a man in the way he should go." (Verse 23. Our saying in this 12 step program "Let go and let God", is the same as the Psalmist's meaning. When we let go and let God take over our life, the Psalmist says, "(The Lord) protects those who please Him. If they fall, they will not stay down, because the Lord will help them up." How great and caring is our God. His love for us is so great that He guides us and, if we slip, He picks us back up and puts us back on the right road. Probably the most difficult part of our recovery is to recognize and to change our self-centered pride. The big "ME" has got to go. I've had too much trouble with the old "ME". When I was on the pedestal of my life, I decided and selected the life I was going to live and look where it got me! Now I understand the problem AND I also know the solution. Each day I must choose who will be on the pedestal of my life. Will my direction come from my old life with all of its problems and addictions, or will my direction today come from the one true God, JESUS CHRIST?

From this day forth, you can never say that you don't know the problem or the solution. Is God running your life, or are you? I pray that you will give yourself to Jesus this day and all the days of your life. AMEN!

SCRIPTURE STUDY:

The following scriptures are provided with respect to Healing Step 7. Please study them carefully and see how they apply to this step in your life:

- ☐ Psalm 10:17
- ☐ Psalm 119:133
- ☐ Psalm 25:8-11
- ☐ Proverbs 18:12
- ☐ Psalm 32:1
- ☐ Proverbs 22:4
- ☐ Psalm 34:4-6
- ☐ Matthew 7:7-11
- ☐ Psalm 34:15
- ☐ Matthew 15:22-28
- ☐ Psalm 37:4-6
- ☐ Matthew 21:21-22
- ☐ Psalm 39:7-8
- ☐ Luke 18:9-14
- ☐ Psalm 51:1-10
- ☐ Philippians 4:19
- ☐ Psalm 79:9
- ☐ James 4:6
- ☐ Psalm 91:14-16
- ☐ 1 John 3:4-9
- ☐ Psalm 103:2-5
- ☐ 1 John 3:22-24

We need to look at the whole forest, instead of focusing on just one tree.
-Author unknown

Real healing takes place through the confession of our soul.
-Anonymous

Life is a road that leads to God for those who follow that road.
-Ray Geisel

Forgiveness and salvation are God's gifts to be received, not goals to be achieved.
-Anonymous

CHURCH FELLOWSHIP

Steps 6 & 7   Lesson 25

Action Words:
INVOLVED IN CHURCH - FAST

ACTIVELY INVOLVED

FELLOWSHIP - CHURCH - WE ARE NOT ALONE

As we have progressed through our steps thus far, we have come to realize that our walk to recovery is not taken alone. In fact, our whole life is not lived alone. Part of our addiction has convinced us that, "I am the only person who counts - ME and ME alone." This of course is not true. Over and over again we have seen that we did not acquire our addiction alone. There were other people involved in the wrongs of our past, which led to the defects of character in our spirit today. We picked up these wrongs from our original family and in the process of living our lives until now. We are part of a society that has influenced us time and again for both good and evil. Our walk, in this 12 step program, is not done alone. There are others who sit right next to us with the same or very similar problems. The AA literature, which is the basis for this program, is used by millions of people throughout the world. Very quickly, we get a sense that there are lots and lots of people around us in the "same boat".

If we go back into the first book of the Bible, Genesis, we find that God did not create just man, He also created woman from man and for man. In this way, God made the very first family. And He told the first man and woman (Adam and Eve) to go forth and multiply and have children. That first family was to multiply and cover the earth. So, from the very beginning of time, man has always longed to be with someone in a physical as well as spiritual relationship. This is a basic human need for all of us.

WE HAVE A SPIRITUAL FAMILY AS WELL AS A NATURAL FAMILY

As a result, you and I were born into a family. We lived in that family for a good part of our early life. Sooner or later, we left that natural family to strike out on our own. Maybe we started our own family since then in one way or another.

We are also part of a larger family however. We are citizens of a great country—the United States of America.

The Bible tells us that an equally important family, next to our natural family, is our spiritual family. This is the family in which we live called the "Body of Christ" or the Church. The early Christian Church is best described in the first few chapters of the book of Acts. There we see that "Church" is the coming together or gathering of the believers to worship God and sometimes, in certain situations, to live together as the community of God. Church is not, and never was designed by God to be, a building, an organization, a denomination, or a pastor, minister, or priest. Very simply, Church is the body of believers, which is also called by Jesus Himself, "The Body of Christ".

OUR NATURAL FAMILY

Now, let's look back to our original family, our mother and father. I am sure you can see how important they were to you being conceived and entering this world. They were the physical vehicles that God used to get you and your body here. They took care of you for many years after your birth (in most cases). They fed you and clothed you. They took care of your medical needs and your education. They loved you in their own imperfect way. They did the best that they could under the circumstances.

GOD CREATED OUR SPIRIT

Without the Spirit of the Almighty God, you and I would never have been conceived. God touched the union of your mother and father and created a living human fetus in conception. So the living Breath of the Almighty Father God created you in spirit. The Bible tells us that you and I were conceived in the mind of God before this universe was created. Psalm 139:16, "The days allotted to me had all been recorded in your book, before any of them ever began."

God waited until this time to place your spirit in your body and cause you to be physically born into this world. You and I, therefore, are not only physical human beings but more importantly, we are spiritual beings. Our bodies will die and return to the earth, but our spirit will live forever and return to the God who made us.

WE ARE CHILDREN OF GOD - OUR FATHER

The Bible also shows us that we are all children of God the Father with Jesus Christ, His Son, our Brother. We have a relationship with God. Many of the readings you have already studied have pointed this out to you. God the Father has made you his son or daughter through Jesus Christ, His Son.

THE "BODY OF CHRIST"

Since we are all members of the one family of God, through Jesus Christ the Son, we become baptized into that family which Jesus calls the "Body of Christ". We are all, therefore, related to each other. God our Father, Jesus His Son and our brother, and those believers who belong to His family who are our brothers and sisters. Therefore, Church to Christians is the celebration of the Family of God. Church is a relationship with our fellow brothers and sisters where we come together to worship and

ACTIVELY INVOLVED

FAST & PRAY
Steps 6 & 7 Lesson 25

Action Words:
INVOLVED IN CHURCH - FAST

give honor and praise to our Lord. We also learn about the Lord in Bible Study; we receive advice and correction in our Christian walk; and we practice and grow in our love relationship to God and His family. We learn who we are and experience that identity in our love relationship with one another called "Church".

This love relationship called Church is essential to the growth and development of our Christian walk. God did not intend for us to do it alone. He gave us to each other and placed His Holy Spirit within each of us. We are called to be Christ to each other and, in so doing, we are called "Christians".

PARTICIPATE IN CHURCH

Active and ongoing participation in our spiritual family called Church is absolutely essential for the success of our Christian life. We need Jesus and we also need each other as we walk with Jesus. It is in this relationship called Church that we help each other along the road to Jesus Christ. It is essential that we attend a good Church along with our family each week. Regular services are a must. Bible study is also a must. You and your family need to be there together. This is God's plan for you and your loved ones. If you do not have a church family, seek one out. Visit several churches and see which one speaks to your spiritual needs. Talk to a friend, your spiritual friend, about it. Ask questions of others and find the church just for you. Be certain that the Bible is preached and taught. Go to a church family that will accept you just as you are. If they will not accept you, move on to another church until you find your home. Keep praying for God to show you the right church. This is VERY important and is essential to your spiritual growth and strength. You cannot live successfully without it. When you find the right church for you and your family, get involved with this new family of God. You need these people and they need you. One word of caution—Don't try to find a perfect church, one without fault or flaw. Remember that church is made up of people, and people, this side of heaven, are imperfect. See the good and push aside the evil. See Jesus in all the people present. They are struggling as you are, so just be patient and work through it. God will bless you immensely.

Beware; however; some people use their AA type of meeting in the place of church. Although this practice may be acceptable at first, it should not be continued indefinitely. You need BOTH your AA type meeting AND Church. At your meetings, you learn about your addiction and how to overcome it. At Church, you practice your overcoming and healing in communion with the family of God. May the Lord be with you and guide you to your Church home.

"FAST AND PRAY" - GOD'S COMMAND

Over and over in God's Holy Word, we are called to "Fast and Pray". He tells us to fast and pray many times in the Old and New Testaments. Here are some examples: 1 Samuel 7:6; 2 Samuel 12:16; 1 Kings 21:9; Ezra 8:21; Isaiah 58:1-12; Jeremiah 36:9; Zechariah 7:5-6; Matthew 4:2; Matthew 6:16-18; and Acts 13:2-3.

When God speaks to us to "fast and pray", He means just that. Fasting is abstaining from food for a certain period of time. You may ask - "What's the big deal about giving up a meal or two?" Please turn to Galatians 5:16-26, and you will read Paul's discussion about the fleshly nature fighting with the spirit nature of man. He calls them "enemies" in verse 17. He goes further to describe our behavior when we allow our flesh to rule our lives. All of us are familiar with these kinds of behavior. He finally ends the reading in verses 24 and 25 by saying, "And those who belong to Christ Jesus have PUT TO DEATH their human nature (flesh) with all its passions and desires. The Spirit has given us life; He (the Spirit) must also control our lives." Fasting is one of the ways that we "put to death our human nature".

OUR SPIRIT MUST CONTROL US - NOT THE FLESHLY BODY

It is quite apparent from this reading that our spirit must control our behavior, not our fleshly nature, the body. Yet, the very reason we have many of our behavioral problems stems from the fact that our flesh is in control rather than our spirit. Our fleshly nature is very strong and our spirit nature is very weak. How do we turn this situation around? The answer is to exercise control over our flesh by depriving it of its strongest need, food. Therefore, fasting periodically from food is essential to teach our fleshly nature who is in control. This process of fasting teaches the fleshly nature to behave and to submit to the control of our spirit nature. All of the growth and strength steps are intended to overcome the fleshly nature in one way or another. But the strongest and most direct way of dealing with our stubborn fleshly nature is to fast. Fasting is our "spiritual push up" which will make our spirit nature much stronger than our fleshly nature. To the person who is addicted, especially chemically, fasting is an absolute MUST.

FOOD - OUR STRONGEST PHYSICAL NEED

The strongest need for our physical bodies is food. The most effective way of bringing the body under the control of our spirit is to deny it food for short periods of time. To those confined to jails or pris-

FAST & PRAY
Steps 6 & 7 Lesson 25

Action Words:
INVOLVED IN CHURCH - FAST

> Humility is not thinking less of yourself, but thinking of yourself less.
> -Anonymous

> Humility is our acceptance of ourselves, just the way we are right now, understanding that we are not perfect, and doing all that we can to improve ME.
> -Anonymous

> I ask that your minds may be opened to see His light, so that you will know what is the hope to which He has called you, how rich are the wonderful blessings. He promises His people, and how great is His power at work in us who believe.
>
> This power working in us is the same as the mighty strength which He used when He raised Christ from death and seated Him at His right side in the heavenly world.
> -Ephesians 1:18-20

ACTIVELY INVOLVED

ons, I recommend that you start slowly by giving up one meal every three or four days. Being confined tends to make a person concentrate on their appetite, so it will be difficult at first. Discipline is required to accomplish fasting. When you pray on rising, ask the Lord to tell you if He wants you to fast today. If you hear the answer "YES" come to you in your spirit, then do it. Skip one meal that day, whichever you choose. Don't make a big deal of it; read Matthew 6:16-18. There you will find the correct attitude for use in fasting. If you can miss the meal without anyone knowing about it, Praise the Lord! If you are required to accept your food tray, then accept it. Very quietly search out the most needy person in your area and take your tray over to him and give it to him. Tell him that you are just not hungry today and would like to know if he would like your food. If he will not accept, go to another person until you give your food away. Then go and pray and read your Bible. A word of caution, it is absolutely necessary for you to drink plenty of water during this time. Never - NEVER deny yourself water while fasting. However, don't drink any other type of beverage or cheat during this time. You will be fooling yourself and you will loose the benefits of fasting if you do.

NOW LET'S SEE WHAT IS HAPPENING INSIDE

When you got up, you prayed to the Lord and He told you to fast today. You informed your stomach that there would be no food for one meal. Chances are good that your stomach served you notice that it was hungry much earlier than usual at that meal. Over and over again your stomach (your flesh) spoke to you saying, "I'm hungry, feed me!" In your spirit, talk back to your flesh and tell it to be quiet. It will be a struggle within you, but you are building spiritual muscle so that you can get control of your flesh with your spirit. This struggle will go on and get much worse as the time goes on. But you must persist in your spirit. Then, at the next meal, your stomach will return to its normal state. "What has been accomplished by all of this?" you may ask. You have taken strong drastic steps to bring your fleshly stomach muscle under the control of your spirit nature. Through prayer and Bible study you have reached out to God and by the power of His Holy Spirit, which He gives you, you have taken control of your body.

Again you may ask, "What's the point of all this?" The answer is simple. The very next time you are put in a position to drink alcohol or use some drug, or become involved in some other out of control behavior, your spirit will demand and take control of your body and force the body to say "NO!" The stronger you become in your spirit nature when joined with God's Holy Spirit, the more controlled your body will become by your spirit. When your spirit, which is in communion with God's Holy Spirit, controls you, you will experience the victory. The result, you will be able to say "no" to drugs, alcohol, or any other addictive behavior, and you will stay sober and in control of your life. This is a very strong and effective tool to overcome all chemical addictions as well as such habits as: depression, fear, anger, improper sexual behavior, stealing, gambling, and many other addictive behaviors.

FASTING IS FOR CHRISTIANS - THEY GO TOGETHER

Fasting is a must for all Christians; the scriptures tell us so. Your goal should be one meal per day, three times per week while incarcerated. Once back in the free world, you may want to try longer periods of time. Let the Lord speak to you in this regard.

PRAY AND STUDY THE BIBLE WHILE FASTING

It is also very important that you pray and study the Word of God while fasting. While you are denying your body its physical food, you must feed your spirit with the Word of God, which is your spiritual food. The Lord said in the scriptures, "Fast and Pray". Think on the Lord especially while you are in your fast. Turn to Him in mind and spirit and give yourself to Him during this time. You will be strongly tempted to break the fast and eat, but your prayer contact with Jesus will help you to be faithful. You will make it; so keep trying.

You may also be tempted to tell those around you that you are fasting. You may want to attract attention to the point that you are "showing" your Christianity. That is why the scripture tells us not to be puffed up with our spiritual practice, to fast and pray in secret. Go into a secret place and pray and meditate on God's word. DO NOT parade around and let the world know what you are doing. Do it only before God who will know the intentions of your heart and reward you. Your reward will be victory over your flesh.

May you find the control of your physical body within the secret of fasting and praying. May the Lord bless you in your determination to overcome your addictive problems HIS way.

STEPS 8 & 9

AMENDS - GOING BACK TO THOSE WE HAVE HARMED

We will now consider Healing Steps 8 and 9, which are concerned with taking the healing which we have experienced thus far to those in our past whom we have harmed. In these two steps, we apply the healing process that began inside of us in Healing Steps 4, 5, 6 and 7. The healing we have received in Step 7 we now proceed to give away to those in our past life that we have hurt or who have hurt us.

SCRIPTURAL BASIS - Matthew 5:23-24

"So if you are about to offer your gift to God at the altar and there you remember that your brother has something against you, leave your gift there in front of the altar, go at once and make peace with your brother, and then come back and offer your gift to God."

Further, in the "Lord's Prayer", we hear, "Lord, forgive us our trespasses as we forgive those who trespass against us." Both of these scriptures concern themselves with broken relationships. When we have a broken relationship in our life, there is separation, pain, and hurt. This situation is completely against God's command of love, "Love God as He has loved you; love your neighbor as yourself." God created us in love to love Him and each other. That is the very central and most important purpose of our existence. When we have a broken relationship with another person, we are out of God's plan for us; we are walking outside of love.

When we are walking outside of God's plan for us, we are disturbed, hurt, and troubled within and so is the other person involved. The above scripture from Matthew chapter 5 calls us to be reconciled to that person, to repair that broken relationship, and come back into a love relationship with that person as much as possible. That process is not only for our healing, but also for the healing of the person affected.

OUR GOAL - TO HEAL BROKEN RELATIONSHIPS - RECONCILIATION

Step 8 calls us to search for those in our life with whom we have broken our relationship. Fault has nothing to do with this situation. The mere fact that we feel badly inside in our relationship to that person means there is hurt and pain connected with that relationship and that needs to be corrected. The Bible calls us to repair all broken relationships, not just the ones in which we were at fault. In fact, the Bible says nothing at all about who is at fault. The reason for this is quite plain. There is hardly ever a broken relationship between two or more individuals in which all parties are not all partly to blame. Fault has nothing at all to do with forgiveness. Forgiveness has everything to do with healing and bringing back together that broken relationship. This is called reconciliation, to heal or mend that which is broken. So, forgiveness and reconciliation are a must for all Christians—the sooner the better.

BROKEN RELATIONSHIPS - THEIR CAUSE

At the very beginning of our program, I indicated the three attitudes we needed to adopt before working with our recovery process. One of these three attitudes was to stop blaming others and ourselves for the problems in our life.

In our every day human relationships with each other, we may have disagreements in thought. These come about as part of our living together. Because we are different people with different ideas and personalities, we find ourselves seeing things differently from those around us. This is basically a healthy situation if handled properly. God did not create us all the same in our thinking. Therefore, we will disagree on certain issues with those in our family and others around us in our daily life. Disagreement is normal and can be very constructive, depending upon how we handle it. However, when we loose control of our behavior as a result of our differences, this can and generally does cause hurt to others and ourselves. We can get angry and demonstrate harsh and vengeful behavior. We can even allow ourselves to get violent or do things to the person that hurt them in some way. This hurtful demonstration of our disagreement is what I am discussing in this step. I am not referring to the disagreement in our ideas, which is very much a part of life.

It is important to learn that it is OK to disagree with another person, as long as we do not demonstrate or act out our disagreement in anger or destructive behavior. This destructive behavior is what causes the pain and hurts within us and requires our reconciliation in Steps 8 and 9.

MAKING A LIST OF THOSE I HAVE HARMED

A question we might ask, "Who should be on the list of people needing our touch of healing forgiveness? Who do we need to approach seeking forgiveness?"

On the following page are some suggestions for making this list.

Steps 8 & 9 Lesson 26

"I made a list of all persons I had harmed, and became willing to make amends to them all"

"I made direct amends to such persons whenever possible, except when to do so would injure them or others"

Action Words:
MADE A LIST- MADE DIRECT AMENDS

Steps 8 & 9 Lesson 26

"I made a list of all persons I had harmed, and became willing to make amends to them all"

"I made direct amends to such persons whenever possible, except when to do so would injure them or others"

Action Words:
MADE A LIST- MADE DIRECT AMENDS

STEPS 8 & 9

Here are some suggestions:

1. ALL PERSONS who have been hurt as a result of our addictive behavior.

2. Most persons included in our Step 4 inventory. We probably owe most of these persons an act of forgiveness.

3. Members of the next generation, our children or any children affected. Whenever our addictive behavior or lack of love has affected them, we need to make amends.

4. We need to consider making amends to the following family groups:

   a. *Our original family: father, mother, step dad or step mom, sisters, brothers, cousins, aunts and uncles; all relatives whether living or deceased.

   b. All members of our created families, the families we gather by marriage or live in relationships.

   c. Those persons we work with.

   d. Our neighbors in our community or state.

   e. Our church family.

   f. **The family of man.

* With regard to item 4-a above, we may owe amends to a highly abusive parent. Maybe this parent had abused us through alcohol, lack of love, over-discipline, violence, sexual abuse or some other wrong, hurtful behavior. Making amends to this kind of parent does not mean that we ignore, excuse, or accept this abuse. No break in the love relationship can ever be right. Rather, we are called to work through the anger, resentment; and hurt of the relationship and to take back any negative input we may have fed into this relationship. We forgive that person for what they did to us and try, by the grace of God, to love that person in spite of the sinful behavior that was present at the time. We also make amends for any wrong, hurtful behavior we may have demonstrated toward them or the resentment we may have carried in our hearts since the time of the event. A letter of amends might sound something like this:

> "Dear Dad, I want you to know that I care for you very much. I know things between us have been very difficult in past years. I am sorry for all of the times that I have been disrespectful and unloving to you; for the times that my behavior has caused you pain and hurts especially during the time of my addictive behavior. I know that this caused you a great deal of hurt and I ask you to forgive me. I want you to know that I also forgive you for anything that came between us to cause problems. Whatever you did to hurt me in any way, I forgive you, Dad. I love you Dad and want to be your son/daughter. Thanks for your patience with me; even when I acted so badly. I'd like to come back some time when you are ready. Let's stay in touch; please. With all my love,"

**With regard to item 4-f above, there are many times when most of us suffer from broken relationships with the family of man. There is prejudice and jealousy against others for all sorts of reasons: race, religion, sex, social standing, financial standing, job status, appearance, political standing, etc. There are all sorts of stubborn reasons why we shove others into "boxes" and then hate those types of people for their differences toward us. How many times did we whites hate the blacks? How many times did we Americans hate the "Japs", who caused the attack on Pearl Harbor, etc.? A close look at our prejudices will show us who we have harmed in our thinking and actions. They need to be forgiven too.

IDENTIFYING THE PERSON NEEDING OUR AMENDS

The bottom line in making amends is this question, "Have I hurt, rejected or ignored another person regardless of the reason?" When we answer that question "yes", we have deep down inside of us guilt connected with this relationship and that causes us to hurt deep down inside. Healing Steps 8 and 9 provide us with the opportunity to rid ourselves of this guilt by setting things right again.

A WORD OF CAUTION

We must be cautioned, though, that WE need to work through and become healed of the underlying resentments, hurt, anger, and pain of these broken relationships before trying to make amends with others. We need to be ready. The frustration and all the rest of the feelings and emotions need to come out before we try to put those relationships to rest. If we do not come to Jesus and bring these problems to Him for healing, we are putting a bandage on a festering, unclean sore, which has not been healed. Healing must take place in us first, and then will come reconciliation and release. Only through Jesus healing power can we release our feelings of guilt, and the complete healing of these relationships can begin.

THE BENEFITS OF MAKING AMENDS

The actual making of amends needs to be approached with caution by us recovering people.

STEPS 8 & 9

There are three things amends can produce within us:

1. A sincere apology for past mistakes and harm done.
2. A wonderful way to rebuild positive and sincere future friendships.
3. A very effective way to completely remove the huge burden of guilt and hurt connected with the memories within us.

ANOTHER WORD OF CAUTION

The one thing making amends should NEVER be is thinking that these amends are installment payments on false guilt or shame. This method is a very destructive path of thinking that can destroy us and worsen our addictive behavior. When we get the idea that we must earn our way back into a person's good graces and life by constantly telling them we are sorry or to constantly try to give them something or do something for them to earn our way back; we are playing a very serious "head game" with them, with ourselves, and with God. When we think that we have to perform or act out some kind of ritual to obtain their forgiveness, we are in deep trouble. You see, forgiveness is for the healing of the person asking forgiveness. It is because Jesus first forgave us that we can ask for forgiveness and be forgiven regardless what the other person thinks or does. James 5:16 states, "So then, confess your sins to one another and pray for one another, so that YOU will be healed." This scripture clearly states that the person doing the confessing is the one to be healed. The Bible also clearly states that all that is necessary is for you to confess your sins and to be sorry for them; the result is healing of your inner self. We do not have to earn forgiveness. Jesus already did that for you and me on the cross of Calvary. Our forgiveness depends only upon our sincere, truthful confession and sorrow. So beware of the idea that you have to earn your forgiveness. Jesus forgave us all and our acceptance and action based on that fact is what is important. The other person may not forgive us. That is his problem, not ours. As long as we have done our best in this process, we have done it all and may rest in that assurance.

POSITIVE RESULTS WE CAN EXPECT

These two steps are very positive ones. There is a group of persons, however, to whom we should NOT offer amends. These are people in our past that would be more hurt than helped by our attempt to make amends. These situations will be discussed later in our study of these two steps.

Let us now take a more specific look at the categories of persons whom we may consider making amends. Remember, if making amends will hurt this person further, then we should not do it. The categories to consider as we think about making a list of people who need our amends are as follows:

1. Members of our own families or spouses who come to mind immediately. If we know in our hearts that we have hurt these people or been hurt by them, we need to consider making amends to them first off.

2. There are those persons to whom we can only partially reveal our past, for to reveal the entire surroundings of our relationship with them would only harm them or their families further. We should deal with only those parts of our past relationship with a specific person that is part of that person's knowledge. Revealing more knowledge than this may be hurtful to him. In that event, we should not reveal anything that would hurt them further or which they may not be aware. We need to be very careful to consider the risks to other persons and their private life. Healing of the past is what we seek, not further hurt or suffering.

3. Sometimes the time to make amends is just not right. Maybe there is still a great deal of hurt or anger present. Maybe the other person still resents us too much for us to approach them. Pray to the Lord Jesus for the wisdom and guidance to know what you should do in this situation. Be careful not to worsen the situation. Remember, we seek healing of our relationships using the love that Jesus has given us and taught us.

4. Those who cannot be contacted directly are people who may be deceased or their location unknown by you. The following methods may help to solve this sort of problem:

    a. If the person in question has moved away or their location is not known to you, try to find that person. Use of the phone directory or the telephone information service may be helpful. Ask others who may have known that person to try to find out where they are presently. Investigate all paths that could lead to their location. Simply excusing yourselves when you do not know a current address is not proper reconciliation. Do ALL that you can to locate that person. If you are unable to find them, please follow one of the steps given below.

    b. The "empty chair" approach. This is where you imagine the person sitting in a chair in front of you. You find a quiet place and

---

Steps 8 & 9 Lesson 26

"I made a list of all persons I had harmed, and became willing to make amends to them all"

"I made direct amends to such persons whenever possible, except when to do so would injure them or others"

Action Words :
MADE A LIST- MADE DIRECT AMENDS

Don't worry about anything, but in all your prayers ask God for what you need, always asking Him with a thankful heart. And God's peace, which is far beyond human understanding, will keep your hearts and minds safe in union with Christ Jesus.
—Philippians 4:6-7

The eyes are like a lamp for the body. If your eyes are sound, your whole body will be full of light; but if your eyes are no good, your body will be in darkness. So if the light in you is darkness, how terribly dark it will be.
—Matthew 6:22-23

Pay attention to what you are taught, and you will be successful; trust in the Lord and you will be happy.
—Proverbs 16:20

Steps 8 & 9 Lesson 26

"I made a list of all persons I had harmed, and became willing to make amends to them all"

"I made direct amends to such persons whenever possible, except when to do so would injure them or others"

Action Words:
MADE A LIST- MADE DIRECT AMENDS

> Do for others just what you want them to do for you.
> -Luke 6:31

> To sin is to love my way more than God's way.
> -Author unknown

> Jesus is life, In Him there is no death.
> -Emmett Fox

"talk" to that person making your amends to them in that manner. This method should be followed by a period of prayer in which you ask the Lord Jesus to deliver the sincere intentions of your heart to that person and to help them to receive your heartfelt apologies for the past.

c. The "letter" approach can be used to contact a person who may be deceased or whose location is unknown. Write a sincere letter of apologies and forgiveness to them and mail this letter to the last known address of that person. If the letter is returned to you undeliverable, destroy that letter in some way such as burning or burying it. In destroying the letter, let go of all the hurts and inner pain that are connected with that relationship and know that you did the best that you could to heal the situation. Prayer along with this process is necessary. The Lord doesn't expect you to do the impossible. Be at peace.

d. The "grave side" approach can be used when a person has died. You can visit their grave side and speak your amends, visualizing that Jesus is there with you—accompanying you in this process. You may include Jesus as you speak your sincere apologies and express your forgiveness. Through your confession, also receive His forgiveness. Ask Him to bring complete healing and peace to you and the life events that have brought you there. It is important to mention that this is simply suggested as a tangible way to make peace if it will help you let go. This is NOT to be confused with necromancy which is communicating with the dead and forbidden by God and His Word.

SITUATIONS WHERE AMENDS SHOULD NOT BE MADE

Our final category in discussing these steps occurs when we find ourselves in a position where contact of that person would cause further hurt and pain. If coming back on the scene of that person's life would hurt them further, then we should not contact that person. This does not excuse us from praying to Jesus for forgiveness and for the spiritual and physical welfare of that person. We should always pray for them. This prayer will help us to heal inside and also bring the peace and healing to the person involved. Our past and theirs will be healed. Before making any attempt to contact a person in a questionable situation, it is most important to pray. Ask the Lord's guidance and discernment. Ask the Lord Jesus to show you what to do and how to do it. Be patient, the answer will come in time.

STEPS 8 & 9

REACTIONS FROM OTHERS IN MAKING AMENDS

These two Healing Steps seem to place all of the responsibility and burden for making amends upon us. We may feel that this is "not fair" since the other person may be just as much or more "at fault" than we are. It is very important to remember that we are the ones who seek recovery from our addiction. Therefore, it is our position to reach out to accomplish this.

It may happen that the other person involved may not accept us or want to speak to us at all when we approach them. They may totally push us away. They may want to hold onto their grudge against us and withhold their forgiveness. What then? Remember, our ideal or example of forgiveness is not how the other person forgives us; rather our ideal of forgiveness is how does Jesus forgive us? Jesus forgives us when we come to Him with a sincere and sorrowful heart. That is the way we must forgive others and seek to be forgiven by others. If they refuse to forgive us in that way, then they are being held bound by their own disobedience to the example of Jesus. The scripture is very clear in this matter. Look up these scriptures and write down key words regarding forgiveness:

- Matthew 6:14:

- Matthew 18:21-27:

- Mark 11:25-26:

- Luke 11:4:

- Luke 17:4:

In John 20:23, Jesus says, "If you forgive peoples' sins, they are forgiven; if you do not forgive them, they are not forgiven." Refusal to forgive another keeps the person refusing locked up in the bondage of unforgivingness. When we are in such a condition, we cannot be healed and will continue to suffer the results of our spiritual sickness, our addiction. Forgiveness is the key to our healing.

MEDITATIONS

Steps 8 & 9 Lesson 27

"I made a list of all persons I had harmed, and became willing to make amends to them all"

"I made direct amends to such persons whenever possible, except when to do so would injure them or others"

DAY ONE - Study Matthew 18:21-35

Step 8 is about responsibility. In this step we try to break our old habits of "hit and run" into a habit of being responsible for "ME" and what I have done.

In the reading for today, the servant who owed millions was brought before the king to become accountable for his debt. He pleaded with the king for mercy and the king forgave him. The servant got what he wanted and "took off". But as soon as the tables were turned and another servant, who owed him money, did the same he refused to forgive the other servant his debt.

The Lord Jesus forgave our sins when we came to Him in the last step. Jesus did not have to forgive us because we were "dead wrong". But He did. And now, Jesus calls us to do the same to others. As Jesus forgave us, so we must forgive others. Jesus is the measure of our forgiveness. Verse 35 tells us we must forgive each other from the heart.

In today's reading, both servants owed the debt. Yet the King (Jesus) forgave willingly while the servant did not. Here is a clear-cut example of how we are to forgive. Broken love relationships cannot be forgiven unless they are done so from our hearts. When God sees such an open heart, totally willing to forgive and let go regardless, then He will reach into that willing heart and remove all the hurt and pain and bless us far beyond our ability to comprehend. Are you willing to become this kind of a person? Are you willing to let God bless you and heal you? Then you must forgive those that have hurt you and seek forgiveness from those you have hurt. Let Jesus walk with you and DO IT!

DAY TWO - Study Luke 6:37-38

The reading today is a beautiful example of the mercy and love God has for us even though we are sinners. If we will not judge others, God will not judge us. If we forgive others, God will be quick to forgive us. If we give to others, God will give to us. How much? A generous helping, all that we can hold. Wow, what a marvelously generous God we have. Even when we are wrong, He does not judge; does not look down and condemn us; He forgives us and gives us more than we can hold of life's blessings. Now, I don't know of any better deal in life. Yet, how many of us know and understand the generosity of God and practice it? Maybe you have never read this verse before or have been touched by its words. Now is the time for you to begin seeing Jesus as your best friend who returns love and mercy for your sin. All that is necessary is that you come to Him, as the servant did, ask for forgiveness and sincerely be sorry for your past.

In Verse 38, the Bible tells us, "The measure you use for others is the one that God will use for you." What a wonderful opportunity for us to change "ME". When we become willing to reach out to others for forgiveness with an open, sincere and sorrowful heart, God will forgive us and heal our past.

Jesus is waiting for you right now. Won't you come to Him and let Him show you how to enter into that healing forgiveness called amends? Now is the time. Don't wait. Jesus is waiting for you to do it. May God bless you in your step forward toward Him.

DAY THREE - Study Luke 19:8-10

In this Healing Step, we uncover the principle of making restitution for the spiritual, physical, and financial wreckage of our past. In the past, we have "burned" many people as a result of our spiritual sickness and resulting addiction. Now is the time to become responsible for that past.

In the reading for today, we see that Zacchaeus was willing to make financial restitution in the conduct of his daily life. In the time of Jesus, a tax collector, such as Zacchaeus, was notorious for collecting more taxes than permitted and for stealing those taxes from both the person and the state. But Zacchaeus was

Scripture :
MEDITATIONS

Steps 8 & 9 Lesson 27

"I made a list of all persons I had harmed, and became willing to make amends to them all"

"I made direct amends to such persons whenever possible, except when to do so would injure them or others"

Scripture:
MEDITATIONS

MEDITATIONS

trying to be an honest tax collector. He had an honest heart, yet Zacchaeus made mistakes. Zacchaeus came to Jesus and the Lord recognized him and came to him. Because Zacchaeus had a "right heart", Jesus came to him and gave him salvation. Zacchaeus was not a perfect man. You and I are not perfect either. We all make mistakes. Our confessing and seeking amends with others is the healing of that broken past. In the past we were lost in our sin. Jesus ends our reading today in verse 10 saying, "The Son of Man came to seek and to save the lost."

Because Jesus comes to forgive us, we must also go and forgive the others in our life. The Lord's Prayer says, "Lord, forgive us our trespasses as we forgive those who trespass against us." Jesus shall forgive us in exactly the same way and to the same extent that we forgive others and seek their forgiveness for our sins.

May the Lord help you to step forward and complete your process of forgiveness soon!

DAY FOUR - Study John 13:34-35

What is the source of the love that we have been speaking about? Our reading today tells us that Jesus is that source. "As I have loved you, so you must love one another." (Verse 34) But you may ask, "How can I love another when I don't know how to love as Jesus loved? I can't do something that I don't know how to do?" These are very good questions and apply to most of us at one time or another. All of us, at some time, did not know how to love as Jesus loved. Yet, we all had to come to Jesus to experience His love for us. After experiencing His love for us, we then learn how to love as He has loved us. As He loves us, we learn to love Him in return and we become lovers as Jesus is our lover.

One of the ways that we "act out" our love, the love that Jesus shows us, is to become accountable and seek forgiveness for our past. All of us have broken relationships in our past. The healing of these relationships through forgiveness will bring about the love that Jesus commands us.

The reading for today is our command to love one another as Jesus has loved us. Jesus is the source of that love. In becoming lovers, we become who Jesus is. We live out the life of Jesus within us. We become His presence in our world today. This is what "my disciples" mean. Are you ready to become a lover as Jesus is? Then begin to clean up your past, now. Jesus will guide you and heal you. You will become the whole and healthy spiritual person He wants you to become.

DAY FIVE - Study 1 Corinthians 13

This is the famous "love chapter" in First Corinthians and probably the most read and preached about chapter in the Bible. In the first two verses of this chapter, Paul tells the "stiff necked" and worldly-wise Corinthians what love really is all about. He tells them that they may have it all, but if they do not have love (God's way) then they have NOTHING. Their life is as empty as a "noisy gong or a clanging bell." They have "missed the boat" entirely. The conditions today are the same, dear friend; nothing has changed since then.

In verse three, Paul tells us that we may have everything in life (in our own eyes). We may lay down our lives for the other guy and do all sorts of "good", but if we do not have love, we have nothing. How many of us are driven in our addiction to helplessly lay down our life for the other guy or blame the other guy for our problem? The Bible tells us that if we do not have Godly love, it does us "no good".

As we meditate on this chapter, let us check ourselves and be sure that we love God first; then ourselves because He loves us; then all others in our lives. Verses 4 to 7 tell us just what healthy God-like love is. Let's make sure that we understand these verses and get ourselves in tune with them. Friend, study each verse of this chapter carefully. Let it soak into your heart. It will speak to you and fill you with the love of Jesus. Jesus stands ready to fill us with His love. So open up, come to the love of Jesus, and give it away to others. You'll be glad that you did.

Walking the 12 Steps with Jesus Christ

MEDITATIONS

Steps 8 & 9   Lesson 27

"I made a list of all persons I had harmed, and became willing to make amends to them all"

"I made direct amends to such persons whenever possible, except when to do so would injure them or others"

Scripture : MEDITATIONS

DAY SIX - Study 2 Timothy 1:7

For most of us, we are frightened by the thought of having to face others and to "come clean" about our past relationship with them. This is not an easy task and takes much determination and courage.

Perhaps young Pastor Timothy was also frightened by the thought of facing others, too. Timothy was like a son to Paul who wrote this letter to Timothy. Paul reminds Timothy that, instead of being fearful, he should release the three wonderful gifts that God has given him: "Power, love, and self-control". Isn't it wonderful that again the Bible reminds us that God's Holy Spirit gives us power, love, and self-control? Remember Galatians 5:22? There we found love and self-control also.

And now, like young Timothy, we also face the challenge to reach out and complete the healing process in our own life and in the lives of those we have hurt. This verse can and should be a great encouragement to us as we embark on this process. Because of the presence of God's Holy Spirit in our lives, we, too, have the power, love, and self-control that is needed to accomplish this task. We have learned that we must seek forgiveness and forgive others in our past in order to become whole and spiritually healthy men and women. In stepping out to do this, let us be assured that we have the mighty power of God's Holy Spirit to guide and direct us. There is nothing to fear; we have everything to gain - total peace and healing of spirit. We are becoming a "new creation" in Christ Jesus, AMEN!

DAY SEVEN - Study James 4:11-12

In this reading and in our study of Healing Step 8, we are called to stop judging others, to give up the bitterness, hatred, and resentments toward those in our past life. We may be tempted to give in to the "stinkin thinkin" that calls us to make amends WHEN AND IF THEY DO IT TO ME FIRST. But the love of Jesus that we have just studied and the whole healing process is based, not on what the other guy does or how he changes, but rather how we change and become the "new creation" that Jesus is calling us to become. And so, we must be willing to let go of our past without any strings or conditions attached.

We may ask ourselves - "How can I possibly forgive another person or seek his forgiveness when I am full of the hurt and pain which is so deep in my heart right now?" The answer must be our willingness to forgive. Remember, Jesus stands willing to forgive you when you come to Him with no strings attached. You and I must be willing to do the same to each other. It is in this willingness and stepping out that we experience the healing process.

Sometimes our willingness to forgive is stopped by the shock, denial, anger, depression, frustration, and sadness of the broken relationship. We must remember that it is OK to experience these feelings resulting from the other person's hurt. This will help us to understand that they may also feel those same kinds of feelings when we hurt them. It is the giving up of these feelings to Jesus, over and over again, that heals the pain and suffering. Only then will we be ready to approach the final step of the healing process, forgiveness, without resentment and with peace and self-control. We will be truly healed.

Dear friend, I pray with all my heart, that you, too, will come to Jesus to experience that healing and that you will also give that healing to those in the "making amends" process. May God be with you!

Walking the 12 Steps with Jesus Christ

Steps 8 & 9 Lesson 28

"I made a list of all persons I had harmed, and became willing to make amends to them all"

"I made direct amends to such persons whenever possible, except when to do so would injure them or others"

Action Words:
MADE A LIST- MADE DIRECT AMENDS

STEPS 8 & 9

OUR GOAL - TO CREATE THE BEST POSSIBLE LOVE RELATIONSHIP

In these two Healing Steps, we become concerned with the relationships between people. In our program so far, we have been concerned only with our relationship with Jesus Christ and ourselves. Now, we expand that walk to the "Body of Christ", all of our brothers and sisters around us whether or not they are believers. Our goal is to bring about the best possible personal love relationship with every person we know.

Now, that is a mighty tall order. You may say to yourself - "This guy is a dreamer! Come on - let's get realistic!" I must say that I agree with you; it is a very tall order and sometimes a difficult one - but it can be done. We may not succeed totally but we can give it "our best shot". And to the extent that we try and are successful will be the extent of the wonder of our new life in Jesus Christ. Remember, dear friend, we are becoming a "new creation" in Christ Jesus. This is a task that requires much effort and patience and one that may take a good long while to accomplish. Learning to rebuild and heal old relationships and develop new peaceful and loving relationships is a moving and fascinating adventure. It can be a very exciting experience; it is all in our attitude.

OUR ATTITUDE - OUR WILLINGNESS

I refer you back to the list of attitudes; there you will note that WILLINGNESS is stressed from the very beginning. Our recovery is based upon our willingness to step forth to change ME, to want to change ME, and to do it, change ME. Making amends to those whose relationship is damaged is a very important part of correcting the past as much as possible and learning to build proper relationships today and in the days to come.

Both the Bible and the AA program teach us that we cannot be successful in building new relationships until we go back and make a sincere and devoted effort to repair the wreckage of human beings that we have left behind us in our past. We now need to take a good look at the people we have hurt along the way in our addiction and the ways in which we have hurt them. Some of us may be against going back over this painful, difficult part of our lives again. We may say, "I suffered enough back in my Step 4 inventory, why do I need to bring it up again?" The answer is clear - the damage done to others needs to be repaired.

A BROKEN RELATIONSHIP EQUALS BONDAGE IN SPIRIT

Broken relationships keep us in bondage deep inside ourselves in our spirit and prevent us from healing our spiritual sickness. We cannot be healed within without experiencing forgiveness, from Jesus, from ourselves and from those others we have hurt in our past. The moment we bring to mind a twisted or broken relationship of the past, our emotions begin to churn inside and up goes our defense. Right off we say - "Well, he/she did this to hurt me, etc." We begin our "head games" all over again and we use this thinking as an excuse for not forgiving that other person. The fact is that we need to forgive them as well as ourselves regardless of who was at fault.

AMENDS - CREATES RESPONSIBLE LIVING

As we make a list of the people we have harmed, we get another severe shock. We are preparing to make a face-to-face admission of our nasty, out of control conduct to those we hurt. It had been tough enough to admit these things to God, to ourselves, and to another human being. But now, visiting or writing the people concerned frightens us, especially when we remember all the "bridges we burned" in the process. Then, there is the situation when we may have to approach a person who does not really know just how badly he was hurt, and we will have to tell him. We can feel the fear take hold of us and then our pride says, "No, I won't do it!" But do it we must. Otherwise, we will stay spiritually sick and our addiction will remain our old "friend".

Another "head game" we play is this. We cling to the claim that while drinking/drugging, etc., we never hurt anyone but ourselves. We worked and paid the bills, we didn't do our "thing" at home, our business didn't suffer much, and we were usually on our job working when required. Few knew about our habit and those that did really didn't care because they were doing the same thing as we were. We ask, "What harm have I really done?" This is clearly an attitude of a convenient lapsed memory. We try to slip out of the real facts of the matter. We don't really have to look very hard to find a string of hurt people who suffered as a result of our behavior. This attitude can only be changed by a deep and honest search of our motives and actions - and a sincere confrontation with those people in a heartfelt and sincere effort to correct, forgive, and heal the problem.

SEARCH THE PAST

Regardless of whether or not we can or must make amends, we still need to make an accurate and searching survey of our past as it affected other people around us. Our attitude in making this list of persons we have harmed should be just as full and complete as our Fourth Step inventory. When we are honest and "above board" about all these

STEPS 8 & 9

Steps 8 & 9   Lesson 28

"I made a list of all persons I had harmed, and became willing to make amends to them all"

"I made direct amends to such persons whenever possible, except when to do so would injure them or others"

Action Words:
MADE A LIST- MADE DIRECT AMENDS

past relationships, they will tell us a great deal about the kind of person that once was "ME" and will also help us to see the kind of person that we are becoming today. Remember, responsibility is our goal. We want to become healthy. We do not want to stay sick.

WHAT DOES "PERSONS I HAVE HARMED" MEAN?

We might ask ourselves, "What do I mean when I say that I have 'harmed' other people?" Let's define "harm" in a practical way. Harm is the result of behavior that puts us in conflict with another person resulting in physical, mental, emotional, or spiritual damage to that person.

Example: If we cheat or steal from another, we take advantage of that person. We cause them to give up what they have so that we can have it and we do this dishonestly in an underhanded way. We cause them to become frightened of us and they lose their trust in us. This creates an extreme dislike for us. Our relationship is broken. After all, "Nobody likes a thief!"

Example: We may have a bad temper and fly off the handle at every little thing. People have a difficult time getting along with us. We tend to drive people away from us. They may have very loving feelings toward us but because of our anger, they cannot be around us. Look at the wives or girl friends that have suffered with this problem. Their response has been, "I love this guy, but I can't stand his behavior!"

This kind of behavior is not, by any means, all that there is in the harm that we do. There are many more ways in which we try to manipulate others and use them to our selfish advantage. Look into your life carefully to see how you used others to your advantage. What were your relationships with those at home, work, at play, and everywhere in your life? Be honest with yourself and you will learn a great deal about yourself. You will also begin to find the people to whom you need to make amends.

IDENTIFYING THOSE WHOM WE HAVE HURT

We have carefully considered the situations and behavior that has caused problems in the past with those around us. Now, we need to search our memory to list those persons whom we have hurt and those who have hurt us. To pick out the "biggies" should be fairly easy. As time goes by and we continue to deal with ourselves in the recovery process, we will come up with those that are not so obvious. When we jog our memory and take this searching look at those who have been hurt, we need to be careful to base our judgment on what WE DID and not what they did. We are responsible for our actions only. We are not responsible for the actions of others. However, we also need to forgive and let go of the actions that they did to us to hurt us. Forgiveness must go both ways. Be fair with them and with yourself in your searching and thinking. Don't over-estimate your actions or theirs. Look up, dear friend; this is the beginning of the end of your isolation from others and from God.

THE PROCESS OF MAKING AMENDS - DOING IT

Now, we proceed to actually put this making amends business into practice. This requires good judgment, careful timing, courage, and much patience. Carefully pray about each instance before taking action and ask God to show you the right way. Wait on the Lord to show you the right time, the right place and the right way to approach the other person involved.

In lesson 26, we have already looked at the various groups of persons we need to approach in making amends. Let us now consider the process of actually going through this face-to-face encounter.

To many of us, we have already begun the making of certain kinds of direct amends when we entered this or any 12 step program. We feel encouraged in having found a place where we can freely talk and learn about our problem and so we want to shout to the world; especially our families, "Hey everyone, I'm in a 12 step recovery program for my problem. I've finally begun to deal with the real 'ME'. We may find ourselves lifted up by the fact that we can now deal with the problem and that someone understands us at last. And so, we want to try to make amends to our families immediately after beginning this process. Many times, a short distance down the treatment road, we are ready to come to our family and admit the damage we have done with our addiction. Almost always we want to go further and admit other defects that have made us hard, very hard, to live with.

SOME POSSIBLE OBSTACLES

This can be a very happy time. It can also be a time of further rejection by our family members. They may say, "I'll believe it when I see it!" This points out very clearly the need for making amends carefully with those who were most hurt by our misbehavior. This is the time to consider the old saying, "Actions speak much louder than words!" It is much more a time of doing than saying. Hurt family and relatives want to see the change, not just hear about it. Even then, they may not accept the change and cling to the "old you" in their minds. They may continue to push you out of their lives. Much love and patience is required in these situations.

Steps 8 & 9 Lesson 28

"I made a list of all persons I had harmed, and became willing to make amends to them all"

"I made direct amends to such persons whenever possible, except when to do so would injure them or others"

Action Words:
MADE A LIST- MADE DIRECT AMENDS

We may find a similar obstacle at our work place. We may think that everyone who knows us at work would like to hear about the "new me". Again, it is much more important to live the change than to talk about the change. Our first consideration should be that we are "on target" with the program and that we stay that way. Sooner or later the opportunity will come to explain, very gently, what has happened in our recovery process. This is an excellent time to admit the damage that we caused others and to ask for forgiveness from them. It would be well to point out what we have learned at this point. It would be proper to share the change in our life and what we may have learned about our past problems and ourselves. Be honest and sincere. Nothing turns a person off as much as another "con job". Most of those we have hurt are upset at the con jobs of our past. When they see a new, sincere, and happy you, they will be able to see the change. It's great to talk about our new-found faith in Jesus Christ. But beware not to give them the idea that this is "Jailhouse Religion". By that, I mean that because you were locked up for a time, you became very holy. Then, after entering the free world, you went back to your old ways. Others may be very skeptical about the new you. Just take it "low and slow", dear friend, and it will work Jesus' way. Be certain that the inside of you, in your spirit, is genuine. Be certain that this new you is real from the inside out.

ADDRESSING FINANCIAL OBLIGATIONS

This is also a time to address financial obligations and debts. More than likely, you will owe others money as a result of your past behavior. In some cases, these amounts of debt can be very large. However, the generous response of most people to quiet sincerity will surprise you. When others see that you mean what you say in recovery, they will meet you more than halfway. When there is a financial obligation involved, it is wise to openly talk about that amount due and offer a payment method. Be sincere and tell the person that you want to make this obligation "good". Your offer to make payment and your sticking to that offer in making payment will speak much louder than your promises. Many times, the other person will forgive the debt or a good portion of it when they see the sincere change in you. Remember, actions speak a thousand times louder than words.

SOME EMOTIONAL REACTIONS

Beware of your emotional reactions at this point. This newfound freedom and joy, this "new you", may create in you a tremendous appetite for more of this "good time" friendship. Or, we may have turned someone off in this process and feel very down and rejected. You may be tempted to argue with the one who does not accept the "new you". Remember, dear friend, that it is not what the other guy thinks, it is most important what you think of yourself, what God thinks of you and what is happening in your life as a result. You are only responsible for your actions, not the actions of others, so be careful of the way you respond to their reaction. Be kind, patient, and loving, even if it hurts a bit. Nothing can be gained in arguing or defending yourself. You are a new person and your only job is to bring that new person out from your inside. Remember what you have been through and how far the power of Jesus Christ has brought you. You are on the road to recovery; so, don't get caught up in "people pleasing". Your new life does not depend on what others think of you. BE YOURSELF and show them the Christ who now lives in you.

After we make the first few encounters with others, we may sense a great feeling of relief, that this whole past is over with. We may get rocked into a sort of dream world where we don't want to remember or consider any of our past again. We may feel secure inside, but deep down we know that it is not all over. We may be tempted to back off of our overcomer meetings, the fellowship, the book learning, the Bible study, prayer, fasting, and the giving of ourselves to others. We may easily excuse ourselves from the discipline we learned in this program. This is a trap that is very easy to fall into; it is a trap of the evil one, the devil. DON'T FALL FOR IT! Remember how we came to the healing and continue strong in that healing by continuing on the road to recovery in the program. That is the RIGHT WAY. Anything short of that will lead us back into our old "rut".

BEWARE OF THE OLD 'HEAD GAMES'

We may get the idea that after making amends to the worst of those we have hurt, that's enough. We really don't have to go any further, we think. Again, this is a "head game". We know, deep down in our hearts, that there are many others we need to consider in making amends, but our sense of new found peace says, "Ah, don't bother!" These are all works of the devil—he is tempting us in a very subtle way. Don't listen to him. Rather, stay on track until the job is finished to the best of our ability. Remember, this process is for our healing as well as the healing of the person we hurt. If we do not confront the person we hurt, we are denying that person the healing that they are entitled to. So keep on working at it.

OPENNESS BUILDS CONFIDENCE AND RESPONSIBILITY

After we get past the first few attempts to talk to someone about our relationship, we will find our-

STEPS 8 & 9

Steps 8 & 9 Lesson 28

"I made a list of all persons I had harmed, and became willing to make amends to them all"

"I made direct amends to such persons whenever possible, except when to do so would injure them or others"

Action Words :
MADE A LIST- MADE DIRECT AMENDS

selves getting more confident in the process. Our fear will have largely left us and we will be able to think more clearly and with less emotion. We will also be able to share with the other person in a more frank and open way. We have made a great step forward by beginning to walk the walk of the twelve steps with Jesus Christ instead of just talking about them. Our behavior has changed drastically; we are now in control of our thinking and our lives instead of being out of control as in the past. By our actions, we are beginning to see that this process of making amends works if we are patient, loving, and faithful in doing it. We are learning to become part of the solution rather than living in the problem.

You also need to confront those who may have been hurt only slightly and even those who may not be fully aware of the damage that was done to them. The only persons we do NOT confront are those who will be hurt further by your going to them.

Example: You may have had a sexual relationship in the past with another that was wrong and hurtful. Going back to that person may (but not always) cause them further grief and harm, which you want to avoid.

When your time comes to talk openly, you need to summon all your courage and, with head held up high, lay your cards on the table, so to speak. There is no need to make a long explanation over the matter. This only prolongs the pain. Say only what is necessary regarding your behavior and MEAN IT FROM YOUR HEART! Allow the other person to respond and listen to their response. DO NOT argue the point. Thank the person for listening, be kind and patient, and let your new self come out into the open. Remember, it is only necessary to talk about what you did to them. Do not judge their actions at all. You are not responsible for their actions. Rather tell them that you forgive them for any wrongs they may have done to you. Make this statement and mean it from your heart. Do not reveal information that would further hurt them or another. Let bygones be bygones.

WHEN IN DOUBT - SEEK ADVICE FROM A COUNSELOR

If there is a question in your mind about some part of the problem which you do not know how to handle, seek the advise of a counselor or clergy. Sometimes these situations can get very "sticky". Pray to the Lord Jesus and seek His guidance as well as the guidance of a competent, qualified person. Most importantly, be willing to make amends.

BEWARE OF THE STALL - "NOT NOW"

In closing these two steps, don't fall prey to the age-old excuse, "Not now". Don't put off making amends because you are afraid to face the "music". Remember, fear is the tool of the devil. He will use your uneasy feelings to frighten you into not doing this step. Rebuke the devil in the precious name of Jesus Christ. The readiness to take the full consequences of your past acts and to take responsibility for the well being of others who you have hurt at the same time is the very purpose and spirit of the recovery process. Remember, you are on the road to recovery. You have given yourself to Jesus so that HE can make you into a NEW CREATION. May the Lord Jesus give you the desire and the strength that you need to seek your healing and the healing of those in your past.

SCRIPTURE STUDY:

The following scriptures are provided with respect to Healing Step 8. Please study them carefully and see how they apply to this step in your life.

- ☐ Psalm 133
- ☐ Romans 12:17
- ☐ Proverbs 10:12
- ☐ Romans 13:8-10
- ☐ Proverbs 14:1
- ☐ Romans 14:7-10
- ☐ Proverbs 14:30
- ☐ 1 Corinthians 4:5
- ☐ Matthew 5:43-48
- ☐ Philippians 2:3-4
- ☐ Matthew 6:14-15
- ☐ Philippians 4:5
- ☐ Matthew 7:1-5
- ☐ 1 Thessalonians 3:12-13
- ☐ Matthew 22:36-40
- ☐ James 5:9
- ☐ Mark 11:25
- ☐ 1 Peter 1:19-23
- ☐ Luke 10:25-37
- ☐ 1 Peter 3:8-12
- ☐ Romans 2:1
- ☐ 1 John 2:9-11
- ☐ Romans 12:9
- ☐ 1 John 4:19-21
- ☐ Romans 12:14

Happy are those who work for peace;
God will call them His children.
-Matthew 5:9

Time wasted in getting even,
can never be used in getting ahead.
-Anonymous

God hates the sin, but loves the sinner.
-Author unknown

Steps 8 & 9 Lesson 29

"I made a list of all persons I had harmed, and became willing to make amends to them all"

"I made direct amends to such persons whenever possible, except when to do so would injure them or others"

Scripture:
MEDITATIONS

MEDITATIONS

DAY ONE - Study Matthew 5:9

All of us want to experience peace in our daily life. Somehow, we feel that peace comes from the outside of us. If our surroundings are peaceful, all is going well and there are no problems to speak of, we think that we are at peace. Yet, when something happens around us to upset us, we very quickly go to pieces and there goes our peacefulness.

Another idea that we acquire quite easily is that we can take our daily troubles and "sweep them under the rug". Somehow, by doing that, the troubles will go away, we think. Both of the above attitudes are "stinkin thinkin". They are just not true. That's the easy way, the compulsive way, of our old addiction.

The Bible teaches that peace is not something that exists outside of us but rather a condition of our inner self, our spirit. We acquire peace by coming into oneness with the Holy Spirit. When Jesus fills our spirit inside, we are at peace from within. That peace will be our strength to handle the problems that come up outside of us in our daily life.

In Galatians 5:22, we see that peace flows from love, the love that Jesus has for us. When we know who we are in Jesus, that we are brothers and sisters to Him, we are in a love relationship with Him and peace flows from that love. Our source of love and peace are from Jesus through His Holy Spirit. 1st John 3:1 says, "See how much the Father has loved us! His love is so great that we are called God's children." Not only do we have God's love to guide us in our peacemaking, John 14:27 tells us that we have the promise of God's own peace resting upon our life. This peace of God's Holy Spirit frees us from fear.

The reading today tells us to work for peace. First we are to be at peace in our own spirit; then we are to bring that peace to those around us. For those of us who have walked the road of addictive past behavior, we need to bring this peace to those in our past who have suffered because of us. As we do this, we build up and heal the family of God and we are healed within our own spirit as well. When our hearts are full of God's love and peace, we can reach out and extend forgiveness to make the necessary amends where needed in our life.

DAY TWO - Study Romans 15:1-6

These two Healing Steps are about building or reconstructing the broken relationships of our past. We seek to repair the bridges that we burned in our past and correct our relationships with those we hurt. In the reading today, we are called to "please our brothers in order to build them up in faith".

The two great commands that Jesus gave us were to 1) Love God with all that we are; and 2) to love our neighbor as He has loved us and as we love ourselves. Love is the great and central purpose of our life as God created us. Love is always a giving up of our life for another. And so, we are called to please those who are our brothers and sisters and to build them up in the faith by bringing them the face of Jesus by the way we act toward them.

Our goal should be the establishment of healthy, loving relationships with those in our past as well as those we meet for the first time today. We are called to be sane, sober, balanced people of God. Healing Step 9 centers upon the making of amends to others as a means to correct the imbalanced self-centered ways of our old addicted past. We now become givers of the love and peace of Jesus rather than takers of things to further the addictions of our past. We seek not only our own spiritual health but also the spiritual health of those in our past. May the Lord Jesus guide you, dear friend, and encourage you to find your spiritual health in Him for yourself and for those in your past.

DAY THREE - Study Philippians 1:9-11

As we walk and work these two steps, our goal is to open up to others in a new way, one that is totally opposite to the way we lived in our addictive past. We may feel totally "wiped out" by what we view as a huge and seemingly impossible task. "How do I know what to say? How do I know how to approach the person? How do I handle myself?"

Walking the 12 Steps with Jesus Christ

MEDITATIONS

Steps 8 & 9 Lesson 29

"I made a list of all persons I had harmed, and became willing to make amends to them all"

"I made direct amends to such persons whenever possible, except when to do so would injure them or others"

If we try to do it by ourselves, without Jesus, we will fail. Our reading today tells us, "Your lives will be filled with the truly good qualities which only Jesus Christ can produce, for the glory and praise of God." (Verse 11) Only Jesus can produce the good qualities in us if we open up to Him and give Him permission to do it. Then, "Your love will keep on growing more and more, together with true knowledge and perfect judgment, so that you will be able to choose what is best." (Verses 9 & 10) This requires us to open ourselves up to His presence in our lives. The entire 12 step program is opening up ourselves to Jesus and giving ourselves to Him. When we do that, this reading tells us what will happen:

1. Our love of Jesus will keep us growing more and more in Him.
2. We will receive true knowledge and perfect judgment.
3. We will be able to choose what is best for us.
4. We will be cleansed from all impurity and blame.
5. We will be in "good shape", saved on our Judgment Day by Jesus Christ.
6. We will be filled with good qualities that only Jesus can produce.
7. We will give glory and praise to our God!

Wow, what an exciting experience we have in store for us. Will you give yourself to Jesus and experience this change? Only you can answer this question. I pray that you will!

Scripture : MEDITATIONS

DAY FOUR - Study Colossians 4:5-6

These two steps are steps toward rebuilding broken relationships. With whom are these broken relationships to be repaired? That's a big question.

First, we are called to rid ourselves of that which tears us apart inside and causes us to feel like less of a person and makes us unhappy with ourselves. The old false guilt and shame has pulled us apart inside and made us very unhappy with our inner self.

Second, we must be put right with other persons. This step gives us a wonderfully loving way that will take us back through the years of bad behavior resulting in broken hearts and dreams to make amends and new beginnings.

Third, and most importantly, as we are put right with ourselves and others; we are also put right with our God. This step allows us to be put back together within our inner self; to be put back together with those in our past and to come into oneness with Jesus Christ from whom our very inner life flows. In this process, we learn how to dump our past feelings of regret, shame and false guilt. We learn to deal with our past destructive behavior. We face up to those we have hurt with a truly sincere "I'm sorry - will you forgive me!" We have died to our old self and become a "NEW CREATION" in Christ Jesus.

How are we to speak these amends? What are we to say? How are we to receive the gift of our new self, to put on that "New Creation of Christ Jesus" inside? A good question to help us visualize that attitude is to ask ourselves, "How would Jesus handle this situation?" We should be calm and full of compassion, for Jesus is our understanding. His peace and healing are our goal. As we seek to be put right with our own conscience and reunited with those we hurt, our words and actions must be sincere and from our heart. We should feel truly sorry for the hurt we have caused and sincerely reflect that sorrow deeply from our heart. We are seeking to have the relationship put back together, if possible. We are not trying to find out who was right or wrong. We are not out to argue or re-try the situation that caused all of this. So a calm, sincere, and peaceful attitude is best. We are out to heal the pain and hurt connected with our differences. The differences may always exist and that is acceptable. However, the pain and hurt are not acceptable. That pain and hurt has made us sick in our spirit and caused our addiction. A calm, sincere attitude is best. In our reading, "Our speech should always be pleasant and interesting." Speak to Jesus first, and then do it! If necessary, seek the advice of a friend.

Steps 8 & 9 Lesson 29

"I made a list of all persons I had harmed, and became willing to make amends to them all"

"I made direct amends to such persons whenever possible, except when to do so would injure them or others"

Scripture:
MEDITATIONS

MEDITATIONS

DAY FIVE - Study Philemon 8-17

This story is a very interesting one. Paul was in prison at the time that he wrote this letter. He wrote to Philemon who was a dear friend and fellow Christian Brother to Paul. It seems that Philemon had a slave named Onesimus and that slave ran away from Philemon. Onesimus came to know Paul and became a Christian as a result. This reading is Paul's conversation with Philemon urging him to take back Onesimus, not as a slave, but as a fellow brother in Jesus Christ.

Paul is in a tight spot here. If you will read this letter carefully, you will see how patient and loving Paul was in trying to resolve this problem. Maybe we can all learn something from Paul with regard to making amends to those we have hurt. That's a tight spot, too.

One of the very difficult results of our addictions is the loss of our responsibility. Yet, our recovery depends on rebuilding this sense of willingness to assume new, healthy self-discipline and self- responsibility.

In this reading, we see a beautiful example of responsibility. In his letter to Philemon, Paul urges Philemon to rid himself of old resentments and differences. Then, Paul cries out to Philemon to accept Onesimus as a follower of Christ (a brother in the Lord); that he be welcomed home and reunited with his family and the Christian Church.

We seek a similar spirit in carrying out this step. We stretch forth our hand of healing forgiveness and friendship to those whom we have wronged or who have wronged us. It makes no difference who was at fault. Chances are, both parties were at fault to some extent. When we let go of the fault issue and seek to heal and make whole in friendship and love for one another, God takes care of the healing; He heals the pain and hurt. And so, we must step out boldly and in good faith as Paul did. Forgiveness and healing are the marks of a true, whole person in Christ. It is a true indication of our spiritual healing and recovery. And we feel good again! How wonderful! AMEN!

DAY SIX - Study Psalm 51:14-17

David was a special man in the eyes of the Lord God. He started out as a humble shepherd whom God made the mighty King of Israel. God calls you and me to be humble, also. When we are humble, we are in touch with our inner self. Humility is an attitude that we have been building since the very beginning of this program. It is an important key to the success in our healing and continued recovery process.

David's words "humble and repentant heart", (Verse 17), describe the attitude that we need to succeed in this step. David also asks God to "help me to speak, Lord." (Verse 15) Why does David ask God for this? Verse 14 gives us the answer - "and I will gladly proclaim your righteousness." When our words become God's words living in us, we proclaim His righteousness; we become instruments of the almighty God. What was God the Fathers' purpose in sending Jesus to earth? The answer: to forgive us, to heal us, break the bondage of our sin, AND to give us eternal life - life without end in Him. When we turn to our God with a humble and repentant heart, we ask Him to help us speak and gladly proclaim His righteousness; we become as the living God who lives in us. This is the way we are called to approach our entire life and the people in our life. It becomes the way we think and act; it is our new creation from the inside out.

The final phase of our coming to Jesus is - "I will praise you." (Verse 15) As we go about the task of making amends to those in our past, let us keep in mind that, in so doing, we give praise to Jesus. Instead of the old selfish me, Jesus has changed me into a new selfless me. We have learned and experienced the newness of life in Jesus. I pray that this will be your experience today, dear friend.

MEDITATIONS

Steps 8 & 9 Lesson 29

"I made a list of all persons I had harmed, and became willing to make amends to them all"

"I made direct amends to such persons whenever possible, except when to do so would injure them or others"

DAY SEVEN - Study Proverbs 16:20-24

Today, we are walking and working in our 12 step recovery process. As we do this, we experience a drastic change in our lives. We become more at peace with our inner self; we increase in knowledge of the Lord Jesus and His love for us and we translate that knowledge into the wisdom that we need to change our lives and to better relate to those around us. Everything we do and say begins to radiate the new "ME". We are better able to see ourselves the way we are - to relate to others and to God. We are on the road to becoming a more healthy and spiritually happy person.

In our reading today, we are called to, "think before we speak." (Verse 23) We are called to "trust in the Lord and you will be happy". (Verse 20) When we trust in the Lord to give us His wisdom and direction for exactly the right words at the right time, we will find the courage we need to be put right with others, to ask for, as well as to extend, forgiveness. Verse 22 tells us that, "Wisdom is a fountain of life to the wise". The pleasant words that we speak will be "like honey, sweet to the taste and good for your health." In this way, we will bring that sweet taste and good health to others as well as to ourselves. Our broken relationships will be healed and we will become healthy and whole persons again. Our reading today gives us a "road map" to successfully go about making amends, the Lord's way. My friend, try it, you'll like it. May God continue to bless you and strengthen you. AMEN!

Scripture : MEDITATIONS

SCRIPTURE STUDY:

The following scriptures are provided in respect to Healing Step 9. Please study them carefully and see how they apply to this step:

- ☐ Psalm 90:17
- ☐ Romans 14:19
- ☐ Psalm 126:5-6
- ☐ Romans 15:5-7
- ☐ Proverbs 3:27
- ☐ 1 Corinthians 8:1-3
- ☐ Proverbs 12:18-20
- ☐ Galatians 6:7-10
- ☐ Proverbs 15:1-4
- ☐ Philippians 4:2
- ☐ Proverbs 16:6-7
- ☐ Colossians 3:12-13
- ☐ Proverbs 25:11
- ☐ Colossians 3:18-21
- ☐ Matthew 5:23-24
- ☐ 1 Thessalonians 5:15
- ☐ Matthew 7:12
- ☐ Hebrews 12:14-15
- ☐ Matthew 12:35-37
- ☐ James 3:17-18
- ☐ Luke 6:27-36
- ☐ 1 Peter 1:22
- ☐ Romans 12:18-21
- ☐ 1 John 3:17-19

> We love because God first loved us. If we say we love God, but hate others, we are liars. For we cannot love God, whom we have not seen, if we do not love others, whom we have seen. The command that Christ has given us is this: whoever loves God must love others also.
> *-1 John 4:19-21*

> If you don't surrender to God you will be captured by the devil.
> *-Author unknown*

> Tears may flow in the night, but joy comes in the morning.
> *-Psalm 30:5*

> God hates the sin, but loves the sinner.
> *-Author unknown*

> The prayer of amends must be a way of life, not just a sad cry at the end of failure.
> *-Author unknown*

Walking the 12 Steps with Jesus Christ

Step 10 Lesson 30

"I continue to take personal inventory daily and when I am wrong, I promptly admit it."

Action Words : TAKE DAILY INVENTORY

STEP 10

THE OVERCOMING STAGE

With this lesson, we begin the fourth and final stage of this 12 step recovery program. This final stage is called "Overcoming in Jesus". The learning, as opposed to the "doing", portion of this program is now complete. Now we begin the actual practice of "walking the walk" with Jesus.

When we entered this program, we were concerned and taken up by our problem. Having gone through this study thus far, we have:

1. Declared and admitted our powerlessness;
2. Believed in the God of Jesus Christ and turned our will and life over to Him;
3. Made an in-depth search of our wrongs of the past in our moral inventory;
4. Admitted our wrongs and gave them to Jesus for healing;
5. Learned the importance of prayer and Bible study;
6. Learned how to go about making amends to those in our past whom we have hurt;
7. Come to realize the importance of fellowship and fasting.

During this process, we have studied our problem with addiction, learned about the cause, studied and practiced the healing process, and we have taken positive steps to correct our past and develop our spirit for today and the days to come. I feel certain, at this point, that you feel a great deal better about yourself. What you thought was an impossible situation, was found to be possible and was also very desirable. In fact, you have probably come to realize that "I don't want the 'old me' back again. I'm through with the old me. I like the new me much better." I want to congratulate you for your determination to find the new you.

If, for some reason, you do not feel "up" or positive about yourself yet, go back over the information we just studied. It probably means that you have not been serious about a portion of your past study and tried to glance over it without applying it to your life. All that is necessary, dear friend, is to do it over again with greater determination and sincerity this time.

Our job, however, is not over yet. In fact, the job will continue until we are called from our bodies by Almighty God to be with Him in heaven. The experience of my life (the past 65+ years) has taught me that finding and growing in the "NEW ME", is a very interesting, challenging, and exciting adventure. It has lasted a lifetime for me and I pray that it will be so for you also. And it is truly EXCITING!

You may ask, "What is this overcoming in Jesus stage of the program all about?" Now that we have learned how to correct our past and are about the business of doing that, it is most important that we learn to live sane, healthy, holy and spiritual lives today and in the days to come. Psalm 118:24 states, "This is the day of the Lord's victory; let us be happy, let us celebrate!" You and I are called to live to the fullest each and every day of our lives, "One day at a time". Jesus wants us to celebrate each day at a time, to the fullest. In this overcoming stage, we learn how to walk in sane, sober behavior each day, one day at a time. This is the stage when all of the lessons and work that we have learned from the start begins to pay off in the present. This is where the "rubber hits the road".

MOVING FROM THE PROBLEM - INTO THE SOLUTION

In the past, we spent much time on our problem. Now we spend our time looking at and living in the solution. It is extremely important that you visualize this transition in your mind. You have left your problem behind you. You are no longer a part of your problem. You now walk in the solution and that solution is your union with Jesus Christ!

Healing Steps 10, 11 and 12 are sometimes called the maintenance steps because they deal with the "how to walk" in the sobriety of our new life. They repeat many of the points which were covered in the previous steps and they emphasize the value of continuing to "work the steps" on a day-to-day basis. We will deal with the information contained in the previous steps in a new perspective - we will be applying them to life today, right now, and in the days to come. We will now learn to walk in the solution to our problem instead of in the problem.

TAKING A DAILY INVENTORY

Healing Step 10 asks us to take a personal inventory DAILY. Just as the 4th Step inventory searches our past all the way back to our conception, so in this step we take a good look at the day that we are about to put to sleep. I would like to refer you back to Lesson 23 when I discussed the function of the mind with you. You will recall how important it was to back up and clean out our subconscious mind, our gut box. All of the past needed to be cleaned out and all the wrongs needed to be confessed and forgiven. The principle of Healing Step 10 is exactly the same. By taking a personal inventory daily, we deal with our day-to-day problems as they happen. We prevent ourselves from piling up these problems over long periods as we did in the past. If you will turn back Lesson 2, you will remember the cycle of addiction in which we found that the basic cause of our addictive behav-

STEP 10

Step 10 Lesson 30

"I continue to take personal inventory daily and when I am wrong, I promptly admit it."

Action Words : TAKE DAILY INVENTORY

ior was PAIN IN OUR PAST. It seems reasonable that if we get this pain healed AND prevent new hurts and pain from creeping into our lives today, we will have eliminated the very reason we act out in addictive behavior. The cause of addiction will be gone and therefore we no longer need our old habits. We no longer have any need to go out and get "drunk" since our inner pain will be gone and the cause of our addiction is gone.

GUIDELINES FOR TAKING A DAILY PERSONAL INVENTORY

At this point, I hope that you will be able to see how important it is to keep that inner spirit clean of any wrongs in the past as well as the present. Here are some of the guidelines for taking our daily personal inventory:

1. "What are my basic needs for love, acceptance and affirmation? Do I understand and recognize these needs and how these needs were met in my life today? If they were not met, why not? How can I correct this situation?"

2. "What about my feelings? Did I allow my feelings to get the better of me today and did I allow them to dictate my actions? Have I acted out those feelings in ways that may have hurt God, another, or myself? Have I looked at what may have caused those feelings and have I taken that situation to Jesus for healing today? Was I rejected or abandoned by another today, or did I reject or abandon some one else today? Have I brought my feelings and actions today to Jesus for guidance?"

3. "Have I fallen back into any of my old addictive habits this day? Did I try to manipulate another today to get what 'I wanted'? Have I tried to 'con' another person today? Did I try to control the life of another around me in any way? If so, how? Am I trying to hide a problem that I may have with another or myself? Am I struggling to get others to accept me by being something or someone I am not? Am I back to playing my old 'head games' to get my own way? Do I see myself slipping back into some old familiar habit or a possible new habit?"

4. "How did I relate to the people in my life today? Did I tend to keep another away from me today or did I avoid that person for some reason? Why? Did I tend to want to 'hang on' to another person today? How did I handle the 'touchy' situations in my life today? Did I say 'NO' or 'YES' when necessary and did I feel secure about my response? Did I feel left out of the crowd today? What were my reactions to all of this? If a 'friend' tried to get me back into an old habit, what were my reactions? How did I feel about that reaction? Did I respect the opinions or limits another person put on me today without getting upset?"

5. "If I need to make a change in my life, can I 'roll up my sleeves'? Am I determined to do it? Have I put off over and over again making a difficult decision? Was I afraid to make that decision? When I had a 'fall out' with another person, did I go back to make amends? Have I talked to Jesus about my relationships with others and what to do to solve these problems?"

6. "Do I admit my wrongs to another promptly? Can I forgive myself for the wrongs I have committed against God, others, and myself? Am I able to accept the forgiveness of God and forgive others and myself? Have I let go of the past guilt and shame in my life?"

7. "Did I spend quality time today with Jesus in prayer and Bible study? Have I been involved today with the 'Body of Christ' in fellowship and love? Did I continue to discipline my physical body and its appetites in my practice of fasting today? Where am I in my relationship to Jesus today? In what areas do I need correction?"

Generally, our daily, personal inventory is a great deal simpler and less difficult than our 4th Step inventory. The reason being, we deal with the present day only. The present day is fresh in our memory. Since we are still feeling what happened today, the process of healing any problems of the day will come much easier and quicker than in the past. Our deep, dark 4th Step is past and healed now. Today we deal with today, one day at a time. We want to stay well today.

The practice of what we learned in the past still applies, however. We still need to stop blaming ourselves and others and we need to bring the problem out into the open and deal with it the Jesus way. Honesty is an important factor in dealing with the present. Remember, lying will only cover the problem up and make it impossible to deal with. Being willing to deal with the problem as it happens is always essential to recovery of today's wrongs. Remember, our goal is to stay clean of the wrongs that hurt us in the past, which made spirit sick and caused our addiction.

Please see pages 138 through 140 for further Daily Personal Inventory Guidelines.

SPIRITUAL SELF EXAMINATION

Our daily inventory should end with an examination of our daily relationship with Jesus Christ. Some questions, "Did I start my day with Jesus in prayer? Have I turned to Jesus each time my life became just a little bit confused? When I got 'stuck' during my day, did I turn to Jesus for the

Step 10 Lesson 30

"I continue to take personal inventory daily and when I am wrong, I promptly admit it."

Action Words : TAKE DAILY INVENTORY

guidance and the answer? How did I handle myself when I got into a dispute with another person? Did I lean on Jesus when necessary? If I 'messed up', did I forgive myself and did I seek forgiveness from the other person? In what ways can I come closer to Jesus? How did what I learned today bring me closer to Jesus and make me a better Christian tomorrow?"

MY DAILY INVENTORY - A LIFE LONG HABIT

The need to take a daily personal inventory is a habit that will continue for the remainder of our lives. This becomes a daily checklist that asks, "How are we doing today in our spiritual walk with Jesus, others and ourselves?" This is the discipline we learn which helps us "WALK WITH JESUS CHRIST" and overcome the old person that we once were.

BEWARE OF THE RITUALS OF THE PAST

This daily check up involves another exercise also. This I call, - BEING AWARE OF THE RITUAL OF OUR PAST HABITS. Here is how it works:

Go back with me to your past addiction and let's take a look at what happened in your daily life at that time just prior to your slip or fall. More than likely, certain events of the day happened to "pull you down" inside in your feelings and spirit. I recommend that you get a clean sheet of paper and make a list of events that commonly happened just before you went off on a "drunk". Maybe someone "pushed you in a corner" in some way to get you "tee'd off" inside. It may have been your wife or husband, your boss, a fellow worker, a policeman, another driver, who knows. Chances are very good that a series of incidents began happening to you that started to quickly pull you down and you began hurting deep inside. You probably began to feel very down and helpless about the situation. Life was not going well and you felt pulled apart inside. And then, your old addiction started to speak to you very loudly and clearly - "Hey man, let's go to it, let's do our thing! After all, you are hurting inside and you need to feel better. This stuff will help you, so let's go!"

SATAN'S TRAP

To illustrate how this works, let's visualize a vacuum cleaner hose with its air suction. All of us have played with a vacuum cleaner hose. How many times have we taken the hose and small pieces of paper and moved the hose closer and closer to the paper until the paper was finally sucked into the vacuum? The suction of a vacuum cleaner hose is fascinating to a young child and all of us have done that in the past. Now visualize yourself as being that small piece of paper. As the vacuum hose is drawn closer and closer to the paper, it will finally reach a point when the paper will begin to move closer to the hose opening. Finally, the paper will be overpowered by the suction and will fly toward the hose opening and into the vacuum.

I describe that process in the following drawing:

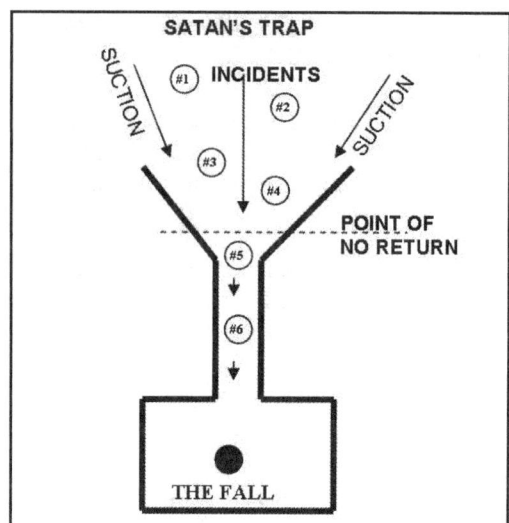

In the drawing, I show a funnel connected to a vacuum hose. This vacuum is always running and will continue to try to draw you back into your old addicted past. The vacuum represents the devil. Each of the incidents that pull you down is shown by dots with numbers. Notice that with the increase of the numbers, the person is drawn closer and closer to that dotted line which is called the point of no return. Once you are drawn past that point of no return, there is nothing you can do to stop yourself from the fall. And we have come back to Step 1 all over again. The point of no return is when you let your hand slip out of the hand of Jesus Christ. It is there that you become lost.

Please, take some time to think about this example. Study your past falls and see if there were not some problems or situations in your life that were very difficult for you to deal with. See how these situations stirred up your "feelings" and see how those feelings caused you to slip closer and closer to the point of no return until you fell again into your old habit. Remember that our feelings are OK, but they are not given to us to dictate our actions. Rather, Almighty God gave them to us simply to indicate and show us what is going on in our life. A good feeling indicates that something is going well and is pleasing to us. A bad feeling indicates that something is "out of whack" and is disturbing us. That usually means that we need to concentrate on the solution to that problem.

STEP 10

Step 10 Lesson 30

"I continue to take personal inventory daily and when I am wrong, I promptly admit it."

Action Words: TAKE DAILY INVENTORY

Make a list of the events that preceded your fall and study them. See how you reacted to them and talk to Jesus about them now. See how He will help you walk strong and stand against that terrible suction of the devil to pull you back down. Jesus is our only defense at this time. We have learned that in the first three steps of this program. Now we can understand why we fell and we can learn from that.

Now, you may ask, "What is the point of all this?" As we check ourselves daily in our personal inventory, we need to become keenly aware of these little incidents which can creep up on us and cause us to be pulled closer and closer into the trap of our old habit. It's VERY IMPORTANT that we recognize them as soon as they begin to happen. If we can see incident number one happening and recognize it, we can do something about it immediately. We can pray about it and bring it to Jesus for help. This becomes a warning sign that we need to come to God for the rescue, for we have learned that we cannot do it by ourselves. Remember Step 1? If we ignore that warning sign and tell ourselves "I can handle it!" we are again fooling ourselves and playing directly into the clutches of the devil, who will tempt us and drive us back into our old habit. If we deal with each incident when it happens or shortly thereafter, we are assured that we will gain the strength and wisdom from our "higher power" Jesus Christ to be able to handle that problem successfully and not let it pull us down. The more we play around with the incidents without proper action, the more apt we are to fall quickly and drastically. When we recognize the first incident and put a stop to it, we will have broken the chain of events that can eventually lead us to a fall.

HOW DO WE DEAL WITH THESE INCIDENTS WHEN THEY HAPPEN?

Here are some helpful suggestions:

1. Immediately STOP what you are doing and change your environment.
2. Talk to someone, preferably a Christian friend.
3. Make a phone call to a Christian friend.
4. Immediately go to prayer.
5. Study your Bible or recall some memorized scriptures to mind and think on them.
6. Go for a walk, swim, or exercise.
7. Take some positive action to stop what you are doing and put your mind on Jesus.

It is essential that you recognize the incident or temptation and immediately stop what you are doing. Change your mind and environment. Then reach out to God and to another for help. Remember Step 5. There we learned to reach out to others for help.

As you learn to recognize the ritual or incidents that lead you to a fall, you will be able to stop them immediately. This will give you a sure and positive way of keeping yourself from falling back into your old habits. The most effective breaking of this temptation is placing your hand more securely in Jesus Christ. Please study Ephesians chapter 6, which is essential to your understanding of and use in overcoming temptations. In my 20+ years of experience with those in prisons and jails, I have found that when we push Jesus out of our lives or ignore Him, we are asking for trouble and a fall. Walking with Jesus daily, moment by moment, is essential for our successful walk daily. This is a discipline that we must learn and practice. It leads to a clean, successful, sober life in Christ. Temptations will always come to us as long as we walk in this fleshly body; however, we have the victory over them in Christ Jesus. Learning to recognize them and applying the action (the blood of Jesus) to them is the answer to a successful, sober walk.

A sincere study and practice of these principles will assure us of a successful walk with Jesus Christ. May you come to Jesus always, dear friend, especially when tempted. May His success be yours. AMEN!

To recognize failure intelligently, is the first step toward building success.
—Emmett Fox

What we go after here, determines where we go hereafter.
—Author unknown

Your word is a lamp to guide me and a light for my path.
—Psalm 119:105

So Jesus said to those who believed in Him, "If you obey My teaching, you are really My disciples; you will know the truth, and the truth will set you free."
—John 8:31-32

The healthier we become, the less willing we become to tolerate disaster in our relationships.
—Mary Catherine North

Step 10 Lesson 31

"I continue to take personal inventory daily and when I am wrong, I promptly admit it."

Scripture:
MEDITATIONS

MEDITATIONS

DAY ONE - Study Mark 14:38

In this reading, we find Jesus in the garden on the night before He was to die. He went to the garden with the apostles Peter, James, and John. He asked the apostles to pray with Him for an hour and went off a distance to pray alone. When He returned, He found the apostles asleep. In verse 37, He addresses Peter as "Simon" which was his name before Peter came to know the Lord. By calling Peter "Simon", Jesus was talking to the old Peter. Maybe Peter had fallen back into his old habits when he disobeyed Jesus and slept rather than prayed. Was the old Peter coming back again instead of the new Peter who believed and followed Jesus? I think so, because it was only a short time after that when Peter denied that he knew Jesus three times.

Do we also have a struggle with our old nature, our old self? Could it be that the moment we let our guard down, the "old me" comes back with a roar? It seems that none of us ever reach the point when the "old me" is completely dead. When we get the urge to return to our old former habits, we know for certain that the "old me" is still alive and we have more work to do. In verse 34 of this reading, Jesus calls His apostles to "Stay here and keep watch". Why did Jesus tell them to "keep watch"? Their hour of trial and testing was upon them and Jesus knew it. Jesus was calling them to watch out for the spiritual warfare that was about to take place and to pray to the Father for strength to see the battle through. Even Jesus was totally dependent upon His Father for His strength rather than Himself. Jesus knew that these three men wanted to follow Him - but He also knew that they would be put through the fire of persecution the following day and for the rest of their lives. He knew that they would need the strength and guidance from Father God.

Jesus also calls us to be with Him, to watch and pray. "Why", you may ask? Jesus knows that we will be faced with new challenges each day as we walk in our new life. He knows that we will be tempted by the devil and how important it is for us to keep ourselves connected to Him for strength and grace.

And so, He tells us to keep watch with Him and pray so that we will not fall into temptation. "For the spirit is willing but the flesh is weak." (Verse 38) We must always remember, our strength and overcoming is in our contact with JESUS! We have the victory, but only when we stay connected to Jesus!

DAY TWO - Study Romans 12:1-3

As we progress through these 12 steps, we may find ourselves with some real success in changing the habits of our past. It feels good to get rid of the old me and find the real me inside. Success in changing our lives and overcoming our addiction is our goal in this or any other 12 step program. There is a very real danger, however, in thinking, "I did it!" We can easily let this success "go to our heads". Our pride can creep in very easily and we can start back to our old "stinkin thinkin". In this reading today, Paul warns us against such a danger.

In verses one and two of this reading, Paul calls you to:

1. Offer yourself as a living sacrifice to God;

2. Dedicate yourself to His service;

3. Be careful not to conform yourself to the standards of this world;

4. Let God transform you inwardly by a complete change of your mind;

5. Then you will know the will of God for you;

6. Then you will know what is good and pleasing to Him and perfect.

In verse three, Paul tells us to be modest in our thinking and judge ourselves according to the amount of faith that God has given us. I think that the key word here is MODEST. To be modest and humble is to be our true spiritual self, the spiritual person that Jesus made us. When we start to climb on our "pride bandwagon", we loose our faith, our humbleness and closeness to Jesus. We become god again and we "blow it".

Walking the 12 Steps with Jesus Christ

MEDITATIONS

Step 10 Lesson 31

"I continue to take personal inventory daily and when I am wrong, I promptly admit it."

Scripture:
MEDITATIONS

So, dear friends, beware that your success does not "go to your head". Instead, keep close watch over yourself on a daily basis with a personal inventory. Keep your spiritual self in proper balance. Keep praying to Jesus and ask Him, "Lord, how am I doing today?" Then stop and listen to His answer and follow it.

Our daily inventory is exactly what we need to keep us "thinking sober and straight". When we have successes in kicking old habits, let us "Praise the Lord!" We should constantly praise God and thank Him for our overcoming. We need Him to walk with us through life. If we have "slipped", let's just admit it and turn to Him again for a new start. Let's try again and just maybe, by the grace of Jesus, we will do it right this time. Our Step 10 personal, daily inventory helps us to keep our eyes on where we are going in life and, most importantly, our need for Jesus in our lives. We are keeping our direction in tune with God's direction for us. May the Lord Jesus bless you, dear friend, as you turn to HIM!

DAY THREE - Study 1 Thessalonians 5:16-24

In the first three stages of this program, we have dealt with the cleansing of our past, getting rid of the "old me". In this step and the steps that follow, we concentrate on building the "new me".

In our reading today, Paul gives us some practical advice for living our "new life" in Christ Jesus:

1. Be joyful, even if we don't feel like it. Jesus walks with us and that's something to shout about.

2. We are to praise God and be thankful to Him. In recovery, we frequently refer to making a "thank you" list in which we list our blessings and thank God for them.

3. Do not push aside the Holy Spirit or restrict Him in any way. Rather, we should open ourselves up to His guidance and strength. We are to talk with the Holy Spirit each day about our success in overcoming.

4. We are to "test all things", keep what is good and avoid every kind of evil. We are to put on our "spiritual radar" which keeps us tuned into the power of the Holy Spirit for the proper direction in life.

In verse 23, Paul gives the people of his day a blessing. Paul's blessing will also fall upon us if we follow the instructions he has given us in the verses above. If we follow his instructions by the Holy Spirit, "God will make you holy in every way and keep your whole being - spirit, soul and body - free from every fault." The Holy Spirit will fill us with His grace. I believe that is the goal for all of us. We all want to live full, happy, and in-control lives. Jesus is the way, dear friend. Let's follow Him by His Holy Spirit within us! AMEN!

DAY FOUR - Study Hebrews 2:1-3

Our reading today calls us to hold on firmly to the truths we have heard so that we will not be carried away. Most of us have been to the beach, at one time or another, when there was a strong under current and rough water. We were warned to be careful of the under-tow. But, we still ventured out and quickly found that it was easy to be carried away by the strong pull of the water's current.

Our new life in overcoming addiction is like that under-tow. It can be so simple for us to "get cocky" and risk getting in over our heads in our daily life. The reading continues by telling us that we need to follow Jesus and obey Him or we will "receive the punishment we deserve". We are to pay attention to our "great salvation" which comes to us in Jesus Christ.

Venturing out into the strong under-tow of life is dangerous business. We need to stay close to Jesus and to each other in the "Body of Christ", the Church. Staying in the program is also an important part of the answer. That is why we "must hold on all the more firmly to the truths we have heard so that we will not be carried away". (Verse 1) Remember, God did not create us to get through this world successfully

Walking the 12 Steps with Jesus Christ

Step 10 Lesson 31

"I continue to take personal inventory daily and when I am wrong, I promptly admit it."

Scripture: MEDITATIONS

without Him. We need Him and our goal is to walk WITH HIM, not by ourselves. Sticking our necks out to the world around us will get us hurt. We will fall again and suffer more. So, dear friends, keep yourselves "Clean in Jesus!" Please.

DAY FIVE - Study 1 Peter 2:11-12

Our reading today is quite clear in its calling. You and I, as Christians, followers of Jesus, are strangers and refugees in this world. This world is not our home, but rather a temporary place in which to come to know Jesus Christ and to prepare for eternity with Him. As members of His Heavenly Kingdom, we are to be very careful how we live in this world. Our old self seems to have a strangle hold on us. We know how much we have suffered as a result of our "old me" and yet, there seems to be a strong pull for us to go back there again. Our old self calls us back to our old habits. This calling is our body, our fleshly nature. Peter warns us not to give in to our old "bodily passions" which are always at war with our spirit. Rather, we are to concentrate on getting our spirit strong and keeping it strong. Keeping our spirit strong requires a constant, daily check up on our spiritual life. This is the very reason for the daily, personal inventory. It's a way to check ourselves daily so that we don't giving in to the old "bodily passions" which war against our spirit. Dear friend, be sure to take this matter of daily inventory seriously. You will grow closer to Jesus if you do and you will overcome in Him! The Holy Word says, "But continue to grow in the grace and knowledge of our Lord and Savior Jesus Christ!" (2 Peter 3:18)

DAY SIX - Study Psalm 85:8-9

What a tremendous promise from our Lord in today's reading. When we listen to the Him, to what He is saying to us, He promises us peace and His saving presence. Jesus calls us, not to go back to our old foolish ways, but rather to come to Him and live in His presence.

As we "count down" in this program, we come to realize the importance of a constant, day-to-day check on our life.

Jesus walks with us, if we will let Him. The taking of a daily, personal inventory is a good way for us to keep Jesus in our life style. By talking with Him daily about each day as we go through life, we maintain that personal love relationship with Him as our Lord and Savior.

The sad fact is that those of us who do not heed this method of a daily check up on our life, will fall. Most will fall very quickly. The experience of many of those who have gone before us in this program has proven this fact without question. "If we don't pray, we'll pay!" When we listen to Jesus, He fills us with His peace. "His saving presence will remain in our land." (Verse 9) Will you continue to walk in His saving presence? I pray that you will.

DAY SEVEN - Study Psalm 103:8-18

Step 10 is a constant check on our daily life. We are constantly looking at the day just past and checking ourselves in our recovery process. Life is shown in the Bible over and over again as a journey. Each day, we grow one day older in the journey. Where are we coming from and where are we going in that journey? Verse 17 today tells us, "But for those who honor the Lord, His love lasts forever, and His goodness endures for all generations." As we come to Him, we experience His love more and more deeply. We find out just who we are in Jesus.

MEDITATIONS

Step 10 Lesson 31

"I continue to take personal inventory daily and when I am wrong, I promptly admit it."

Scripture: MEDITATIONS

Our daily practice of Step 10 gives us an on-going check on our walk with Jesus. Have we been truthful to Him—honoring, obeying and serving Him humbly today? Have we done our part in our relationship to Him so that He can do His part? Are there any areas of our life today where we see ourselves slipping back into our "old me"? If we are faithful and come to Him, He will do His part, "As high as the sky is above the earth, so great is His love for those who honor Him." (Verse 11)

Our God is also merciful. If we do "mess up" and sin, He is quick to forgive us. "As far as the east is from the west, so far does He remove our sins from us." (Verse 12) So, if we do sin, we must come to our Lord immediately for that loving forgiveness that He gives us so freely.

Each day of our lives, we face a new challenge. Each day is a new day for spiritual growth and strength. Each day is a new day to learn more and more about "Who I am!" Even if we make a mistake, we can always come back, be forgiven, and start again. All is not lost. It is not the end of our life but just a bend in the road along the way. Again, the Lord reminds us, "But for those who honor the Lord, His love lasts forever, and His goodness endures for all generations." (Verse 17) Healing Step 10 is our daily checkup to be sure that we are walking with Him and are honoring Him. I pray that you will be sincere and faithful in your practice of this step. In that way you will receive the Lord's goodness and love. He will truly bless you. AMEN!

SCRIPTURE STUDY:

The following scriptures are provided with respect to Healing Step 10. Please study them carefully to see how they apply to this step:

- Psalm 24:3-5
- Galatians 5:13-15
- Psalm 68:5-6
- Ephesians 4:26-32
- Psalm 101:2-4
- Ephesians 5:15-16
- Proverbs 12:1
- Philippians 2:14-15
- Matthew 5:8
- Colossians 3:1-3
- Matthew 26:71-75
- 2 Thessalonians 3:3-5
- Luke 6:41-42
- 2 Timothy 2:4-7
- Luke 14:25-35
- 2 Timothy 2:20-26
- John 17:15-17
- Hebrews 3:7-13
- Romans 12:16
- Hebrews 10:35-38
- Romans 16:19-20
- Hebrews 12:25
- 1 Corinthians 3:11-16
- Hebrews 12:28
- 1 Corinthians 6:12
- James 1:13-14
- 1 Corinthians 10:6-13
- James 1:19
- 1 Corinthians 10:23-24
- 2 Peter 3:17-18
- 2 Corinthians 10:17-18
- 1 John 2:3
- Galatians 4:9
- 1 John 2:15-17
- Galatians 5:1
- 2 John 8

I love the Lord, because He hears me; He listens to my prayers. He listens to me every time I call to Him.
—*Psalm 116:1-2*

Search out shortcomings and correct them.
—*Author unknown*

Repent then, and turn to God, so that He will forgive your sins. If you do, times of spiritual strength will come from the Lord, and He will send Jesus, who is the Messiah He has already chosen for you.
—*Acts 3:19-20*

To err is human, to forgive divine.
—*Alexander Pope*

No one is so good that he can save himself. No one is so bad that God cannot save him.
—*Author unknown*

Walking the 12 Steps with Jesus Christ

Step 10 Lesson 32

"I continue to take personal inventory daily and when I am wrong, I promptly admit it."

Action Words : TAKE DAILY INVENTORY

STEP 10

THE TEST - CAN I DO IT? CAN I WALK SOBER?

Up to now in our study, we have been dying to our "old me" and going about the business of building the "new me" the Jesus Christ way. Now, in this step, we learn how to walk in this image of the "new life" in me in a very practical way. The acid test will come soon when we ask, "Can I stay sober and in proper balance today?" It is then that we will face the true test of our learning and our faith in Jesus Christ. If we have followed the Healing Steps and Growth/ Strength Steps of this program, we will "OVER- COME" successfully.

WHERE HAVE WE BEEN?

Let's look back to where we have been since our walk with Jesus started. So far, we have dealt with our past problems; we have confessed them to God, to ourselves, and another human being; we have asked God to heal us and believed that He has when we gave our wrongs to Him; we have made amends to others whenever we could; and now we have decided to keep a constant check on ourselves day-by-day as we take a daily inventory. In the Growth/Strength Steps, we have learned how to pray; how to study God's Holy Word; the importance of fellowship with others in the "Body of Christ"; and we have learned the importance of bringing our body under the control of our spirit in the practice of fasting.

All of this past learning and experiencing has been our preparation for the day of testing, when we will be back "on the streets" in the old world. But we must remember, we are no longer the "old person" we once were. Remember, dear friend, "I have been made into a NEW CREATION by the mighty power that Jesus Christ gives me in His Holy Spirit." I can do it, not by my power, but by the power of CHRIST WHO LIVES IN ME! (See Philippians 4:13)

And so, we must continually look at what we have learned; we must study it over and over again until it becomes a part of us. This is the key to our growth and overcoming. We must always have a desire to learn and a longing to become "better persons" in Christ Jesus. When we understand and begin to live in the Christ within us, then we will become better persons day-by-day as we go through our lives. Remember, dear friend, we have not arrived at our goal as yet. Rather, we are on a journey into eternal life. Each day, Jesus reveals and gives to us a greater portion of the abundant life that He promises in John 10:10. Look up this reading again and, if you have not already done so, memorize it so that you will never forget it. Jesus wants you to have abundant life, not tomorrow, or next week, or when you die, but RIGHT NOW. All that is needed is to open up to Him and receive that abundant life from the inside out. Be open and patient and Jesus will show you the way.

OUR DAILY SELF SEARCHING INVENTORY IS A MUST - TODAY I WILL DO IT.

Our inventory is a must and should become a regular daily habit. Daily we need to find and admit our wrongs and persistently work to correct them. No longer will we allow them to pile up and go unattended. Remember, it is in admitting these wrongs and bringing them out into the open that we find the key to our recovery and overcoming. Our past wrongs in all the yesterdays before today have been exposed and healed by the saving power of Jesus. They are forgiven. Now we are concerned only with "today". Today, I will keep my life clean, in order and in check. Today, I will not fall into my old habits. Today, I will stay sober by the power of Christ within me. Today, I will love God, others, and myself. Today, I will keep my eyes on Jesus, who is my strength and salvation. Today, by the grace of Jesus Christ, I WILL OVERCOME!

In this process of "daily inventory taking", discipline is the key word. It must be done regularly, making a habit of doing it each day at the same time. Once in a while it would be good for you to search out your Prayer Partner or a spiritual advisor and do it with that person as in Healing Step 5. Remember, your successful overcoming depends on it.

BUILDING OUR NEW SELF IMAGE

At this point in our spiritual walk with Jesus Christ, it is very important for us to look at our self-image. The old "you" has been shed and a "new you" is now born afresh. We are new persons now, so it is important to begin to dump the old ideas of who we once were. The "addict", "drunk", or "druggie" images are now a part of the past. WE need to begin thinking this way, right NOW. Maybe others, who have known us in the past, may not agree for the moment, but we are out to show them the new me in a very humble, sincere, and real way. So let's grab onto the "new you" and let's bury the "old you".

This is exactly why it is so important for us to take a daily inventory. What we are doing is asking ourselves, "Dear Jesus, how am I doing at the job of bringing about the new me?" This should be a very exciting time, not one of dragging out the old memories of the past. This should be a time with exciting new things happening in our lives to show us the right way. We are on the path to becoming whole, happy, emotionally and spiritually healthy persons. Our healing has taken hold and we are now well on the way of being that "NEW CREATION".

STEP 10

Step 10 Lesson 32

"I continue to take personal inventory daily and when I am wrong, I promptly admit it."

Action Words : TAKE DAILY INVENTORY

In our over-all self-image, we need to remember that we are looking for spiritual growth and progress not for perfection. Our goal is to become the best Christian person that we can with the help of Jesus Christ. It is a journey, not one big jump. We get there one step at a time, one day at a time. If we can make each day better as we go along in our spiritual walk, soon we will hardly remember the person we once were. That's exciting news and should make us all eager to experience that change.

SELF-CONTROL

In walking this new walk, it is important to exercise self-control. Let's not go charging off into the future like a "bull in a china closet". Rather, let's take it "low and slow", building carefully as we go along. We are trying to build a new house on a solid foundation one block at a time. If we should back slide for a moment into the "old me", let's recognize that immediately and take the steps that we learned to remedy that situation. If we are tempted to go back "then", remember that we now have the grace and strength of Jesus Christ to sustain and help us. When the devil comes at us in some of our old "stinkin thinkin", remember that the name of Jesus will quickly kick him out. So let's call on Jesus when the old self wants to come back.

Jesus is our help and our salvation. Let us act with thought and firmness in our new life, neither in haste nor rashness—without thought. No snap judgments, no impulsive behavior, just total, firm self-control rooted and grounded in our faith in Jesus Christ. Remember, dear friend, He walks with us. We do not walk alone unless we choose to. Control of our tongue and temper are attitudes. We must avoid, at all cost, quick-tempered criticism and furious power-driven arguments. The same goes for sulking and silent "licking of our wounds." The "woe is me" attitude is not for us. Let us beware of the traps that we once fell into. When we are tempted by a situation, we must train ourselves to STOP, "cool it", step back, pray to Jesus and think. Ask yourselves, "What would Jesus do if He were in this spot now?" We cannot act in good behavior without Jesus while under the pressure of the moment. It is very important for us to exercise self-control at all cost.

GIVE JESUS THE CREDIT FOR OUR RECOVERY

Another "beware" is the matter of success. Some of us can get "drunk" quickly when success comes our way. We seem to get that "big head" very easily. Let's remember that success belongs to Jesus, not to us. He is the one who saves us and gives us the new life. Remember when we first came into the program, we were powerless over our addiction and our life was unmanageable. Never forget that time from Step 1. Jesus is the one who saves us and gives us new hope and a new life. Certainly we should feel very happy about our newfound life and success. But let us not "let it go to our heads" for we will be sure to fall again if we do. Remember, "I didn't do it, Jesus did it for me."

AS WE ARE HEALED, WE BEGIN TO UNDERSTAND OTHER PEOPLE'S PROBLEMS

Finally, as we travel through our "new life", we will become more aware of other people and what they think and how they act. Soon, we will begin to see that the people around us have problems in their lives just as we did. As we struggle to keep our self-control, we will quickly see that it is pointless to become angry or loose our self-control. It is pointless to get hurt by another or angry with that person since they, too, suffer from the same kinds of pains deep inside that we suffered. Such a radical change in our thinking will take time, but it will come. This is the beginning of true Godly love. When we recognize that the other guy is struggling just as I did, then I see clearly that nothing but love and patience can help the situation. Anger and fighting does nothing but make it all worse.

The only Godly and loving solution is to reach out to that person in love and patience. In helping that person, we begin to experience the true meaning of love, the Christian way. We have finally begun to understand that hate and all the feelings connected with this emotion will only destroy us and hurt the other person. But love will build us up and give us true peace and a healthy life. Therefore, the goal of our new life is to love: love God, love ourselves, and love those around us even when they seem down right unlovable.

HANDLING DIFFICULT RELATIONSHIPS WITH GODLY LOVE

Love says, "I accept you just where you are! You don't have to change for me. I will love you regardless." When we can see this concept and begin to do it to the best of our ability and mean it from our hearts, we will stop making unreasonable demands on those around us. We will begin to like that person and deal with them just the way they are. This will lead us into a frame of mind where we will want to help that person rather than hurt or condemn him. We understand that we ourselves were once in that state of mind. Now that we have been healed by the power of Jesus Christ, we can extend that same healing power to our fellow brothers and sisters. When we have a "fall out" with another person we will be quick to

Step 10 Lesson 32

"I continue to take personal inventory daily and when I am wrong, I promptly admit it."

Action Words : TAKE DAILY INVENTORY

Finally, build up your strength in union with the Lord and by means of His mighty power. Put on all the armor that God gives you, so that you will be able to stand up against the Devil's evil tricks. For we are not fighting against human beings but against the wicked spiritual forces in the heavenly world, the rulers, authorities and cosmic powers, of this dark age.

So put on God's armor now! Then when the evil day comes, you will be able to resist the enemy's attacks, and after fighting to the end, you will still hold your ground.
-Ephesians 6:10-13

I forget what is behind me and do my best to reach what is ahead. So I run straight toward the goal in order to win the prize, which is God's call through Christ Jesus to the life above.
-Philippians 3:13-14

STEP 10

make amends and try to heal that relationship. We do not give love to get it back, rather we give it because that is who we have become. This new attitude is a reflection of the Christ who now lives within us. It is our joy to love others as Jesus has loved us. We will be living godly love when we can say, "Lord, your will be done, not mine." We must check ourselves by asking, "Lord, am I doing to others as I would have them do to me?"

LAYING OUR HEADS ON THE PILLOW TO SLEEP EACH NIGHT

As we lay our heads on the pillow to close out the day, let us come to the Lord Jesus in prayer. Let us look at our day just past, the good things and the not-so-good, difficult things. Let us talk to our best friend Jesus about them. The good things should cause us great joy and thanksgiving. The failures should cause us to look back to see what went wrong. Even in the failures, we should feel confident that we tried but, for the moment, we did not succeed. We should examine the situation and see how we can correct it. Amends should always be uppermost in our minds and hearts. We know that the next time we try, we will succeed by and in the power of Jesus Christ within us. Even in the days that seem disastrous, let us thank Jesus for getting us through them clean and sober and ask Him to help us learn from that experience. We need to continue to go forward on our journey.

TAKING DAILY PERSONAL INVENTORY

The following are suggestions for taking a Daily Personal Inventory. You may use whatever methods help you personally.

1. Set aside a quiet time to be alone with God—at the end of your day is best because the events of your day and your reactions are fresh and can be kept from slipping into your "Gut Box" undetected.

2. Items you might like to have with you: a Bible, your journal, paper, pen, highlighter, and "My Daily Inventory" checklist sheet.

3. Quiet yourself in a way that works for you. Ask the Holy Spirit to reveal anything hidden in your mind and heart. Ask Him to reveal not only what needs correction, but also what is positive, good, and already aligned with Him. You might choose visualized prayer for this.

4. Option 1: Examine your inventory carefully. Use an "x" to note negative attitudes. Use a "checkmark" to note positive attitudes. Option 2: Rate yourself on a scale of 0 to 4 for each attitude for that day. (0=Poor 1=Fair 2=Average 3=Good 4=Excellent).

5. Meditate on any "x's" or below average attitudes. Identify how they build on each other. Examine any offenses of the day. Focus on your own reactions and attitudes to situations. Avoid blaming others. Identify any unhealthy thoughts related to lies the enemy would like you to believe. For example: I am not good enough, no one loves me, God doesn't hear me, etc. Ask the Holy Spirit to reveal why you have these negative attitudes and where their roots are.

6. Find scripture to replace any negative thinking and meditate on it. Maybe write the scriptures several times in your journal and put them on notecards posting them where you will see them every day. Practice visualized prayer—invite Jesus into the events of the day that troubled you and ask Him to minister healing to you in those areas. Break any ungodly Soul Ties you identify. (See Soul Ties in Step 7.)

7. Caution: tackling all of these attitudes at once can be overwhelming. Choose what you feel you can begin working on successfully. For this exercise, quality is more important than quantity. As you practice this daily evaluation and become more aware of yourself, you will be able to process more at one time.

8. It may be helpful to keep a daily journal to record the insights the Holy Spirit gives you. Date each entry and try to be as specific as you can. His insights may have come as thoughts, scriptures, songs, ideas, strategies, words you recently heard from someone, etc. Keeping a journal is a tremendous tool to help you visualize how active the Lord is in your life and the progress you are making. This can be very encouraging.

STEP 10

DAILY INVENTORY DEFINITIONS

Self-Pity: exaggerated feelings of sorrow or regret for yourself (poor, poor me!)
Self-Forgetfulness: unselfish; ignoring one's own interests

Self-Justification: justifying/rationalizing your own actions, beliefs, or motives (excuses)
Humility: being aware of your own defects/shortcomings; not prideful; not asserting yourself

Self-Importance: exaggerated feelings of your own importance
Modesty: having a moderate opinion of yourself; not boastful

Self-Condemnation: feeling like you have no value or worth; punishing thoughts toward yourself
Self-Valuation: believing you have value and worth; feeling you can learn from a mistake and move on

Dishonesty: lying; deceiving; cheating; stealing
Honesty: being truthful, sincere, and fair

Impatience: not being able to bear or endure pain or trouble without complaining or losing self-control; being provoked or angered; not being able to calmly tolerate delay, confusion, inefficiency, etc.
Patience: being able to bear or endure pain or trouble without complaining or losing self-control; not being provoked or angered; being able to calmly tolerate delay, confusion, inefficiency, etc.

Hate: strong feeling of dislike or ill-will towards
Love: see 1 Corinthians 13

Resentment: strong feeling of displeasure or anger coming from feeling hurt
Forgiveness: giving up resentment against someone; giving up the desire to see them punished; giving up being angry

False Pride: thinking too highly of yourself
Simplicity: seeing yourself as you are

Jealousy: very watchful or careful in guarding or keeping your rights; resentfully suspicious of a rival; requiring exclusive loyalty
Trust: belief or confidence in another's honesty, integrity, reliability, etc.

Envy: desire for something that someone else has; feeling discontent and ill-will towards someone because of their advantages or possessions, etc.
Generosity: freely giving and sharing

Laziness: not eager or willing to work; slothful
Activity: willing to work; willing to be active to achieve your goals, dreams, and desires

Procrastination: putting off or postponing things
Promptness: quick to act and ready to do what must be done

Insincerity: not being honest, sincere, truthful, genuine, or in good faith
Straightforwardness: direct, honest, frank, open, or clear

Criticizing: looking for the bad; finding fault; disapprovingly judging someone/something
Looking for the Good: focusing on the good and positive; not finding fault

---

Step 10 Lesson 32

"I continue to take personal inventory daily and when I am wrong, I promptly admit it."

Action Words: TAKE DAILY INVENTORY

Step 10 Lesson 32

"I continue to take personal inventory daily and when I am wrong, I promptly admit it."

Action Words : TAKE DAILY INVENTORY

STEP 10

MY DAILY INVENTORY

Month _____ Year _____

LIABILITIES
Eliminate the Negative
Watch for -- X

ASSETS
Accentuate the Positive
Watch for - ✓

Liability	1	2	3	4	5	6	7	8	9	10	11	12	13	14	15	16	17	18	19	20	21	22	23	24	25	26	27	28	29	30	31	Asset
Self-pity																																Self-forgetfulness
Self-justification																																Humility
Self-importance																																Modesty
Self-condemnation																																Self-valuation
Dishonest																																Honesty
Impatience																																Patience
Hate																																Love
Resentment																																Forgiveness
False Pride																																Simplicity
Jealousy																																Trust
Envy																																Generosity
Laziness																																Activity
Procrastination																																Promptness
Insincerity																																Straightforwardness
Negative Thinking																																Positive Thinking
Criticizing/Finding fault																																Looking for the good
Sexual Fantasy/Thinking																																Sexual purity
Sexual acting out																																Walking with Jesus
Chasing old habits																																Living in recovery
Seeking the wrong																																Proclaiming the right
Failure to pray/study Bible																																Prayer/Bible study
Forgetting God																																Looking to Jesus
Out of control																																Self-control in Spirit
"I can do it"																																Only Jesus and I can

Walking the 12 Steps with Jesus Christ

STEP 11

Step 11 Lesson 33

"I seek through prayer and meditation to improve my conscious contact with God, as I understand Him, praying only for knowledge of His will for me and the power to carry that out."

Action Words:
IMPROVE MY CONSCIOUS CONTACT WITH GOD

In this step, we seek to strengthen our daily spiritual maintenance and growth by developing a closer, more intimate relationship with God. This process began in Lesson 15 under the title of prayer. At that time, prayer was discussed to get you in the "habit" of praying. We studied the essentials of prayer at that time which is our conversation with God. In this step, we will study how to come into a closer relationship to Jesus using a process called meditation and contemplation, which is a deeper encounter with the Lord. It may be good at this time to go back to Lesson 15 and review the elements of a sound prayer attitude.

MAINTAINING OUR SPIRITUAL WALK

During our walk with Jesus Christ in this program, we have used our experience and our meetings as the means to our spiritual growth and strength along with the practice of the 12 steps of the AA program and the four steps of our spiritual program. As a result of our study thus far, I sincerely pray that you have come to see the importance of coming to Jesus and making Him your constant companion and friend. Over and over again, it was emphasized that you cannot survive and overcome alone. From the very first step, we learned that we are powerless over that which controls us and only, ONLY Jesus can help us to get sober, remain sober, and overcome successfully.

This realization should cause us to long for a deeper and closer relationship with Jesus. Our hearts should hunger and thirst for a deeper friendship with our best friend, Jesus Christ. This is where a church fellowship, Bible study, and meditation become important tools for lasting spiritual growth. Many millions of overcomers have used the fellowship of brother and sister Christians and the Bible as their tools to maintain their Christian walk.

And so, taking quality time in prayer is the food necessary for our spiritual life to grow and prosper. We need to set aside a specific time to come to our friend Jesus to pray and meditate each and every day. There must be NO excuses. Even if we don't "feel like it", we still must come and be with Him each day in the best way that we can for the moment.

Studying the Bible helps us to know Jesus better and to learn what He wants for us in our daily life. How can we know someone if we pay little or no attention to Him? If we seek to build up a friendship, we spend time with that person. Jesus is calling us to do that now. If we have neglected this practice, now is the time to correct that.

Throughout this study guide, many scripture references have been used to help you get into the Bible and to learn from it. They have been provided for you to use over and over again. Please take the time to study each reference carefully and think upon it. Let it sink into your mind and heart. Read around the reference, before and after, to get the full meaning of the verse. Let your Bible study become a form of prayer for you. It truly is a time to think on the Lord.

Earlier in this program, I discussed prayer in depth. At times, we prayed together as a group and we also shared. Prayer is simply our conversation with God. Remember, our best prayer is to say "yes" to Jesus and to become one with Him in mind, body, and spirit. We grow in our method of praying as we do it. Deeper prayer will follow each time we come to Jesus. Our concept should be my oneness with Jesus. It should be a pleasant time of being with our best friend. We begin in a simple fashion and keep working at it. No fancy words are necessary. Just tell Jesus what is in your heart. He loves you right where you are right now. Don't try to solve your problems, rather give them to Jesus. See yourself letting go of the problems one by one. Then, listen to His "still small voice" and feel His healing touch. You will never experience anything like it anywhere in the world.

Remember to pray regularly throughout the day. It does not have to take long and it makes no difference where you are. It may take the time that you are sitting and waiting for a traffic light to change while driving. It may be a difficult time when you cannot seem to get a mechanical situation to work. It may be a purely mental problem that does not seem to want to be solved. Jesus walks with you and is at your side. See Him and open up to Him. That's prayer. Simply speak a few simple words to Him. He hears you even though you may not utter a sound. Jesus is your silent friend.

Also remember, never go to sleep at night without giving Him your day, your successes, failures, and sins. Be sure to take your daily, personal inventory and ask Him to forgive you for the sins of the day. Speak to Jesus, for He loves you and cares for you. Give yourself to Him and listen for His answer.

Another prayer might be reviewing the program in your mind. Remember Step 1 when you admitted that by yourself you could not overcome. Then, in Steps 2 and 3, you came to know Jesus in a more intimate way and gave your will and life over to Him. Think of His presence with you in Step 4 as you made your inventory and then gave that to Him in Steps 5, 6 and 7. See how He met you and entered your house of prayer when you came to Him sincerely. See how He revealed Himself to you in the Holy Word and how you came to know Him better in the fellowship of Church. See how you began to train your body in the self-control He gave you in your practice of fasting.

Step 11 Lesson 33

"I seek through prayer and meditation to improve my conscious contact with God, as I understand Him, praying only for knowledge of His will for me and the power to carry that out."

Action Words:
IMPROVE MY CONSCIOUS CONTACT WITH GOD

This is the same Jesus who now calls you to allow Him to be your best friend, not just for the moment, but for the rest of your life. When you take the self-examination, the confession, and the healing of this program and put them together with Jesus, there is a new life created deep within you. Jesus is the strength that causes this new life. Without Him, we could never have gained that new life. Without Him, we will lose that new life. So our prayer life is essential to staying "plugged into" that new life which is ours in Christ Jesus.

MEDITATION - WHAT IS IT?

In prayer, we talk to God. In Bible study, God talks to us. In prayer, we pour our hearts out to Him. In Bible study, He reveals Himself to us in thousands of different ways. Meditation is putting this process of speaking and listening together. We talk to God, and then we listen to Him. Meditation allows the good in us, however small that may be, to be watered, to grow and flower by the grace of God. Meditation allows us to step out into the "sunlight" of God and to allow this new creation within us to grow and develop. Meditation is taking time to allow God to speak to us and to HEAR HIM.

In meditation, we take a written prayer or a portion of scripture and we read it over slowly. We allow each word to sink deep into our spirit. Then we listen for God's "still small voice". We concentrate on being with Jesus, nothing more, nothing less.

A typical prayer is the one given below, the Prayer of St. Francis:

Lord, make me an instrument of your peace; where there is hatred - may I bring love; where there is wrong, may I bring your spirit of forgiveness; where there is discord - may I bring harmony; where there is error - may I bring your truth; where there is doubt - may I bring faith; where there is despair - may I bring your hope; where there is darkness - may I bring light; and where there is sadness - may I bring your joy;

Lord, grant that I may seek rather to comfort than to be comforted; to understand - rather than to be understood; to love, rather than to be loved.

For it is in giving and forgetting self that we find the answer; it is in forgiving that we are forgiven; and it is dying to our self that we enter into Eternal Life. AMEN!

EXPERIENCING MEDITATION

To experience meditation, is to take the above prayer or a similar scripture reading and re-read it slowly several times. It is not necessary that we use the above prayer. Any good prayer or scripture will do. Let each word sink deep into our spirit as we soak up every word from God. Let the deep meaning of each phrase and idea sink deep into us. Hear the Lord speaking to us through these words. If we hear the Lord speaking in addition to these words, stop and listen carefully. Rejoice that Jesus is speaking to you and you are hearing Him in your spirit. Drop all outside thoughts and resistance from your own mind and spirit. Let your spirit be IN Christ Jesus, not in the world or your own thoughts.

As we lie in the "sunshine" of God's word speaking to us, let us relax and deeply partake of the spiritual goodness which this prayer gives us. Let us become willing to receive and be strengthened and lifted up by His tremendous spiritual touch, the power and love of Jesus, which these words bring to us. Let us look deep into the presence of Jesus who is within us and is speaking to us. Let us visualize becoming the person that this prayer describes. Like little children, let us look into the Father's eyes through the eyes of Jesus. We are in the Holy Presence of the Eternal God and Father through Jesus Christ, His Son. We are allowing that presence to remake us into the "New Creation" of the Bible. God is touching us in a deeply spiritual way. Let us give our spiritual imagination over to our God. Let Him speak to us and transform our mind.

This is meditation. It has no boundaries and is a very individual adventure, something that each one of us works out in his own way. It is a very private time of listening to Jesus within us. Its object is always the same, to improve our conscious contact with the grace of Jesus and receive the touch of His wisdom and love. Meditation is a very practical and strengthening exercise. Its fruit is emotional balance and control because it helps us to walk arm in arm with the Master. We are building a new relationship with our new friend and Lord, Jesus Christ.

In prayer and meditation, we are in constant union with our Creator and Best Friend Jesus. It is in this union with Him that He gives us the "knowledge of His will for us and the power to carry that will out". We have "turned on" the light of His Spirit. We no longer walk by ourselves in darkness; rather, we now walk in union with Jesus who is the light. The responsibility for overcoming our old self is no longer ours alone. It now rests with Jesus AND us. We can now go about looking forward to each day as a new adventure in a new life with Jesus. We can plan each day so that it will come

STEP 11

Step 11 Lesson 33

"I seek through prayer and meditation to improve my conscious contact with God, as I understand Him, praying only for knowledge of His will for me and the power to carry that out."

Action Words:
IMPROVE MY CONSCIOUS CONTACT WITH GOD

out right. Our thinking is no longer ours alone, but it is in union with Jesus.

This new way of thinking brings us to a new awareness of Jesus and how He fits into our life. We now know that we must consider Him in all that we do. Our mind set will now go like this, "Lord, not my will be done—but Yours!" We will constantly ask the Lord what He would have us do in a certain situation. We will be aware of and seek after His will rather than our will.

When we have a disturbance in our day that clogs up our communication with the Lord Jesus, we stop and remember who is our strength and guidance. Just repeating the name of Jesus over and over will unclog our anger, fear, frustration, or whatever is "messing us up". We can deal with those regular temptations in the same manner. Let us submit to our "Higher Power", Jesus, to do His will rather than our own. That's how we overcome.

A WORD OF CAUTION

Let us be certain that the word that we hear in our mind and spirit is the word of Jesus and not our own imaginings. How do we do that? By simply waiting and allowing our spirit to tell us to act. A good word to remember, "When in doubt, wait on the Lord Jesus to give a clear affirmative answer". If doubt is still present, pray with a friend and listen, LISTEN for His "still small voice" inside.

Another caution. Be concerned only for what is going on inside of us, for our own moral and spiritual guidance. NEVER tell another that the Lord has given you the cure for his or her spiritual life. Always remember to pray for that person in God's will, not ours. May the will and presence of Jesus be done in him, neither his will nor ours. This should be our prayer.

CONTEMPLATION

Before closing our discussion of meditation, I would like to comment briefly about another type of meditative prayer called contemplation. Contemplative prayer is a form of prayer where we simply "sit with Jesus". This type of prayer uses the visualized form that was discussed previously.

The following is an example of a contemplative prayer that I have used many times in my own personal life. It is personal to me and I use it here as an example only:

I visualize myself being in the woods very early in my life when I was a boy. I see myself climbing a mountain path at which time I come across a mountain stream. As I sit on a rock next to the stream, I look up the path leading to the top of the mountain and I see a man coming toward me. He comes near to me and stops in the path looking at me. I see him as a very big and strong man dressed in cut off jeans and tee shirt with worn sneakers full of holes. I begin to study him and see that he has scars on his wrists and ankles and around the forehead. I notice his peaceful smile and finally come to recognize him as Jesus, my Savior. He is calling me to come closer to Him. Finally I get up and go to Him. He hugs me and whispers how much He loves me into my ear.

To end the prayer, I see myself walking up the path arm in arm with Jesus into eternity. This visualized prayer has been a favorite of mine for many years. I use it regularly to come close to my Jesus. I find great peace in being with Jesus during this time together. It is our favorite meeting place - Jesus and I.

I recommend that you develop a visualized prayer such as this with Jesus. Close your eyes and go to your favorite place in nature. It may be the seashore, the countryside, or a mountain. It may be scuba diving, or skydiving, or fishing. Just go to the place you love the best, your retreat with Jesus. Then visualize seeing Jesus there. Put Him into a human body form - draw near to Him and let Him touch you. Let Him put His arms around you and love you just as you are. It's a beautiful experience, one you will use over and over again whenever you need it. Try it; you'll be pleasantly surprised.

THE RESULTS OF THE AA EXPERIENCE

Those who have persisted in the AA 12 step experience over the years have found strength far beyond their own capacity. They have found wisdom beyond themselves and have increasingly found a peace of mind, which can stand firm in the face of any difficulty or addictive habit. They have discovered that they receive guidance for their lives to the extent that they stop making demands upon God to "give it to me on my orders and on my terms!" Any successful overcomer who has walked these steps will tell how his affairs have taken remarkable and unexpected turns for the better as they tried to improve their conscious contact with God through prayer and meditation. Even when times "got tough", or when God seemed to come down hard on them, they were able to stand in the trial by the power of Jesus within them. They had learned new lessons for successful living and coping with the problems of life. They had new courage and determination to go on and overcome in the mighty name of Jesus. Finally, the overcomer came to understand that, God truly does "move in strange and mysterious ways and that He does care and work miracles".

Step 11 Lesson 33

STEP 11

"I seek through prayer and meditation to improve my conscious contact with God, as I understand Him, praying only for knowledge of His will for me and the power to carry that out."

Action Words:
IMPROVE MY CONSCIOUS CONTACT WITH GOD

My sheep listen to My voice; I know them, and they follow Me.
I give them eternal life, and they shall never die. No one can snatch them away from Me. What my Father has given Me is greater than everything, and no one can snatch them away from the Father's care. The Father and I are one.

-John 10:27-30

We are only as sick as our secrets.

-Anonymous

"My sheep listen to My voice; I know them, and they follow Me."

-John 10:27

The task ahead of us is never as great as the POWER behind us.

-Anonymous

Forgiveness is a gift I give myself.

-Anonymous

Remain united to Me, and I will remain united to you. A branch cannot bear fruit by itself; it can do so only if it remains in the vine. In the same way you cannot bear fruit unless you remain in Me.

-John 15:4

All of this should convince us, beyond a doubt, that there is nothing but a new and exciting life ahead of us. Maybe we won't feel like it, or even come to a time when we just can't stand to pray. But pray we must or we will die spiritually. The Lord recognizes us, especially during those times of difficulty, and gives us the special touch we need to get back "on track". He shows Himself to us in a most miraculous way.

Perhaps one of the greatest rewards of meditation and prayer is the sense of BELONGING that comes to us. That sense of doing it alone or being totally alone in this world is gone forever. We know that, even if the whole world is against us, Jesus is for us. We truly "have a friend in Jesus!" We no longer live in a completely hostile world. We are no longer lost and frightened and purposeless. The moment we grasp the presence of Jesus in our lives and give ourselves over to Him, we begin to see truth, justice, and love as the real and everlasting moments in our life. We are no longer totally overcome by the hopelessness and sin of the world around us. So then, prayer and meditation lifts us from the depths of this world and our sin into the very arms of God the Father through Jesus Christ, His Son. We know that God lovingly watches over us. We know that, when we turn to Him, all is well with us in our spirit, now and in the hereafter.

May the Lord Jesus richly bless you and give you the strength and determination to stay in constant contact with Him and His all-sustaining grace through prayer and meditation. AMEN!

SCRIPTURE STUDY;

The following scriptures are provided with respect to Healing Step 11. Please study them carefully and see how they apply to this step:

- Psalm 1:1-3
- Galatians 5:22-26
- Psalm 50:14-15
- Galatians 6:14
- Psalm 55:22
- Ephesians 1:17-19
- Psalm 105:1-4
- Ephesians 3:14-20
- Matthew 5:6
- Ephesians 5:19-21
- Luke 6:20-26
- Ephesians 6:10-18
- Luke 6:46-49
- Philippians 1:20-21
- Luke 12:27-34
- Philippians 1:27-29
- Luke 17:7-10
- Philippians 3:7-14
- Luke 22:42
- Colossians 2:6-10
- John 3:30
- Colossians 3:14-17
- John 8:31-32
- Colossians 3:23-24
- John 14:12-21
- 1 Thessalonians 4:9-12
- John 15:4-11
- 2 Thessalonians 2:16-17
- John 16:23-27
- 2 Timothy 1:12-14
- Acts 20:28-32
- 2 Timothy 2:15
- Romans 5:3-5
- 2 Timothy 3:14-17
- Romans 12:10-13
- Titus 3:14
- 1 Corinthians 10:31
- Hebrews 13:1-16
- 1 Corinthians 14:20
- James 1:22-27
- 1 Corinthians 15:58
- 1 Peter 4:7-11
- 1 Corinthians 16:13-14
- 1 Peter 5:8-10
- 2 Corinthians 3:17-18
- 2 Peter 1:2-8
- 2 Corinthians 5:6-9
- 1 John 1:7
- 2 Corinthians 5:14-15
- 1 John 5:4-5
- 2 Corinthians 9:6-15
- 1 John 5:18-21

MEDITATIONS

Step 11 Lesson 34

"I seek through prayer and meditation to improve my conscious contact with God, as I understand Him, praying only for knowledge of His will for me and the power to carry that out."

Scripture :
MEDITATIONS

DAY ONE - Study John 4:13-14

As we journey through life, most of us find ourselves "thirsty" for the love, peace, security, and sense of purpose in our life. Life produces hurts in our spirit. We long for completeness and wholeness. We long for a healthy life inside. We long to find out exactly who we are and how life "fits together" for us.

As we collect so many hurts during our lives, these hurts build up in us from our early childhood. Most of us try to put out the fire of these hurts through some addictive misbehavior. Sometimes, we struggle with this addiction for years until finally, in desperation, we begin to search for the answer. It is in this search, we may come across a 12 step program and we are introduced to God in a new, life saving way.

The story of the Samaritan woman at the well in today's reading is an example of a hurting, mixed up, sinful person coming to Jesus. The woman discovers Jesus at the well and strikes up a conversation about water. Jesus offers her "His water" and she is confused a bit. Finally, He clarifies what He means in today's reading. Jesus says, "The water that I will give him will become in him a spring which will provide him with life-giving water and give him eternal life." (Verse 14)

When we come to Jesus and accept Him into our lives as our personal Lord and Savior, we, too, receive His life-giving water unto eternal life. Jesus washes us clean of our sins by His life-giving water. (See Ephesians 5:26-27) As we are washed in the cleansing water of Jesus, we receive His Spirit and the fruit of His Spirit, which is: love, joy, peace, patience, kindness, goodness, faithfulness, humility, and self-control. (See Galatians 5:22) In short, as we receive Jesus into our lives, through His Holy Word the Bible, we are filled with His life. In receiving His life, we are healed from our past hurts. Are you ready for that healing?

DAY TWO - Study Romans 8:26-28

This Healing Step 11 shows us quite clearly that our overcoming, our sobriety, is dependent on the state of our relationship with Jesus. If we remain closely connected to Jesus, we will walk a successful, sober, and spiritually healthy life. If we get sloppy in our connection with Jesus, we will fall right back into our old self. Our principle connection with God (Father, Son, and Holy Spirit) is through Jesus Christ by the power of His Holy Spirit living in us each day. This connection is brought about through prayer and Bible study.

Our reading today gives us confidence that we can approach our God through the power of the Holy Spirit, which is the living presence of Jesus and the Father in our lives today. The Holy Spirit is the connection, the "phone line", between us and Jesus and the Father. In addition, the Holy Spirit prays to Jesus and the Father in accordance with the will of the Father. (See verse 27) He, the Holy Spirit, translates our prayer into God's language for us. As a result, we pray not according to our will but according to the will of God himself. The Holy Spirit living in us makes our prayer perfect. What a blessing to know that we can come to our God who will always understand us even if we can't say it the way we should. His Spirit does it for us.

Are you willing, dear friend, to give this Holy Spirit a try in your life today? I pray that you will.

DAY THREE - Study Galatians 2:20

A famous AA saying is - "Let go and let God!" In our walking the twelve steps with Jesus Christ, we have learned this principle over and over again. We no longer walk by ourselves through this life, now we have learned and practiced walking with Jesus Christ. In this process, We have given up being god in our lives, instead we have made Jesus Christ the God of our life. We have learned that by making ourselves the god of our life, we have failed miserably; but when we make Jesus the God of our life, we can and will overcome and be healed. We can and will walk a sane, sober, happy, healthy spiritual life. In short, we have "put to death" our own control and given the control to Jesus.

Paul states clearly what we have learned when he says, "It is no longer I who live but it is Christ who lives in me!" (Verse 20) We have become "born again" into the Spirit of Jesus Christ, the Holy Spirit. We are no longer the same spiritual person we were before; rather we have become a "new me" through the power of the Holy Spirit.

How do we live this new life? The latter part of this verse tells us, "This life that I live now, I live by faith in the Son of God, who loved me and gave His life for me." Finally, finally in our lives, we let go of our

Step 11 Lesson 34

"I seek through prayer and meditation to improve my conscious contact with God, as I understand Him, praying only for knowledge of His will for me and the power to carry that out."

Scripture: MEDITATIONS

old self and begin to let God. We finally begin to experience this rebirth in the Spirit. What we could not do for ourselves before (remember Step 1), the Holy Spirit is now accomplishing for us. We now know how to handle the problems of our new life as they "come down the pike". We are now overcoming that addiction which once drove us insane in misbehavior.

Have you begun to experience your "new life" in Jesus Christ? I pray that you have and that you will continue to grow in that new life.

DAY FOUR - Study Philippians 4:5-9

Healing Step 11 deals with prayer; not just ordinary conversation with Jesus, but rather a new more intimate and meaningful relationship with Him. There are many methods to accomplish this new conversation with Jesus in meditation and contemplation. Simply put, this reading gives us a new attitude that helps us to make this "holy connection" with our God. Here are some suggestions from today's reading:

First - We are to quiet our inner self with all its anxieties and stress. The reading says, "Show a gentle attitude toward everyone." - "Don't worry."

Second - We are to "ask God for what we need, always asking him with a thankful heart". Be thankful for God and our new relationship with Him.

Third - Receive the peace that He wants to give us. Verse 7 tells us that His peace "will keep your hearts and minds safe in union with Christ Jesus"! Take time to open up our inner self to His peace. We don't need a whole bunch of words; just visualize Jesus touching us.

Fourth - We are called to "fill your minds with those things that are good and that deserve praise, things that are true, noble, right, pure, lovely, and honorable". (Verse 8) We are to push out the evil things of the past in our minds and fill our minds with the "things of God".

Fifth - In verse 9, we are called to "Put into practice what we have learned: both from my words and from my actions". We are to live what we have learned.

Above all, we are not to be anxious or "up tight" about anything in our lives. We are to place ourselves in the loving arms of Jesus our Savior. Have you placed yourself in the arms of Jesus? I pray that you have.

DAY FIVE - Study Titus 3:2-7

The description of our spiritual sickness causes us to think that we can "save ourselves". Over and over again, we have tried to heal the hurt of our spiritual pain by the use of our addiction, and over and over again we have failed. There is just no way that you and I can "save ourselves". If we could, Jesus would not have had to die on the cross of Calvary to set us free from our sins and addictions. The fact is, that, by ourselves, we have no power over that which "bugs" us. Remember Step 1?

As we progress in our recovery process, we still find ourselves thinking that we can somehow "work our way into heaven" or that we have to earn the "grace of God" by self-works, or doing things we think will heal us.

The simple fact is that our healing is a gift from God who loves us beyond our wildest dreams. We don't have to earn it. In fact, we can't earn it. There is just nothing we can do to pay the price for being saved. The only thing that God asks of us is to come to Him and to say, "Yes, Lord, I give myself to You, just as I am. Save me Lord, please!"

In verse 3, our reading describes our former state of life, "We ourselves were once foolish, disobedient and wrong. We were slaves to our passions and pleasures of all kinds. We spent our lives in malice and envy, others hated us and we hated them." (Verse 3)

But in verse 4, we find the saving power of Jesus who saved us. "It was not because of any good deeds that we ourselves had done, but because of His own mercy that He saved us through the Holy Spirit, who gives us new birth and new life by washing us."

MEDITATIONS

Step 11 Lesson 34

"I seek through prayer and meditation to improve my conscious contact with God, as I understand Him, praying only for knowledge of His will for me and the power to carry that out."

Scripture :
MEDITATIONS

This miracle of salvation shows us clearly that we walk, not by ourselves, but now we walk with Jesus WHO SAVES US! This walking with Jesus is a day-to-day situation in which we are saved moment-by-moment. As long as we walk with Jesus, we experience and receive that salvation. When we leave Him and proceed to walk alone, we will fail.

Meditation in prayer is one of the important and necessary ways in which we maintain that walk with Jesus. It is a time set aside alone in which we refuel our spiritual life with the mighty power of the Holy Spirit who sustains us and keeps us walking straight. Are you willing to give this special time to the Lord Jesus each day for the rest of your life? It is the insurance of your sobriety and self-control.

DAY SIX - Study Psalm 84:5-12

In the days of the Psalmist, the Jews journeyed to the Temple at Jerusalem for their special time of "in-filling" from the Lord. They believed that they had to go to the Temple to receive the strength, forgiveness and blessings from the Lord.

In the New Testament, Jesus tells us in Luke 17:21, "No one will say - 'look here it is, or there it is!', because the Kingdom of God is within you." You and I today do not need to go to the Temple of Jerusalem because you and I are the temple of God's Holy Spirit.

Yet, our travel through daily life takes us over lots of rough roads and dangerous paths. As the Jews searched for God in the Temple, we have only to turn within to find Him. If we open up to Him in these special times of prayer, we will be prepared for anything we may meet along the "road of life". Jesus walks with us, so let us PRAISE HIM! This Psalm today is a beautiful way to turn to Jesus. Let us "stand up at the gate of the house of God". (Verse 10) For "The Lord is our protector and glorious king, blessing us with kindness and honor." (Verse 11)

The result, "Lord Almighty, how happy are those who trust in you!" (Verse 12) Have you turned to the Lord Jesus? Have you given Him your total self and trusted in Him so that He can make you happy? I pray that you have.

DAY SEVEN - Study Psalm 127:1-2

Some of us have grown up in life to think, "Hard work is the measure of our success in life". We seem to get the idea that if we want something, all we have to do is work hard enough and we will get it. Our whole life seems to be measured in money and wealth. Now there is nothing wrong with good honest daily work. God commands that we work so that we can receive His blessings. What about working to heal our spirit? In today's reading we learn that "If the Lord does not build the house, the work of the builders is useless". (Verse 1)

Those of us who have walked this program or any AA program, know how useless it is for us to try to "rebuild our shattered house" by ourselves. We just cannot heal or rebuild that aching spirit within us. In our reading today, we find that our source of supply is the Lord Jesus. He takes care of our spirit, our body and the total of our life, if we will let Him.

As we complete our study of meditation and contemplation, let us see clearly that the way that we rebuild our lives is to come to Jesus. He is the "Master Builder" and only when we let Him rebuild our lives can we succeed. Verse 2 tells us, "For the Lord provides for those He loves". All that is necessary is for us to turn to Him and yield ourselves to Him. Our God will supply our every need and show us the way if we do.

Have you turned to Jesus in prayerful meditation? He is the source of your strength and guidance. I pray that you have and will continue to do so. AMEN!

Walking the 12 Steps with Jesus Christ

SERVICE

Lesson 35

Healing Step 12
"Having had a spiritual awakening as a result of these steps, I try to carry this message to others with my addiction and to practice these principles in all my affairs."

Growth & Strength Step 8
"I make a daily effort to give the healing and strength which I have received from the Holy Spirit to those in my life around me. I make a sincere daily practice of loving others as Jesus loves me."

Action Words:
CARRY THE MESSAGE - LOVE

Let us hold on firmly to the hope we profess, because we can trust God to keep his promise.

Let us be concerned for one another, to help one another to show love and to do good.
-Hebrews 10:23-24

SERVICE STEPS

VICTORY IN JESUS IS IN MY HAND

At last, we have come to the final step. We may think, "Now I can sit back and relax, I'm healed and done. My addiction is part of my past." However, the truth is that we have just begun to really understand what walking each day with Jesus looks like.

WE WALK NO LONGER ALONE

We have learned that we are not alone in our walk. Not only is Jesus with us, but a whole bunch of brothers and sisters as well. All of a sudden, a new world of people is around us, people we never saw before in this light. In the past, we saw them only to take advantage of them, to "use" them to get our way in our addictive behavior. Now, we begin to see them as fellow brothers and sisters in Christ Jesus, people who are struggling to overcome the same or similar kinds of problems that we have. All of a sudden, we find ourselves with new friends, most of whom are sincere about their recovery and overcoming. And all of this is very exciting, and it should be.

As we progress in our spiritual healing and growth, we begin to recognize that - "Hey, if Jesus lives in me, then Jesus lives in the other guy, too!" As Jesus is my healing and my overcoming friend, so is He the same with the others around me. We say to ourselves, "Wow, I'm no longer alone in this search for the solution. I don't have to walk it alone anymore. There are people all around me who are seeking the same overcoming solution, and that solution is a personal relationship with Jesus.

WE EXPERIENCE THE JOY OF JESUS

Living life in Jesus is our challenge for the rest of our lives. Not only are we called to accept and rejoice in the miracle, we are also called to live it AND to give it away to those all around us.

GIVE IT AWAY - WHY?

"How can that be?" you may ask. "How can I give away what I have found in Jesus and still keep it? That does not seem to make any sense." And that, dear friend, is the true miracle of Jesus. You see -Jesus is love. And love is not love until it is given away, unselfishly and with no strings attached. The miracle is the more you give it away, the more you open yourself up to God's love and the more He will fill you. God will not be outdone, dear friend. He is the eternal source of love. We must open up to that love, receive it, and give it away. In that way, we become instruments of His love. The more we give the love of Jesus to another, the more we are filled with His love. This is exactly what Jesus was talking about in John 4:14, when He said, "The water that I will give him will become in him a spring which will provide him with life giving water and give him eternal life." Jesus has filled us with His life giving water, not to keep, but to give away to those around us so that they can drink and be filled with the presence of Jesus also. In that way, we keep filling ourselves with the fresh clean life giving water of Jesus Christ.

THE JOY OF "LIVING IN JESUS"

CARRY THE MESSAGE - LOVE OTHERS, are the action words for these steps. We must give away what we have received to those around us. Jesus calls us to turn outward toward our fellow brothers and sisters in the Lord who struggle around us. They may have a similar problem to ours or they may have a totally different one. Regardless, we are now in a position to "give away what we have received". The solution to their problem is exactly the same regardless of the type of problem. That solution is Jesus Christ. Here we begin to practice the kind of giving that is totally selfless, which asks for no rewards and with no strings attached. We seek no favors or repayment in any way. Jesus gave to us freely. We give to others in the same way in His name. We begin to practice all 12 steps of this program in our daily life so that those around us may find their way, as we have.

OUR SPIRITUAL AWAKENING

In these steps, we refer to what has happened to us as a spiritual awakening. Our spiritual awakening is a very personal experience and will probably be somewhat different for each of us. But we certainly have something very special in common for all of us. We now have the control over our lives that we did not have back there "when". We also feel a new strength within us that guides us and protects us each moment of each day. We have been given a gift which amounts to a new state of consciousness and being, a new inner self. We have been set on a new path that tells us we are someone that God loves and we are going somewhere. In addition, we now find ourselves being able to love "me" and to love those around us. Our life is no longer dead and without purpose. In a very real sense, we have been transformed, made new, because we have laid hold of a source of strength which we had never known before. We have acquired new habits in place of the old ones. We have received a new honesty, tolerance, unselfishness, and peace of mind that we had never known.

LET GO - AND LET GOD

By allowing the hurts and wrongs of your past to come out, you should have experienced a sense

SERVICE STEPS

of relief inwardly. The burden of those hurts and wrongs should have lifted. Does this mean that everything will be perfect and that we will no longer have any troubles? Does this mean that there is never a chance that our old life will return again like a bad dream? Of course not. Life is never perfect for anyone. Troubles will come and challenge us. We may even fall back into our old ways for a time. But now, there is one big difference. Now we know, we have tasted the solution. We know who the answer is and His name is Jesus Christ. We may let go of His hand and fall back temporarily, but we also know that as Jesus saved us once, He will do it over and over again. It sometimes takes many tries to totally overcome. His hand is always there, waiting for us.

THROUGH GIVING, WE RECEIVE

Acts 20:35 says, "It is more blessed to give than to receive." Through the process of giving to others, we are further filled with the grace we need to continue to be strengthened to overcome. A spiritual principle is at work. The more we give love away, the more we receive God's love in return. When we meet another person suffering from addiction, we may gladly share our walk with Jesus that has restored our sanity and transformed us. If it worked for us, it will work for them.

OUR GIFT - TOTAL HEALING

When we first came into the program, we expected to be healed of a particular addiction. Now, we have found that, not only have we been healed of that addiction, but also we have received far more than a specific healing. Instead, we have received the gift of a profound spiritual awakening, a new life. In a sense, the addiction, the pain, the healing of the addiction all have only been stepping-stones to a spiritual transformation and renewal.

A powerful tradition of the AA program is, "You can't keep it unless you give it away." That tradition is very true. This giving away part of the recovery program provides a bridge between the 12 step program and the Christian Church.

WE ARE THE PRESENCE OF JESUS TO THOSE AROUND US - CAN WE SEE THAT AND ACT ON IT?

The scripture which is so very important to us in these lessons is Matthew 28:18-20. Jesus drew near and said to them, "I have been given all authority in heaven and on earth. Go, then, to all peoples everywhere and make them my disciples, baptize them in the name of the Father, the Son, and the Holy Spirit, and teach them to obey everything I have commanded you. And I will be with you always, to the end of the age."

As part of the "giving away" process in this program, Pastors, Ministers, Counselors, and Psychologists have learned that there is a very important need for fellowship among those sharing the same or similar problems. That is why the founders of the AA program encouraged 12 steppers to help others with the same types of problems. These founders were Christians and knew very well the verse in Matthew given above by Jesus. Therefore, it is most important that we obey the Bible and traditions of the AA program and do the same. We must reach out to those who are hurting and tell them about Jesus and what He did for us. That is the principle, which Jesus gave us in the above, quoted verse from Matthew 28. We are to bring the message to "all peoples everywhere". We are to bring the healing water of Baptism; we are to help them to believe that none should be lost. "Believers will be given the power to perform miracles; they will drive out demons in My name.... they will place their hands on sick people and these will get well." Study Mark 16:15-18, to seek the power that God gives to us believers.

THE OVERCOMING STAGE

In this stage, we gather together all that we have learned and experienced in our walk with Jesus Christ and practice it for the rest of our lives. This means, if we have been spiritually transformed, others will begin to observe that in our financial, family, work, and personal lives. Our new spiritual selves will be very apparent in all the areas of our lives. Others cannot help but take notice of the new person in us. Be certain that you show them what Jesus has done for you, but be certain that you do this in a humble manner—with no pride or puffed up attitude. Remember, the Bible teaches that pride comes before the fall. Our attitude as Christians is to humbly serve others as Jesus came to serve us.

One last word. It is a recognized fact that those closest to us are most often the ones who understand our addiction and the process of recovery the least. It is very important to patiently encourage spouses and older children to become involved in the 12 step recovery process of AA. Of course, it is imperative that such learning includes the presence of Jesus Christ, for without Him, there is little or no lasting healing possible.

SERVICE Lesson 35

Healing Step 12
"Having had a spiritual awakening as a result of these steps, I try to carry this message to others with my addiction and to practice these principles in all my affairs."

Growth & Strength Step 8
"I make a daily effort to give the healing and strength which I have received from the Holy Spirit to those in my life around me. I make a sincere daily practice of loving others as Jesus loves me."

Action Words:
CARRY THE MESSAGE - LOVE

The measure of our success in life is our ability to love others as Jesus loved us.
For love is not love until it is given away; freely and unselfishly with no strings attached.
-Ray Geisel

Do not conform yourselves to the standards of this world, but let God transform you inwardly by a complete change of your mind. Then you will be able to know the will of God -what is good and is pleasing to Him.
-Romans 12:2

Walking the 12 Steps with Jesus Christ

SERVICE STEPS

SERVICE
Lesson 35

Healing — Step 12
"Having had a spiritual awakening as a result of these steps, I try to carry this message to others with my addiction and to practice these principles in all my affairs."

Growth & Strength — Step 8
"I make a daily effort to give the healing and strength which I have received from the Holy Spirit to those in my life around me. I make a sincere daily practice of loving others as Jesus loves me."

Action Words:
CARRY THE MESSAGE - LOVE

This can be done by taking this course or by attending AL-Anon meetings or similar meetings for dependents of those addicted. In this way, those close to us can come to understand the nature of our addictions and the process of healing and recovery. Not only will they come to understand this process more completely, but they will also be healed in their inner selves as well.

"FORGET YOURSELF - CARRY YOUR CROSS AND FOLLOW JESUS"
- Mark 8:34

In conclusion, I would like to offer you an example that might be your goal for the days and years to come. In the scripture quoted above, Jesus says, "If anyone wants to come with Me, he must forget himself, carry his cross and follow Me. For whoever wants to save his own life will lose it; but whoever loses his life for Me and for the gospel will save it." Jesus clearly declares that we are to lay down our life for Him and for the cause of His Word. You see, He created us for Himself - and we will never be happy until and unless we come to HIM. It is in denying our selfish desires and ourselves and giving ourselves to others that we come to Eternal Life. These two steps give us the challenge to do that. We have received the healing touch of Jesus. Now it is our turn to give that touch to another person and to keep giving it away. Throughout the life of Jesus, He gave Himself totally to others, healing, casting out demons, raising the dead, calming the storm, feeding the five thousand, and on and on. His whole life was spent in giving. We are called to do likewise. Then we will be complete and whole Christians who can walk the road of life in a healthy, happy, and sober manner.

May our God and Father Himself and our Lord Jesus prepare the way for us to come to you! May the Lord make your love for one another and for all people grow more and more and become as great as our love for you. In this way He will strengthen you, and you will be perfect and holy in the presence of our God and Father when our Lord Jesus comes with all who belong to Him. AMEN!
-1 Thessalonians 3:11-13

Hold close to your heart the love of God, Let go of the wrongs that hurt you.
-Ray Geisel

SCRIPTURE STUDY:
The following scriptures are provided with respect to these last steps. Please study them carefully and see how they apply to these final steps.

- ☐ Psalm 22:22-26
- ☐ 2 Corinthians 5:18-20
- ☐ Psalm 40:1-8
- ☐ Galatians 6:1-2
- ☐ Psalm 78:4
- ☐ Ephesians 2:10
- ☐ Psalm 106:1-3
- ☐ Philippians 1:6
- ☐ Psalm 107:1-2
- ☐ Colossians 1:9-13
- ☐ Psalm 107:21-22
- ☐ Colossians 1:27-29
- ☐ Psalm 111
- ☐ 1 Thessalonians 1:2-4
- ☐ Psalm 145
- ☐ 1 Thessalonians 2-3-4
- ☐ Matthew 5:16
- ☐ 1 Thessalonians 2:10-12
- ☐ Luke 12:35-40
- ☐ 1 Thessalonians 5:14
- ☐ John 4:34-36
- ☐ 1 Timothy 1:5
- ☐ John 16:33
- ☐ Titus 2:7-8
- ☐ Romans 1:14-17
- ☐ Hebrews 10:24-25
- ☐ Romans 10:14-15
- ☐ James 5:7-8
- ☐ 1 Corinthians 16:9
- ☐ James 5:19-20
- ☐ 2 Corinthians 2:14-17
- ☐ 1 Peter 2:9-10
- ☐ 2 Corinthians 4:1-2
- ☐ 1 Peter 3:15-16
- ☐ 2 Corinthians 5:10-11

Walking the 12 Steps with Jesus Christ

MEDITATIONS

DAY ONE - Study Mark 5:18-20

We have come to the end of our study of the 12 step program. Like the demon-possessed man, we may feel the wonderful healing touch of Jesus within us. We may want to go to the top of the mountain and just worship Jesus and live for Him each day for the rest of our lives, in peace and quiet, separating ourselves from others. But Jesus calls us to do differently, as He did the healed man in today's reading. Instead, Jesus calls us to go back out into the world and "spread the Good News". Now that we have been healed, He sends us forth to heal others in His name.

"Just how do we go about bringing this message of Jesus to others?" you may ask. We do this simply by being a witness for the Lord each waking moment of each day. We become a living example of Jesus to those around us. We are walking and talking proof that Jesus can and does heal our addictions for those who come to Him and surrender their lives to Him. Sharing our lives with others and helping others to find the answer is what we are called to do.

DAY TWO - Study 1 Corinthians 9:22-27

The miracle of the "born again" experience is that we are freed from our past. We become a "new creation" in Jesus. That is, we are no longer the old me, but rather the old me has died and is buried, gone forever. We have now become the new me. With the death of the old me, we have been set free from our old addictive life style. How do we keep this "NEW ME" alive and well? The answer is simple, we walk as Jesus walked, in a spirit of service and love toward others. Because we are dead to our old self and have now come to life in Jesus, we are free from our old habits - free from the control of others. Only Jesus has power over our lives, because we have chosen that way. Since we now belong to Christ, we can live and act as Christ would act. We actually become followers, imitators of Christ to do as He did - heal the sick, raise the dead and preach the Good News. We have now become Christ to each other.

DAY THREE - Study 1 Corinthians 15:10

"But for God's grace I am what I am." (Verse 10) What a wonderful declaration of what Jesus had done for Paul and for those of us who follow Him. If it were not for His grace, we might still be "stuck" in denial or the fear of our past addiction, totally dependent on a substance or some out-of-control habit. Another gift of God is the 12 step recovery program.

If it had not been for His grace, we would have never found this AA recovery program. If it had not been for His grace, we would still be at the "bottom" of our addictive habit. We would still be wallowing in the misery of our addiction. Finally, if it were not for the grace of Jesus, we might not have found Him at all in our recovery process. We may have missed finding the "new me".

We may ask, "What is this grace of God anyway?" Grace is unmerited favor. It is Divine help from God placed within the spirit of man. It is the provision that God gives us to handle matters that are impossible or difficult to handle without Him. As we traveled this road called the twelve steps, Jesus has filled us with His grace. Now, we come to the time to "pass it on". Giving it away simply means touching another person and being a friend to that person as they struggle with their addiction problem. When we do that in love and caring, Jesus blesses us many times over. We truly walk with Him and are strengthened in our own life. Are you willing to begin giving it away for Jesus?

DAY FOUR - Study 1 Timothy 1:12-16

In this reading, Paul gives his living testimony. He tells about himself, who he was and who Christ made him to be. Paul was a persecutor of Christians. In his past life, as a Jewish Pharisee, he went around getting people arrested and put to death for their belief in Jesus. After he met Jesus, he was completely changed to the greatest apostle in the church. He does not claim the change on his own, "God was merciful to me... Our Lord poured out His abundant grace on me and gave me the faith and love which are ours in union with Christ Jesus." (Verses 13 & 14) Paul acknowledges that Jesus changed him totally by His grace. He takes no personal credit at all.

Paul's attitude should be our attitude. The healing and success in overcoming our addiction belongs to Jesus, not to us. It is by the grace of Jesus that our lives have been turned around. Jesus is calling us this day and all the days of our life to "follow Me"! We have been saved, rescued from our past and changed by His power.

SERVICE

Lesson 36

Healing Step 12

"Having had a spiritual awakening as a result of these steps, I try to carry this message to others with my addiction and to practice these principles in all my affairs."

Growth & Strength Step 8

"I make a daily effort to give the healing and strength which I have received from the Holy Spirit to those in my life around me. I make a sincere daily practice of loving others as Jesus loves me."

Action Words:
CARRY THE MESSAGE - LOVE

SERVICE
Lesson 36

Healing
Step 12
"Having had a spiritual awakening as a result of these steps, I try to carry this message to others with my addiction and to practice these principles in all my affairs."

Growth & Strength
Step 8
"I make a daily effort to give the healing and strength which I have received from the Holy Spirit to those in my life around me. I make a sincere daily practice of loving others as Jesus loves me."

Action Words :
CARRY THE MESSAGE - LOVE

MEDITATIONS

Many people around us go through life pulling themselves down as they struggle with their addictions. Their attitude is one of, "Oh, I'll never amount to anything. I'm just a good for nothing drunk. God doesn't love me unless I'm good and I can't be good."

It is this type of person who needs Jesus the most. They need to hear the story of our healing and recovery. They need the touch of Jesus. As we share our story of recovery with them, Jesus uses us as the key that opens the door to their life. Jesus can enter their life with His love and healing. We become the "example for all those who would later believe in Him and receive eternal life". (Verse 17) In this way, Jesus uses us to bring the "Good News" to those hurting around us.

DAY FIVE - Study Psalm 92:1-4

Oh, what a wonderfully joyous song in our reading today. The Psalmist is praising God for the wonderful blessing that he has received. This Psalm should also be our song today as we near the close of our walk in this study guide. What a miracle has happened and continues to happen in our lives. How wonderful is God, to have rescued sinners like us and saved us.

The wonderful gift of Jesus in our life is now the center and driving goal in our life. We no longer walk alone buried under the junk and troubles of this world; rather, we walk with Jesus and we have the victory, the joy and happiness of knowing Jesus and living and walking with Him. He is our best friend.

We can truly sing with the Psalmist, "How good it is to give thanks to You, O Lord - to sing in Your honor, O most High God!" (Verse 1) We learn quickly in this reading that our walk with Jesus is not "here today and gone tomorrow." Rather we - "proclaim your constant love every morning and your faithfulness every night." (Verse 2) Our new life with Jesus is on-going and never ending.

We have been healed and we are so happy in this new life that all we want to do is to tell others, and in so doing, "give it away" only to receive more abundant life from our God who will never be "out done". Our life has become a constant love affair with Jesus. And because of Him, we are in love with those around us in His name.

DAY SIX - Study Psalm 96

Each day, as we walk the 12 steps with Jesus Christ, becomes a day of healing and overcoming in HIM. What a privilege to "Proclaim every day the good news that He has saved us". That is our calling as overcoming Spirit-filled Christians.

Our proclaiming the good news happens in several ways:

First - People will see the new person in us as we go about our daily lives. We will be living the life of Jesus. This new life will become evident by our actions.

Second - We will have the opportunity to tell others about what Jesus has done in our lives. We become living, breathing examples of the miracles of Jesus within us.

Maybe we might be a bit afraid as we step out in the new "ME". Let us read and reread this Psalm to strengthen us and give us the boldness and courage to walk and talk for Jesus. When we have Jesus, there is no fear in us. We walk with Him and by His grace we are overcomers.

DAY SEVEN - Study Proverbs 31:26-31

In this Proverb, we see that parents have a mighty influence on their children. That influence is reflected in their words, actions and their relationships with that child.

We are now a new creation in Jesus, therefore our total self reflects a new way about us. We become:

1. Filled with "gentle wisdom". (Verse 26)

2. Our actions show caring as we "look after our family's needs". (Verse 27)

3. We gain the respect of others around us. (Verse 28)

As we walk and live in these last steps as a regular part of our lives, we can, with the constant help of Jesus, become like the woman described in Proverbs 31. Our lives can and will become Christ in our presence today.

POSTSCRIPT

Congratulations on the completion of this study! You may be wondering, "What's next?" Growing in the Spirit continues until our time on earth is through. We will always need to be on guard, doing all that we can to never fall back into the "old me."

You should now be concerned with maintaining all that you have gained. Use the following steps over and over again from now on:

1. Continue taking a daily personal inventory and promptly admit when you are wrong. (Step 10)

2. Continue improving your conscious contact with God through prayer and meditation. Pray for the knowledge of His will and the power to carry it out. (Step 11)

3. Make a daily effort to study the Bible for at least one hour.

4. Become involved in a church community, attend Bible study and worship services each week.

5. Continue making efforts to fast at least one meal three times a week.

6. Look for opportunities to carry this message of recovery through Christ to others. Continue practicing the principles of this study in all your affairs. (Step 12)

In addition, you may want to remain in some sort of Christian AA type 12 Step recovery program. Like you, people involved in leading 12 Step recovery groups are usually in the maintenance stage. Their desire is to continue addiction free through Jesus Christ and to help others do likewise. We suggest you contact some of the larger local churches in your area to ask about Christ-centered overcomers programs. The local AA inter-group office may also be able to direct you to these programs.

A word from our founder, Mr. Ray Geisel:

"I, too, struggled with my addiction for many years. But now, at age 70+, I know that those old temptations are not nearly as strong as before. I found that the solution to those temptations is the mighty power and presence of Jesus Christ. It is this humble knowledge that I have tried to pass on to you over and over again in the study guide. I call upon that power and presence daily in my life and I urge you to do the same. I have succeeded with this program and I pray you will to. Never give up! Even if you should fall, come back and try again until you win."

May the Lord Jesus Christ bless you and keep you in His constant care. It gives us great joy, at Christian 12 Step Ministry, Inc., to know that God has used us in some way to help you draw closer to Him. In the name of Jesus, may you be filled with the mighty power of God's Holy Spirit.

Walking the 12 Steps with Jesus Christ

The 12 STEPS

REFERENCES

Corn, J. (n.d.). Spiritual Strongholds. Retrieved October 17, 2016, from https://www.christianarmor.net/spiritual-warfare/3-spiritual-strongholds (Davis, 2014) (Corn)

Davis, S. (2014, February 20). Strongholds : Tony Evans Mobile. Retrieved October 18, 2016, from http://tonyevans.org/mobile/tag/strongholds/ (Davis, 2014)

Strauss, L. (2004, June 14). 2. Man A Trinity (Spirit, Soul, Body). Retrieved October 18, 2016, from https://bible.org/seriespage/man-trinity-spirit-soul-body (Strauss, 2004)

Durrance, R. L. (n.d.). Healing of Memories. Retrieved October 17, 2016, from http://durrance.com/FrAl/healing_of_memories.htm (Durrance)

Durrance, R. L. (n.d.). Tract on Sexual Bondage. Retrieved October 17, 2016, from http://durrance.com/FrAl/tract_on_sexual_bondage.htm (Durrance)

Durrance, R. L. (n.d.). Article on Sexual Bondage. Retrieved October 17, 2016, from http://durrance.com/FrAl/article_on_sexual_bondage.htm (Durrance)

Durrance, R. L. (n.d.). FEAR AND THE ROOTS OF SIN. Retrieved October 18, 2016, from http://durrance.com/FrAl/fear_and_the_roots_of_sin.htm (Durrance)

Savelle Foy, T. (2010, October 1). Breaking Soul-Ties. Retrieved October 17, 2016, from http://www.terri.com/breaking-soul-ties-2/ (Savelle Foy, 2010)

Savelle Foy, T. (2012, July 1). 4 Indicators Of Wrong Soul Ties. Retrieved October 17, 2016, from http://www.terri.com/4-indicators-of-wrong-soul-ties/ (Savelle Foy, 2012)

Nee, W. (1993). The Finest of the Wheat: Selected Excerpts from the Published Works of Watchman Nee (Vol. 2). New York: Christian Fellowship. Pages 52-64 (Nee, 1993, pp. 52-64)